Raising A Son

Raising
A Son

*Parents and the
Making
of a Healthy Man*

Jeanne Elium
Don Elium

Celestial Arts
Berkeley, California

We are extremely grateful to our clients, colleagues, friends, and families who, in our workshops, classes, parenting groups, and Don's private psychotherapy practice, shared personal accounts of their lives with us. To protect their privacy, names, anecdotes, and case histories have been changed and, in many cases, woven together. We acknowledge those whose courage to tell their stories allows us all to benefit from their tragedies and triumphs.

Celestial Arts
P.O. Box 7123
Berkeley, California 94707

Cover design by Soga Design

Text design by Victor Ichioka

**The Library of Congress has
catalogued an earlier edition as follows:**

Elium, Don, 1954–
    Raising a son : parents and the awakening of a healthy man / by Don
Elium and Jeanne Elium
        p.   cm.
    Includes bibliographical references.
    ISBN 0-89087-844-7 (hardcover)
    ISBN 0-89087-811-0 (softcover)
    1. Parenting. 2. Boys. 3. Fathers and Sons. 4. Mothers and sons.
I. Elium, Jeanne, 1947–   . II. Title.
HQ777.E45   1992
649' .132—dc20   91-42856
                                                              CIP

Library of Congress card catalog number 96-084976

First published by Beyond Words, 1994

First published by Celestial Arts, 1996

First Celestial Printing, 1996

        3   4 / 99   98   97

Gratefully dedicated to our children
Heidi Ann Dunbar and Matthew Guy Elium
our greatest spiritual teachers

Acknowledgments

Writing *Raising a Son* has been a time of discovery, joy, challenge, cooperation, stress, and loving support. The "Can we really write a book together?" doubts led us to new levels of cooperation and communication in our marriage relationship. We could not have achieved it all without the support of loving friends, colleagues, family, and each other. We especially thank the following people from the tops and bottoms of our hearts:

Marilyn Hough, who got the whole thing started; our publishers, Cindy Black and Richard Cohn, whose confidence in us from the very beginning propelled us into the realization of a lifelong dream; the entire staff at Beyond Words Publishing, who answered our telephone calls so cheerfully; Sara J. Steinberg, whom we know only by telephone but who feels like a kindred spirit, and whose editorial expertise, wisdom, and way with words helped us say what we really wanted to say; Loyd Auerbach, whose publishing experience and expert guidance helped us ask for what we needed; Liz at the Contra Costa Central Library in Pleasant Hill, California, who went out of her way to find needles in haystacks; Gail at the Music for Little People catalog store in Redway, California, who did the same; Lew Powers, wise old man who taught us what boys really need; Bob Brownbridge, for reading our first rough chapters with his wise, critical eye and cheering us onward; Sherry Glueck for her support of our work and for always asking how the book was going; author and therapist Ruthanne Olds, whose encouragement and "bookwise" advice helped us avoid endless problems; the entire staff at Touchstone Counseling Services for their unfailing support of our work; Don's clients, whose courage inspired us to write this book; our friends and neighbors Sue Gates and Carolyn MacKenzie, for sharing what living with sons is like for them; Shepherd Bliss, a man in touch with the deep masculine, who taught us through his vulnerability, wisdom, power, and poetry; Michael Mayer, teacher, Tài Chi master, friend, and trusted guide on the mythic journey of self-discovery; Bruce Silverman, Audrey Silverman Foote, Elana, and Naomi for their loving friendship and parenting support; Dr. Gary Jordan for teaching us about family life and our places in it; Bob Kliger, eternal friend and essential member of our spiritual family, whom we trust to tell us the truth; Laura Kennedy, for her willingness to ponder any weird question and come up with an answer, and Wally, Elizabeth, Michael, and little Rosie, too, for being our lifelong friends; and Polly and Preston Elium and Bill and Ruth Guy for parenting us.

For this second edition, we give a special thank you to our agent, Peter Beren, a rock in the middle of the storm; David Hinds and Phil Wood at Celestial Arts/Ten Speed Press for their generous confidence in our work; Veronica Randall and Kathryn Bear, whose insightful criticisms and gentle nudgings were paced just right to help us get through; Jackie Miskel and all the staff at Bonanza Street Books, who always have time for us amidst the glorious stacks of old books; Robert McEleese for his bottomless wealth of expert information; and Lynn Bowen for her talent, time, and telephone.

CONTENTS

The Quest for
A New Humanity

What we call the beginning is often the end
And to make an end is to make a beginning.
The end is where we start from.[1]

—T.S. Eliot, *Four Quartets*

There is room for debate about how far our economy and technology will take us. The immediate future for our sons is clearly marked, however. No longer can we afford to live, "every man for himself." Men, alone, cannot continue to believe that they hold the world on their shoulders. The task is too great, and we are losing them to alcoholism, drug abuse, violent crime, illness, and early death. Never before in human history have we faced such an opportunity for growth. Men are no longer masters of the world of work, and women no longer own the world of the home. Humans, both male and female, are challenged to stretch to our full size—assuming the proficient skills of the hunt and the nurturing ways of the hearth. Nothing less than strength, boldness, a sense of adventure, insight, courage, and leadership joined with gentleness, sensitivity, caring, kindness, and understanding will see us into the future. Let us not make the mistake of simply trying to make our sons more feminine; we must parent to channel *all* their gifts into serving life.

It is time to teach boys to love women and to strengthen the mother-son bond—that vital link which teaches caring for others and loving themselves. Having fathers become full partners in family life provides sons with new models of male nurturing and love. Learning to cook for their families offers a perfect metaphor for teaching boys to care for a larger society, with all its needs, ills, differences, and values. How would a son's vision of manhood change if he saw movies, TV programs, newspaper stories, and ads about boys and men cooking for their families, bathing babies, planting trees, and settling disputes peacefully?

Single mothers *can* raise good boys, and all parents need the help of an entire village to grow boys into healthy men. Parents must reassume authority in the raising of sons. The responsibility to be firm-but-kind leaders of their growth and behavior is ours. We must require boys to lift, tote, build, *and* to cook, serve, and clean up. Through these tasks they learn the skills of listening and seeing through another's eyes. They master the craft of leadership in all its broad aspects. They discover the wonders, excitement, and pride of accomplishment in the Hunt—the world of work. They savor the joy and sense of belonging at the Hearth—the world of home and relationship. They learn how important it is to spend time alone, to listen for guidance, and to replenish their spirits.

A new humanity is awakening, where little boys do not have to cut off parts of themselves to fit the cultural expectations of what it means to be a man; where men can fully feel and express their feelings without shame or fear of being seen as weak; where boys no longer have to sever their ties to their mothers and distance themselves from their families to become men; where fathers instinctively care for their babies; where women and men work equally, side-by-side in partnership, each valued for their unique gifts; where boys learn to solve human problems through love and care rather than violence; where boys learn to love women, to cast aside misogyny and the objectification of females; where boys reclaim their connection with Nature; where boys feel responsible for the welfare of the whole.

An old king was challenged by his enemy to a test of wits, the loser giving up his kingdom to the winner. His enemy won the right to choose the game. "Oh, King," he bellowed. "In the hand behind my back I hold a dove. Is the bird alive or dead?" The king immediately realized his predicament. If he answered, "Alive," his enemy had only to tighten his hand and kill the dove. If he answered, "Dead," he would merely open his hand, and the dove would fly free. Everyone tensely awaited the king's answer. The king replied, "The decision of our life or death lies in your hands."

—Source unknown

As we move beyond independence to an inter-dependence based not on gender roles but on needs, we help boys grow into a new and healthier manhood. The development of a new, more compassionate humanity is in our hands.

No man is an island, entire of itself;
every man is a piece of the continent,
a part of the main; . . .
any man's death diminishes me,
because I am involved in mankind;
and therefore never send to know
for whom the bell tolls;
it tolls for thee.[2]

—John Donne, Holy Sonnets

End Notes

1. T. S. Eliot, *Four Quartets* (London: Folio Society, 1971).

2. *The Complete Poems of John Donne*, Roger E. Bennett, ed. (New York: Packard, 1942).

Part I:

Boys and Men—
The Puzzle of
Being Male

CHAPTER ONE

The Trouble with Boys

*My mother had a great deal of trouble
with me, but I think she enjoyed it.*[1]

—Mark Twain

The title of this book, *Raising a Son*, may have caught your eye because you are expecting a boy, or because you are in the midst of raising one now, and want to scream "Help!" at the top of your lungs from the highest steeple in town. The trouble with boys is that no one knows how to parent them today. They are left to find out for themselves what it means to be a man in our culture.

"Boys want to know three things," says seventy-two-year-old Lew Powers, a twenty-year veteran Boy Scout director. "One, who's the boss? Two, what are the rules? And three, are you going to enforce 'em? To have a strong relationship with a boy, you have to be the boss, and a very kind one. Only set rules that you can enforce, and always enforce them. Then you have the basis for a relationship. From here comes respect and more importantly, trust. Then you can be kind, he'll listen, and he knows that you are on his side."

Scoutmaster Powers, a tall, silver-haired gentleman with a look in his eyes that says "old, wise man," has held every position there is in the Boy Scout organization. Boys are attracted to him like bees to honey. "While I was on the board of directors for our area Boy Scout troops, I visited one that was having trouble," Powers recalls. "I quickly saw the problem. The leader let the boys wrestle and fight till it was time to go home—that was their program. I asked him why he didn't teach the boys anything; he told me that if I thought I could do better, to go ahead. So I did. I announced to the twenty-five boys that I was coming back the following week to teach them how to tie knots, and that if anyone didn't want to learn, he could stay home. Twelve boys showed up the next week. That night they learned to tie knots. In twelve months, we were up to seventy-five boys.

"Other members of the board asked the boys why they preferred to be in my troop over the others. Almost every boy said, 'Because we get things done, and I learn how to do things.' In other words, they got discipline—not the hard and cold variety, but clear, firm, and kind.

"I always listened, too. When we were camping, I would have 'sick call' right before dinner. I would bandage all of the hurts and scrapes the boys got playing, and talk to them. They would tell me all about their troubles—at home, at school, and with girls. One boy waited for sick call all day with a long splinter in his hand, just to talk with me. I had him lie down in my tent to rest, and he talked to me for an hour. I listened and tried to help them all solve their problems. They knew they could trust me."

The voice of this wise mentor cuts to the core of the trouble with boys today: they lack consistent, kind, and firm leaders with rules that make sense. Because we are so busy trying to "make it" financially or trying to "find ourselves," we have delegated the parenting of our sons to the institutions of culture, and we are all suffering because of it. Everywhere we see the influences of media violence and sexual "come-ons," the availability and temptation of alcohol and other drugs, the loss of authority and discipline in the schools, the erosion of crafts-manship and pride in one's work—even the desire to work at all—and the lack of respect for the law. We are all too familiar with the effects on our sons of growing up too fast in a technological age. Yet instead of leading them firmly by the hand into manhood, we are leaving the job to day-care workers, teachers in overcrowded classrooms, TV writers, movie and rock stars, gangs, the neighbors, and sometimes even the courts, juvenile hall, and probation officers.

Parenting is harder today than it used to be. The world has changed; families have gotten away from the authoritarian mode, whereby parents were in charge, decisions were nonnegotiable, and kids followed the rules with little thought to the contrary. Child psychologist and author Louise J. Kaplan, Ph.D., describes the family of the past in her insightful book, *Oneness and Separateness: From Infant to Individual*: "When the emotional structure of the family was more certain, children accepted parental authority out of a sense of obligation and devotion. And from their parents they acquired the firm and rigid ideals that later allowed them to act, albeit inflexibly, with confidence and inner authority toward their own children."[2]

In the child-centered family of today, parents try to be in charge, but how to do so is unclear. Inevitably the rules, when there are any, are casually broken and chaos reigns. Because the position of the family as central to American life has given way to the rights of the individual, parents have relinquished their authority with their sons for fear of infringing upon those rights. These changes in social structure have left both parents and children doubtful and confused. We push our children to make choices too early, set limits and boundaries that are too vague, and we do not follow through with the consequences that we set.

Scoutmaster Powers and Dr. Kaplan would seem to agree that our sons need firm but kind authority figures to guide them. As parents we know this too, but our good intentions seem to be no match for the obstacles we all face in raising boys today. Single mothers are crying out for men they can trust to be part of their sons' lives. Fathers experience the frustration of being locked out of their families because of work obligations, financial pressures, and the lack of training in how to parent. Mothers know that overcompensating for the absence of a father is woundinf to their sons, but how can a mother encourage her son to become a man when there are no adult males in his life?

> *I wish I could put my son in the Army. That would shape him up! The boy doesn't respect me, his things, or his mother. He won't work unless I push and push. His room is a mess, and he just won't take care of his responsibilities. At least with the Army he would come out changed!*
>
> —*Bob, father of Mason, fifteen*

Although the father quoted above was being facetious when he talked about sending his son to the Army, he spoke to a real concern.

He was referring to the male energy of his fifteen-year-old son. Parents of sons come to know this energy well. It is forceful, willful, and determined. Sometimes we also call it lazy, wild, and crazy-making. Often in our fast-paced, tightly scheduled lives, we view the masculine birthright as an inconvenience. Usually at the worst of times for parents, sons succumb to the male drive to explore, to investigate, to push ahead, to tear apart. No matter what their son's age, parents come running to the counselor's office with troubling questions: Is my son normal? What have I done wrong? How can I make him more sensitive? How can I get him to cooperate? How can I tame him? Why does he do the things he does?

Why We Wrote This Book

People ask us why we wrote a book on the specifics of raising sons. We each have our own answer to the question.

JEANNE I, Jeanne, have never understood men. My father, who was a loving, insightful, caring man, remains a mystery to me. My brother is charming, witty, intelligent, warm, and an enigma. My husband is my partner in many areas of our life together, but a part of him stays just out of reach—foreign, alien, different from myself. And now I have a son, and I often wonder who he is, and who must I be as his mother to start him on the path to a healthy manhood.

My relationships with men have been both awful and wonderful—some more awful than wonderful. The women's movement gave me permission to rail at men and to rage at "The Patriarchy" for my being trapped in feminine stereotypes, debilitating fears, and limiting roles. Later on, with the support of other women, I learned to know myself as a woman, to feel proud of my feminine nature, and, eventually, to let go of my anger toward men. My work with the environmental movement helped me see that blaming men for the state of the world is working with only half of the problem.

We must all be held accountable for the conditions of the technological world our children will inherit.

This very feeling—that it is time for men and women to reach out to one another to heal our planet—led me to my work in conjunction with the men's movement. From all over the country, men are quietly coming together in the woods, in the dark: to drum, to dance wildly, to weep, to comfort each other, to tell their fatherless stories. Men are beginning to support one another, as women did in the sixties, to discover what it is to be a man in today's world. I have been privileged to witness their courageous struggles, and to hear the stories of some of these men. They have helped me understand the uniqueness of a male's journey into manhood, and for that, I am grateful. I have chosen to write this book with my husband, Don, so that my son may grow up free to be the beautiful male that he so naturally is.

◅ ◅ *DON*   When I, Don, came of age during the height of the women's liberation movement, I was given a picture of the man I was supposed to be—cooperative, in touch with my feelings, and sensitive to the feelings of others. So I rejected the "John Wayne" model, but I noticed an odd trend—I had women friends, but no dates. Most women I knew were going out with men who were like the "Duke"—harder, more self-assured, and sometimes more stubbornly aggressive than I was. What I was calling a "sensitive man" was really a passive-aggressive man, who didn't say what he felt, didn't take a stand, and said yes when he really meant no. My marriage and the birth of my son backed me even further into a corner. I started looking for a better way. I did not want my son to grow up without a strong father figure.

Before, I had looked to women to define my maleness. Now I began to search out other men. It was then that I discovered the powerful, masculine force that is within me, and within all males. Left unattended, it can be destructive; nurtured to maturity, it gives life. The turning point for me was when my therapist, Dr. Gary Jordan, said, "Don, this is what it's like to be a man." I was shocked. Here was a man who believed that men have unique challenges—to be strong and sensitive, and to act on what they feel is right. We are not just like women. We are a different sort. I discovered that as a man, I have a powerful mission and a role to play in this life, and that it was time for me to embrace it, live it, and redefine it for a modern world. It is this challenge, in partnership with my wife, Jeanne, that makes me speak bluntly and squarely to the issues of raising sons. There is a difference in parenting a boy, and that difference has a purpose: the making of a healthy man.

End Notes

1. *A Mother's Journal* (Philadelphia, Pa.: Running Press, 1985), last page.

2. Louise J. Kaplan, *Oneness and Separateness: From Infant to Individual* (New York: Simon & Schuster, 1978), 25.

CHAPTER TWO

What Are Little Boys Made Of?

Sugar and spice and everything nice,
That's what little girls are made of.
Snips and snails and puppydogs' tails,
That's what little boys are made of.

—Old nursery rhyme

When our son was a baby he epitomized the sugar part of this classic rhyme. But starting around the age of four, he became someone else altogether. He was still sweet and sensitive and nice to be around—most of the time—but a new fierceness was emerging. He had a budding sense of himself as a powerful person to be reckoned with in his own right. In those moments when our ideas did not match his (such as, now it's time to pick up toys), we were confronted with a furious storm disguised in the shape of a small boy.

As boys grow they often amaze and confound us with their ferocity. Aghast and thoroughly dismayed, we look at our sons and think, "What do we do now?!" Then we wonder, who is this baby that has become so big, so aggressive? Only yesterday, he was happy to be tickled and cuddled and carried around. Who is this boy-man that stands before us, defiant and surprisingly wise? What strange forces have been changing him?

To understand what boys are "made of," we must consider what shapes them: the powerful forces of biology, the uniquely masculine psychological tasks, and the moist, dark, mysterious call of the masculine soul.

The Biological Force

Boys are biologically driven via a drug-like hormone that is one of the most powerful manipulators of behavior the world has ever known. It is this force that pushes boys to be aggressive and inspires them to win at all costs. It compels them to wear out the furniture, knock over lamps, and make us parents glad that we have good home, health, and car insurance. A minute drop of this potent substance, administered over a brief period of time, empowers the smallest, weakest male in a group of monkeys to challenge the dominant male for his throne. The previously "wimpish" monkey not only wins the struggle, but goes on to dominate and rule the entire group—females, babies, and the other males.[1] The same stimulus turns a playful nine-year-old human into a fourteen-year-old "Incredible Hulk." From conception to manhood, this force triggers the human male body and brain to take a masculine form. It is the hormone testosterone.

The Masculine Plan

Although it may be hard for us to imagine that our cute and cuddly six-month-old son is under the influence of such a powerful force, testosterone is already at work, orchestrating the intricate development of a baby boy into a man. Keep in mind that each boy grows at his own rate, yet he develops according to a well-defined plan that determines his sex, shapes his body, and influences his temperament. Biologically, he will unfold before our eyes no matter what we parents do. This miracle is beyond our control—and his. He is growing into the man that his hormones predetermine him to be.

Please bear with us now, as we review some basic biology that will shed a little light on how this takes place. As we may all know, hormones are secretions produced by the growth regulators of the body's glandular system: thyroid, pancreas, pituitary, thymus, ovaries in females, and testes in males. They are under the control of a biological intelligence that holds the perfect plan for every boy's development. Both boys and girls have the major sex hormones, testosterone and estrogen, but boys have a greater abundance of testosterone, and girls produce a greater level of estrogen. The differences in their ratios and in the strategically timed release of hormones create the uniquely feminine or uniquely masculine plan of development.

The intelligence in charge of this plan operates through genetic coding. In our sons these instructions are carried by a "Y" chromosome. All embryos begin life as female, so during the first few weeks after conception the "Y" chromosome has an important mission: to signal the production of testosterone, which will change the biological template to male. From this moment on, the baby is a boy. The first part of the plan is now complete. Too often we forget what a miracle it is that a small mass of undifferentiated flesh can grow into a magnificent and vital male being. This is the goal of the masculine plan.

This masculine mission has been researched carefully to determine just how different males and females are. Camilla Benbow and Jullian Stanley, researchers at Johns Hopkins University who studied more than one hundred thousand children, created intense controversy when they proclaimed that the differences between genders, without a doubt, have a biological basis. Benbow reported, "After 15 years looking for an environmental explanation and getting zero results, I gave up.... We're just beginning to have evidence that when there are two equally valid approaches to a problem, via words or via images, females tend to choose the approach through words and males the approach through images."[2]

Brain studies by pioneer endocrinologist Roger Gorski, Ph.D., show marked differences in the brain structures of girls and boys. These variations may account for differences in higher brain functions, such as memory, imagination, and control of bodily movement, and in how men and women think, feel, act, and perceive things.[3] For example, a man tends to fix problems first and consider his relationship with his spouse or partner later, whereas most women consider the relationship in the solution. Men tend to focus on one problem or task at a time (as at a bull's-eye on a target) and see any other occurrences in their lives as distractions to ignore. Women focus on a goal with the broader picture in mind.

Some researchers in biology, psychology, and sociology strongly question these findings, with good reason. Nineteenth-century gender-related research was used in a sexist way to prove that women had no place in the world other than as mothers and housewives. Author Susan Davis writes, "Anthropologists, biologists, and other researchers looked at everything from brain size to appetite to justify the Victorian notion that men are smarter, more aggressive, and (therefore) should have more political rights than the weaker sex."[4] The pendulum then swung to the other side, whose strong opinion was that there are no basic biological differences (other than reproductive function) between men and women. This group argued that development of those qualities we think of as male or female is all determined by family and cultural socialization. This long-standing disagreement over the importance of heredity and environment is known as the "nature vs. nurture" argument.[5]

The truth is that many factors influence male and female development. Biologically, females and males do march to the beat of divergent hormonal balances, corresponding to their differing dispositions, bodies, and styles of communication. A boy's being vibrates to the rhythm of testosterone.

As we have learned, the first spurts of testosterone ensure that a fetus begins the development of the masculine plan. Another strong release at six months of fetal growth signals the second stage of the developmental plan. Then the secretion of testosterone levels off until puberty, when this powerful hormone increases in quantities from ten to twenty times over the usual amount received by girls.[6] Here again, testosterone levels and age of the onset of puberty vary among boys. But it is no surprise that the adolescent male has trouble walking without bumping into things, needs more sleep, loses his temper easily, becomes moody, and cannot concentrate on his homework. The boy is confronted with an amazing, often confusing, but powerful sequence of changes: increase in body hair, refinement of the muscles, eightfold increase in genital size, deepening of the voice, expansion of fantasy life, and an awakening interest in sex.

This testosterone rush brings an intoxicating feeling of power and invincibility. The teenage boy feels he can do anything. Auto insurance companies know he is a bad risk. School principals know he may have trouble with rules. Mothers know he can be a challenge to understand. Fathers know he can be hard to communicate with. He is under the spell of the masculine biological plan.

Around the age of twenty, the dramatic upswings in testosterone levels stabilize, unless a man becomes affected by disease or physical debilitation. There is some new evidence that testosterone levels rise temporarily when a man needs its thrust for action: when he or someone he loves is in danger, when he becomes angry, when he participates in competitive games.[7] But never again after puberty will we see the remarkable increases in his hormones to spur the creation of a strong, resilient, adult male body.

Testosterone and Male Behavior: Three Tendencies

As we have seen, the "Y" chromosome has an agenda to create an adult male body. It uses testosterone to accomplish its developmental plan— to change the fetus to male, develop the young boy's body, and add secondary sexual characteristics. Result: a mature masculine physique.

In equally powerful ways, testosterone also affects masculine behavior. Although each boy grows according to his own style, three themes emerge: a tendency toward aggression and dominance, a strong urge for impulsive risk taking, and the repeated experience of short-term cycles of tension and release.

Aggression and Dominance

> *He's so different from my daughter. She fights and yells too, but he zooms in a way I don't understand. He's always pushing, and he has to have his way about things. His first instinct is to hit and yell. He doesn't do it to be mean; it just erupts out of him.*
>
> —*Yvonne, a frustrated mother*

Hormonal research links high levels of testosterone in males with aggressiveness and the drive to dominate others. According to James Dabbs, Ph.D., researcher at Georgia State University, "It has to do with dominance in the human herd...." Males with greater than usual amounts of testosterone, says Dabbs, attempt to influence and control other people, to dominate in social and home situations, and to express opinions and emotions freely.[8]

These tendencies result in positive or negative behaviors. The drive to be socially dominant can lead to positions of leadership in school, on the basketball court, in business and politics. On the other hand, over-aggression can give rise to delinquency, substance abuse, promiscuity, and violent crime.[9]

Vying for "king of the hill," engaging in win-lose competition, and challenging authority are marks of the biological force of testosterone. Boys express their masculine drive in different ways, but hitting, kicking, and verbal aggression are commonly found among young boys in diverse cultures all over the world.[10] Some boys are extreme in their physical use of aggression, as evidenced by the growing number of male juveniles convicted of violent crimes and assaults. Other boys more habitually express aggression verbally, as in dead-end arguments at home or, more creatively, in speech class at school.

> *My son is quiet and sensitive. He doesn't go in for rough-and-tumble play with the other boys. But he is like a madman when he turns on his computer.*
>
> *—Sam, father of a ten-year-old*

Certain behaviors we may not recognize as aggressive, such as working to solve a computer problem. Aggression can be acted out vicariously through such vehicles as computers, building blocks, cars, and skateboards. As researcher Camilla Benbow observes, "Let's face it, human males like to manipulate things—from Tinkertoys to the cosmos."[11]

> *I don't know where I'm going, but I'm on my way!*
>
> *—Stymie, "Little Rascals," in his wagon racing down a steep hill out of control*

If we visualize this biological force of testosterone as an arrow, and then observe male behavior, many actions have an underlying (or extremely obvious) straight-ahead push. Out of a group of fifty men who attended a discussion group at a conference on men's issues, most could identify with this push. One man said, "It doesn't necessarily have a particular direction. Sometimes I feel like a rocket. I just go off. In conversations I might push an agenda that is not really important to me, but I push anyway. If I don't disengage and reflect on what I want to say, I get going and end up in places that I really didn't intend to go."

Linguistic studies by Deborah Tannen, Ph.D., indicate that a male's argumentativeness and logic are geared more toward dominating a situation than toward the actual content of a discussion.[12] As parents, we have all probably observed that whether the subject is bedtimes, curfews, chores, or allowances, a boy notes who is in charge and whether he can dominate the situation. Instinctively he is responding to the testosterone force.

Impulsive Risk Taking

> *I was driving with five other guys in the car. It was raining, and we were on a scenic ocean road. Suddenly a curve came out of nowhere. I ripped the steering wheel around, and the car went up on two wheels, tipping toward the edge of the cliff. We could see the ocean and jagged rocks below. We all screamed, and I don't know how it happened, but the car pulled itself back and landed on four wheels in the middle of the road. I slammed on the brakes and stopped. In the shocked silence that followed, my first thoughts were: Let's do it again!*
>
> *—Ted, a sixteen-year-old boy*

These stories drive parents crazy. It is hard enough to protect one's son from others; it's doubly hard to protect him from himself. The biological force not only drives the boy's body to develop physically, it also pushes a boy to test limits, especially those that everyone else takes for granted. Bandage companies succeed on the knowledge that young boys will test gravity. Stores spend good money on two-way mirrors and video cameras to catch those who try to see if the hand is indeed quicker than the eye. The makers of hang gliders, motorcycles, mountain climbing gear, skateboards, fast cars, and so on, prosper because they know that males will inevitably test fate. Later in life, when a son shares with his folks what he really did when he was younger, they are usually glad that they didn't know.

Studies conducted by Frank Farley, Ph.D., a University of Wisconsin psychologist, linked high levels of testosterone with risk-taking behavior. Males with "rather high testosterone levels" he called "Big T" types. Those whose testosterone levels were more normal were termed "little t's." The "Big T" subjects either tended to score high creatively or were prone to delinquency. Sometimes they showed both tendencies. Furthermore, whether creative or criminal, "Big T's" exhibited more self-destructive behavior. Along with a much higher incidence of drug abuse, smoking, and alcoholism, they had twice as many accidents as males in the "little t" group.[13]

Dr. Farley suggests that boys and men described as "Big T's" typically break new ground, challenge authority, and love to make the rules. They take charge, create something new, then usually move on to another project that challenges them. "Little t's," though also aggressive, prefer to follow the rules, bring order and stability, and manage projects rather than create them. All organizations need the genius and power of both groups: the power hitters and the sacrifice hitters of baseball, the creative corporate president and the reliable manager, the theater's leading man and the chorus line.

Risk-taking behavior ranges from dangerous, life-threatening stunts to milder forms of pushing the limits. A young teen rigged the main office computer at his high school to automatically adjust his grades to passing status whenever anything below a C was entered. He then extended this "service" to other students, turning it into a very profitable business until a secretary found the programming notes he inadvertently left in the computer room. One savvy high-tech computer firm actually found a way to profit from the young male hacker's propensity for doing the unauthorized—it employed a thirteen-year-old boy as a program tester. His job was to break into computer programs to find holes in their security systems. If you don't recognize either of these risk-taking extremes in your own son, think back: as a pre-schooler, did he ever build a five-foot tower with his table and building blocks, drape a towel around his shoulders, and jump to see if he could fly like Superman?

Testosterone predisposes males to seek out risky ventures. They expend a great deal of energy trying to beat the system, test their abilities, and challenge the limits of what is possible.

Tension and Release

The instant when the hunter makes the kill, the thrill of the long touchdown pass, and the closure of a big sell are all moments that live in the dreams of men from prehistoric times through today. Central to these moments is a powerful cycle of energy, fundamental in the makeup of a man: a short buildup of tension followed by a quick, gratifying, and decisive release. This short-term, immediate-gratification cycle (see figure 1) prepares a male's body to act.

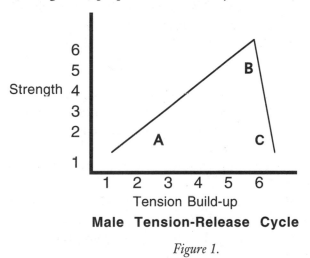

Male Tension-Release Cycle

Figure 1.

When he is under threat or extreme stress, a male's body is put on major alert to act; whether called upon to fight for his life, protect his family, or solve a problem, he is poised for a swift, decisive action that brings relief and resolution to the situation confronting him.

> *A young boy played quietly with "Legos," those small, plastic building blocks that snap together. He had carefully constructed an intricate sculpture, when suddenly he burst out with "You dumb thing!" and*

threw the piece to the floor. He then quietly resumed his work as though nothing had happened.

Alec worked furiously at his computer, eyes focused, shoulders tensed, fingers flying. No distraction pried his attention away until he had solved the problem. He then threw up his arms, jumped up, and yelled, "I did it!"

The men crowded around the TV set, faces tensed. Their bodies mirrored the motion of the quarterback as he rolled and zigzagged out of reach of defensive hands. A groan arose from the group with the long, slow lob of the pass downfield. The lament swelled into a shout of triumph, as the men leapt to their feet in unison with the catch. They fell back in their seats, limp. Ahhhhhh, "Miller Time!"

This tension-release loop is most easily seen in male sexual behavior, which is dominated by this powerful cycling of energy. A man's sexual role in the life cycle is much narrower and simpler than a woman's role. His biological task is to successfully "plant the seed." When this is completed, his body tells him to move on to another challenge— tension and release.

Though shaped by the culture, this biological compulsion to experience tension and then quick gratification originates and is deeply embedded within a man's being. It shows up in young boys' run-and-tackle play, but during the teen years the cycle reveals its power. The preoccupation with masturbation, the life-daring stunts to impress the girl of his dreams, and the need to feel the thrill of competition and victory are examples of this biological force at work. Competitive sports are positive channels for the tension-release urge. Other outlets use brainpower rather than muscle:

⊰⊱ ⊰⊱ DON | Tom, a seventeen-year-old client, was depressed and saw himself as a "wimp." His parents and teachers considered him lazy. He came to counseling because he was flunking out of school and refused to explain why to anyone. I told him I knew his laziness was a cover, and that I thought it was working great. Then I asked him what project he was so frantically working on in his mind. (I was taking a shot in the dark, but figured that testosterone must be working his mind overtime, since his body and attitude were so dulled.) Tom gaped at me in surprise and blurted, "A spy novel. I love law-and-order stuff!" He admitted that he had been afraid to tell anyone about his book for fear of being ridiculed. Eventually Tom summoned enough courage to read a portion of his writing to his English class. He reported, "I got so nervous that I almost chickened out, but I stood there and read it. When everybody clapped, I felt like the most powerful person in the world. It scares me to think about it, but I want to do it again!"

The nervousness of the preparation, the buildup of performance tension, and the release that brings resolve don't have to be violent or illegal in nature. However, what we see on the streets and read in our newspapers makes us believe otherwise. Suspense-laden drug deals, shoplifting, clever computer scams, and organized cheating are common arenas of masculine expression in our modern world.

It's the rush I get right when I lift the candy bar in the store. The feeling is awesome. Am I good enough to pull this off? The moment when I know I've done it— there ain't nothing like it!

—Nate, twelve-year-old risk-taker

A male's day is ruled by the constant cycle of tension-release: the rise and fall, the respite, and the urge to do it again. If he finds no creative, legal way to get the thrill, this compulsion will go underground to angrily lash out later in destructive acts. Or it will grow within him into depression, torturing self-criticism, or painful feelings of hopelessness.

The Psychological Force

*I complained to a friend that although I had completed
six years in therapy, my mother still wouldn't let me go.
He replied, "She's not supposed to let go of you.
Your father is supposed to come and get you."*

—Richard, a thirty-five-year-old man

We have examined briefly the male biological force as a physically
generated push that propels a son to follow a developmental path
beyond his conscious control. The domain of the psychological force is
in relationships. Its drive comes from the unseen world of developmental stages and teachable moments. Today we parents are armed
with many good books about childhood psychological development,
but a key step has been underemphasized: the journey over the bridge
that every son must take—the bridge from Mother to Father. Men do
not talk much about relationships, but when they do a common theme
emerges: they feel stuck with Mother, estranged from Father, and
unclear about a man's roles and identity in the world. Most modern
men are stuck on Mother's side of the bridge.

Mother's Side of the Bridge

When a boy is born, it is perfectly clear that he is his mother's son. He
looks to her for the milk of life; to be close to her is heaven, and to
separate from her is agony. He and she are one being. The life force
that cements this relationship is extraordinary in its power, love, and
influence. Tiny women, barely able to pick up their own weight, have
been known to lift an automobile off their threatened child. A mother
knows her own baby's cry in a group of hundreds, and a child knows
the minute the mother lifts the receiver to make a telephone call that
he no longer has her undivided attention. This is a boy's first
relationship. Whether it is a positive or a negative one, his emotional
framework begins here. Mother is primary.

Where is Father during this love affair between mother and son?
Father is definitely in a secondary position (in spite of recent inventions, like the artificial breasts that he can strap on to nurse his infant

son). Father's role must be to protect and to encourage this vital mother-son connection. However, we do not mean that a father should not be involved in the care of and bonding with his infant son. Many a father experiences great loss and loneliness after the birth that he and the mother had anticipated together for so long. The father may suddenly find that he and the mother no longer share the closeness they had before their son was born. There never seems to be the time nor the energy. Every moment goes to the care and feeding of a tiny interloper—wanted and loved, but an interloper nonetheless.

> *When he came out, he was a miracle. No matter how hard it gets, I think of that moment, and my commitment to my son returns.*
>
> *—John, a father who assisted in the birth of his son*

A father must persevere to maintain a close connection with the mother and to join her in bonding with their new son. The father who is active with his son in the early years is making a huge investment for the future. Its return will multiply as the years pass and bridges are to be crossed. His support during the birth, his long nights of rocking his son and walking the floor with him, and his continued efforts to support his family financially are anything but secondary. In this season of a boy's life, however, he must first identify with his mother.

The Transition

Between the years of five and eight, the psychological force moves the son into transition. The primacy of identification now begins to shift from Mother to Father. This is not a conscious choice made by the son. The inner urge of the male plan of development nudges him out of the nest of the mother over a precarious bridge to the world of the father. The transition, then, between the dreamy, symbiotic world of childhood and the development of an individual male self is often challenging for a boy and his family. This does not mean that a boy no longer needs, wants, nor pays any attention to his mother. He may seek her out even more than before, craving her attention, understanding, and approval. This is a precious and precarious time for a son and his mother. His inner inklings that the fantasy life of childhood is fading behind him causes profound sadness and pain. He experiences a push-pull feeling toward his mother, which is often confusing and frustrating but, at the same time, compelling and poignant. By age nine, he challenges Mom's authority in earnest. He is slow to dress and dawdles over any small task. Easily frustrated when projects don't go smoothly, he shouts in anger one minute and is reduced to tears the next. Every suggestion is met with scorn, sarcasm, or "You just don't get it, Mom."

Mother and boy, at this point, face a more grown-up world of reality that warns them their relationship must change, even hints that it must end. Modern society, education, psychology, and literature admonish mothers against spoiling or coddling their boys for fear they will grow up unable to deal with the harsh business of being real men.

Don | This transition took a dramatic turn with one of my clients. Nathan, aged ten, lived with his mother and younger brother. Dad lived on the other side of town and visited only occasionally. One evening Nathan argued with his mother over where he would sit at the dinner table. Suddenly Nathan threatened to hit his mother. She grabbed him to sit him down, and Nathan fought her to the floor. Both mother and son were stunned, as if the event had happened to two other people. The mother later told me, "I'm a pacifist. I can't believe I grabbed him like that!"

I assured her that two important changes needed to happen. First, she must rethink how to set limits with her now-stronger son and how to deal with her own anger. Second, it was now imperative for Nathan to spend lots of time with his father and other adult males. Later, the mother told me that Nathan's dad had refused to become more involved, so she arranged for Nathan to stay often with a favorite uncle and with neighborhood friends whose dad spent lots of time with them. She said, "I was so relieved to know that his pushing against me was a normal outburst for his age. More importantly, though, I have found that the more he is with older men who invest their time and interest in him, and won't tolerate his 'stuff,' the less angry he is with me. I am amazed at the changes in him."

These encounters between mothers and sons are normal signs that Dad needs to be "front and center" in the family picture. Whether he is married or divorced, his role is clear, and his presence and investment in his son sets in motion the making of a strong and healthy boy. If Dad hasn't been active before, now is the time to begin. He must reach out to other fathers and health professionals for help and support.

Fathers are amazing in their ability to commit to their sons, once they get the right information and training. Many nine-, ten-, and eleven-year-old boys from divorced families are with their fathers most of the time. This requires tremendous sacrifice of mothers in letting go of their sons, and much time, money, and loss of personal pleasures for a father.

> *I can't believe it. I have cut my work week in half. My son stays with me for five days out of seven. I cook for him, help him with his homework, tuck him in at night. When he's at his mom's I thought I'd be delighted. And I'm glad I have the break. But the truth is, I miss him and can't wait for him to come back. I thank God that I heard about how important my role as father is at this time of his life. That's why I have this chance. But I never, ever, thought I would be into it this deep.*
>
> *—Jack, a forty-four-year-old divorced father*

When he starts to crave adult male attention, it is time for a boy to cross the bridge between the world of the mother and the world of the father. Any man who comes near him will be teased and punched and wrestled for contact. He will begin to ask for more time with his father —mowing the yard, washing the car, working on a model, planting a garden, camping, playing or watching sports, and in hundreds of other ways that fathers and sons connect in our modern world.

The boy of eight to ten will try to please his father at all costs. Even if he appears to hate his father, deep down he craves his approval. A compliment or an "atta boy!" from Dad does wonders to create self-worth and self-acceptance in the son, and cultivates cooperation as well. At this tender age any negative comment or "put-down" hurts to the bone. If we recognize the signs of a son's readiness to identify with his father in the world of men, we can relax our parental tendencies toward feeling guilty, frustrated, or angry about our son's difficult behavior. He is simply ready to "cross the bridge."

However, he will not cross this bridge by himself. He will stop at the edge and wait. Why would anyone want to leave the mother's world by his own choice? This world has been his universe since he was born. Here he was fed, bathed, rocked, sung to, tickled, protected, nursed, held. Mother reassured him when he fell, laughed at his jokes, admired his achievements. No boy would leave this comfort lightly. And it is at this juncture, perhaps, that our modern culture makes an error in the developing life of a small boy. All models of healthy development assert that a boy must separate from his mother, but we have interpreted separation to mean severance. Because of the intense bonding between most mothers and sons, the boy has become part of the mother, and the mother is part of her son. From the boy's perspective, to separate completely from this most important person means to dismember or to cut off a part of himself. No wonder so many men today, even into their forties, still feel chained to their mothers.

Jean Shinoda Bolen, M.D., in her book *Gods in Everyman*, writes that "the stereotype of what a man is expected to be does violence to men's psyches. A man then becomes cut off from parts of himself that don't fit…. Men are expected to leave their mothers and renounce any sameness with them. Fathers are distant and withholding of themselves…. Psychological dismemberment results…."[14]

For our sons to weather this transitional period without becoming thus scarred, we parents must allow our sons to separate from Mother in a more gentle and natural way. A son's developmental task while crossing the bridge between Mother—or Woman—to Father—or Man—is to internalize his relationship to his mother. From the mother-bond, a boy develops the seeds for his emotional life, his world view, and his way of connecting with others. The seeds are planted in his heart by his mother, and he carries them with him as he crosses over into the world of his father. As his relationship with his mother matures, those seeds will sprout and flourish into the boy's ability to create satisfying relationships with others, to nurture himself and others, to feel and to express his emotions.

Father's Side of the Bridge

During transition a boy's biological force pushes him, and the psychological force leads him, but his father must come carry him across the bridge to the other side. Now the father is primary in the boy's psyche. His absence or presence powerfully influences a son's behavior. Whether their relationship is active or passive, the son soaks up from his father what it means to be a man. If the father is away at work most of the time, and remains detached from his family when he is home by leaving the care of his children to the mother, chances are that the son will one day relate similarly to his own family. If a father is abusive, alcoholic, or has deserted his family, statistics suggest that the son will follow his father's lead.[15] The following situations are common among fathers and sons:

> *I swore that I would never become like my father. He always tried to shove his ideas down my throat, and I opposed him at every opportunity. When I was eighteen, I left and formed my own ideas. The real quirk to this whole thing is that now I'm trying to cram my ideas into my son. The ideas have changed, but the behavior lives on.*
>
> *—Robert, a young father*

> *I spent my teenage years arguing with my father about his opinions, prejudices, and politics. From my left-wing radical position, his ideas seemed pretty outdated and conservative. Now I am employed in the*

state capital as an administrative assistant, and I find myself leaning to the moderate, conservative side of the hall. I remember when our relationship began to change. I got my first computer in college, and for the first time I was showing an interest in something that Dad loved. He came to my dorm room to help me set it up. We sat for hours fooling around with it, and we haven't stopped talking since. I had always sided with my mother against him, but now I better understand this man who has been such an enigma to me.

—Burt, a twenty-seven-year-old man

While the content of a son's life often varies from his father's, his patterns of behavior may parallel his father's. The fact that he has followed in his father's footsteps (or taken what only looks like an opposite direction) usually occurs to a man in his thirties. He looks in the mirror (or, perhaps, really listens to what his wife has been saying), and he finds that no matter how hard he has tried not to, he is becoming like his father in one way or another. There is a lesson here for fathers: making peace with your own father and accepting the truth about yourself will prepare you to encourage your son to cross over the bridge. Sensing this acceptance in you, your son will accept more easily his masculine lineage, and you, in turn, can welcome the eager attempts of your son to be just like you.

Boys have to be pulled into the responsibilities of the adult male world with compassion, firmness, and father-love. It is a frightening walk away from Mom. To a boy, Dad's world view and actions are attractive yet scary, comforting yet challenging. This side of the bridge holds a strange paradox: the boy's body is male—like Dad's—but he came from Mom's body, which is very different. From Dad the son learns not only about his male body, but about the masculine workings of his mind, soul, and spirit. He learns how to reach out and to make a difference in the world. Even silent contact with the father fills a waiting heart.

I had broken my leg, and after it healed I decided to go backpacking to prove to myself that I could still do it. I took my twelve-year-old son along as an afterthought.

I don't remember our saying one word the whole time.
For me it wasn't a trip that stood out for any reason.
My son is now twenty-seven, and he still talks about
that trip as one of the high points in his life.

Edmund, a fifty-year-old doctor

Single mothers and sons are in a bind during this transitional time. A mother can tell her son about his differences, his roles, and the growing forces within him, but because she is not a man, she cannot communicate the innate awareness of what it means to be male. Her body reaches out to her son in a different way than a father's would. If Dad isn't available, for whatever reason, Mom must find opportunities for her son to be with older men who can give him attention and show him how to use the powerful forces that urge him into manhood.

The Bridge to the World

Eventually, a boy must internalize his father's world, too. In our culture this process can begin at sixteen or seventeen and last until age twenty-eight or older. The son germinates the seeds of self-worth and self-understanding that time with his father planted within him. But one man is not enough to satisfy the drive of a boy's soul, so, with his father's help, he must cross over into the world at large. There he meets older men who help him further discover the many possibilities of his destiny as a man.

 DON | I spent just one day with such a man. His name was Carlye Marney; he was seventy years old and still at the top of the profession I sought. I asked him, "How can you stay at the top and be as honest and straightforward as you are?" He looked at me, blew smoke from his pipe, and growled, "Never get in a position where they got something you have to have." I have never forgotten.

It was my Uncle Bruno who saved me. My father and I were okay; I worked in his store, but I wasn't the business type. I loved to talk about things you couldn't see, like how things felt, or how my mind could imagine the strangest things. Uncle Bruno would listen to me for hours. Sometimes he would respond to my musings; most of the time, he would merely listen and nod his head occasionally. My father just did not understand anything that you couldn't put on a shelf. Uncle Bruno made it easier for me to work in the store. I always knew we could walk and talk when I needed it. It's that side of me that became a psychologist.

—*Thomas, a forty-five-year-old clinical psychologist*

The strength of a boy's alliances with male mentors greatly affects his transition into manhood. Vital to his maturity is the presence of other adult males. The stories he hears and the lives he observes will sink in deeply and become subconscious models for what he will seek to become. Many boys meet older men when in trouble—probation officers, counselors, and judges. In problematic relationships between fathers and sons, a male therapist can serve as the "extra" male. Other relationships develop more informally with bosses, older men down the block, male schoolteachers, coaches, uncles, and grandfathers. However these relationships are created, both Mother and Father become secondary, and the world becomes primary as the boy finds his way and purpose in it.

The Soul Force

Walk your path or be dragged.

—Paraphrase of Carl Jung

We often marvel at how a boy who experiences the worst of life—poverty, abuse, hardship—can grow up to give his life for the sake of others. And we wonder how a boy who has had the best of everything can turn and take the life of another. Is the cause his biology, his psychology, his parenting or schooling? We usually take the middle road: the answer is all of these influences. But there is another force in the making of a boy's life. In the end, biology, psychological development, and the influence of culture (which we will explore in chapter 3) are overshadowed by the profound, numinous power of the masculine soul.

Much of how we raise boys today focuses on shaping behavior. Certainly, we must mold our sons into civilized beings. After reviewing the powerful biological and psychological forces at work in our sons, we can understand why they need strong limits and love to help them develop to their fullest potential as life-givers and life-affirmers in today's world. But a key part of the boy has been lost in the modern shuffle—his soul. When the soul force is acknowledged, nurtured, and honored, it serves as the guiding power of the other three forces. Without this guidance, a man is like a "loose cannon"—under the influence of a power-hungry army with no general at its head.

Most of us are aware of a sense of self that seems beyond our upbringing and environmental influences. All religions and philosophies speak to this core, selfhood, or center. The language of the soul is best captured by the generations of philosophers and poets who have written about this elusive human essence. Fifteenth-century master poet Kabir said that "if you can't find where your soul is hidden, for you the world will never be real."[16] James Hillman, contemporary analytical psychologist and author, believes that modern people have become de-souled. He asserts that "the world and the Gods are dead or alive according to the condition of our souls."[17]

The soul manifests itself in our dreams, our hopes, and our despairs. It urges us to follow our own paths in life, but it never makes our decisions for us. For some reason, those choices are always ours to make. We can temporarily ignore the call of the soul, but its presence will haunt us in our dreams and daytime fantasies. We often feel its urgings most strongly when faced with "fork-in-the-road" decisions. In quiet moments we pray to God, the gods, or The Goddess, and then we follow our "gut feelings." Years later we look back, and it all makes sense. Like radar that homes in on the intended object, the soul force is with us, guiding us, without pushing, into the decisions we must make.

Those of us who saw the movie epic *Star Wars* will always remember the tense moment when Obi-wan Kenobi reminds Luke Skywalker, "Remember the Force, Luke. Follow the Force." Luke relaxes, stops trying so hard to will his craft through the dangerous maze, and allows his inner being, his "soul force," to take over. We have all experienced those times when we finally give up the struggle to solve a problem: an inner force in us takes over, and the solution falls neatly into place.

Our sons have this force. Like the tiny bit of salt that seasons a meal, the masculine soul is a powerful, unseen catalyst that flavors a boy's life to bring out his uniqueness.

While our sons are young, we parents are the caretakers of their souls. We can help instill a trust in the inner guidance system of feelings and intuitions, and in the voice that some call "soul," to assist our sons on a path in life that is life-giving, rather than life-taking, and life-affirming, rather than life-denying. To aid them in being true to themselves, we have the difficult task of helping our sons learn how to use feelings as guides to solutions, instead of seeing them as emotions to be denied and ignored. It is no simple task to be true to one's soul, as parents well know. Soul urgings are not always clear, and our children's here-and-then-gone-again floods of feelings make the signals hard to interpret. Like "hide and seek," messages from the soul usually flash at the strangest of moments.

> *I wanted to get that jerk for making me look like a fool in front of my girlfriend. I had the chance when I saw him cheating on the final exam. I wanted to rat on him and really set him up, but my stomach felt sick when I thought of turning him in. I let it go. I don't want to be the jerk I'm accusing him of being.*
>
> —*Philip, a sixteen-year-old-boy sorting out his ethics*

During the teenage years, the quest for soul fires up, as teens seek to find out who they are as whole individuals, and to explore the unique direction of their destinies. When boys reach their twenties, either they develop a clear vision of the soul's direction, or their forties will become the "land of depression." The mid-life years offer yet another opportunity to deepen into the call of the soul and to follow its urgings.

As parents, we can detect our son's special way of meeting life. The more we help him accept himself, the more chances he has of taking the risks needed to build his own life, and to put his positive stamp on the world around him.

The Soul and Its Positive Intent

Imagine for a moment this familiar situation: A therapist is asked to find the motivating factors behind a client's behavior. Together, client and therapist travel through the client's inner world strata of biological, psychological, and cultural influences. It is not until the soul level is reached that the deepest desires and urges are unearthed. Take as an example the mother who is genuinely moved to care for others; she can end up with a legion of people depending on her, exhausting her with their never-ending demands. They may begin to depend more on her than they do on themselves. If this is a problem for her, the solution is not that she reduce her caring. That would violate her soul's deepest urge; she would resist, and rightly so. The solution lies in helping her learn to care in a way that makes others stronger. This frees her to care more for herself. Going against the soul's desire is futile; working with it can bring astonishing results, as the following therapeutic story illustrates.

DON

Terry, eighteen, came to counseling because he was flunking his senior year of high school, despite the fact that all he had to do was to show up and complete the daily homework in class. His mother called him lazy, uncaring, and weak. She was an alcoholic in denial and refused to be part of Terry's counseling. I asked him, "How long have you held your family together?" His eyes widened in disbelief behind his long hair. "How did you know?" As the oldest of four children, he had been helping his younger siblings to deal with their alcoholic mother. He was flunking his senior year to get revenge on her. "Don't tell her what I am doing with my brothers and sisters. I hate her guts. I want to embarrass her." I said, "Your way of embarrassing her—flunking out of school—is hurting you more than her. How can you keep your cover and not jeopardize your own future?" He solved the problem by waiting until the last day of school to turn in an entire semester of homework; he then appeared at the graduation ceremonies without telling his mother. He said, "It was so great to see her eyes pop out when I walked across that stage. I'm not gonna waste my life because of her."

To many tribal peoples the world over, a son's unique soul urging had to be carefully identified by specified adults. This soulful dimension of the boy was praised, honored, and developed over time. If he was shy and fascinated by his inner world of thoughts, feelings, and dreams, he might be known as "He Who Looks Inward." Perhaps he was not the fiercest warrior, but when a fellow warrior was depressed or emotionally confused, he could go to "He Who Looks Inward" for help in sorting out his troubles. This second "name" brought forth a boy's dominant qualities in the most meaningful and positive light. His warrior shield carried a symbolic form of his second name—a tree, an eagle, a fox, or a mouse, for example.

The wisdom behind these customs still speaks to our needs as parents in this technological age. When the soul's urge has acknowledgment and room to grow, a boy's inner life and outer life are congruent, and he can be more at peace with himself and with the world.

DON | When I first met John, he was thirteen. I feared that his "second name" was "Boy Who Destroys All Adults' Sanity." He had a string of probation officers, counselors, teachers, and social workers a mile long behind him. After a long time of trust-building between us, I finally put it to him as clearly as I could. I called him "powerful." Then I told him, "You move mountains when you want to. Your only problem is that you keep moving them in your way instead of out of your way. That's why you end up in places like my therapy office with people like me, whom you hate being with. Are you interested in getting us out of your life?" This became our running joke: "What mountains have you moved in your way this week, and what mountains have you moved out of your way?" In time, John learned how to stay out of needless trouble and to create a life more of his choosing. He is still as cagey and crafty as ever. "He Who Moves Mountains" is now applying to law school. Pray you don't meet him in court!

Touching His Soul

Naming the qualities of a boy's soul touches him deeply. Not merely a "labeling," it is both a recognition and a blessing that moves his soul to develop and bloom. The word psychology can be defined as psyche, meaning "soul," and ology, meaning "movement of." This makes psychology's meaning and purpose more clear—the "movement of the soul." It is this movement that makes us feel alive, connected to others, and in touch with ourselves. This movement of the deeper self empowers us to tackle great challenges.

So often when boys are put down for their aggressiveness, inattentiveness, and unruliness, their souls get lost in the constant coping with their biological drives. It is amazing how spending time with a son, getting to know him, naming his deeper qualities, and taking his concerns seriously, calms him and gives him a sense of being real. Though he doesn't always want to hear us name his best qualities, deep down he wants to hear them a thousand times. Cooperation blooms if we give him meaningful opportunities to display his innermost drives and abilities. He feels a satisfaction that goes far beyond his biological need for instant gratification.

Sons are starving for adults to see in them what they feel but cannot quite name. It requires time, the ability to really look and listen, and trial and error, to name a son's soul qualities truly. The effort and attention required can bring the most persistent and patient of parents to their knees, but when we name them rightly, our sons will bloom. We will see how deeply they are touched—in a glance, a nod, or an expression of glee. We can all remember times when this happened to us. For a moment we felt seen, heard, and known. There is no better feeling. When we fathers and mothers side with our sons' souls and continue to parent their behaviors, they know they are loved in the deepest ways that anyone could love another—touching the soul.

Son: I want to be an artist.

Father: You can be an artist and more, if you like.

Son: I'll be an artist in the mornings, and a football player in the afternoons.

Father: You really want to do things that make you happy.

Son: Dad, do you do things that make you happy?

We cannot block the powerful forces of biology, psychology, culture, and soul. Nor would we want to stop them, because through them, boys and men feel most alive and inspired. These masculine forces fuel the stories of older men when they tell about a time when life was worth living. Author Carl Sherman in his article, "Raging Hormones," writes that the complexities of a man—his hormones, experience, background, intelligence, and opportunities—all determine whether he ends up in the Statehouse or in a jailhouse. "On one block testosterone power might express itself in drug wars; across town, in leveraged buyouts.... It's what you do with it that counts. And what you do with it is up to you...."[18]

Every known culture, except our modern one, has been aware of the influence of the four forces—biological, psychological, spiritual, and cultural (whose story we tell in the next chapter). Ancient peoples wisely anticipated the first show of testosterone's power. When the boys became unruly, hard to handle, aggressive, and difficult, community members knew the time was ripe. It was time to make a boy into a man.

End Notes

1. George Gilder, *Men and Marriage* (Gretna, La.: Pelican, 1986), 25.

2. Michael Hutchison, *The Anatomy of Sex and Power* (New York: William Morrow and Co., 1990), 170.

3. Roger Gorski, interview by Douglas Stein, Omni, Oct. 1990, 72.

4. Susan Davis, "Ruled By Hormones?" San Francisco Chronicle Examiner, Sunday, 28 Oct. 1990, sec. D.

5. Ibid.

6. Gilder, *Men and Marriage*, 25.

7. Hutchison, *Sex and Power*, 202.

8. Carl Sherman, "Raging Hormones," San Francisco Chronicle Examiner, This World, Sunday, 19 Nov. 1989, 9.

9. Daniel Goleman, "It's Hormones That Make Men Rage," San Francisco Chronicle, 19 July 1990, sec. B.

10. Max Gates, "Coming of Age a Health Hazard to U.S. Males," San Francisco

Chronicle Examiner, Sunday, 6 Aug. 1989, sec. A-3.

11. Hutchison, *Sex and Power*, 200.

12. Deborah Tannen, *You Just Don't Understand* (New York: William Morrow and Co., 1990), 38.

13. Hutchison, *Sex and Power*, 207-9.

14. Jean Shinoda Bolen, M.D., *Gods in Everyman* (San Francisco: Harper & Row, 1989), 281.

15. Edmond G. Addeo and Jovita Reichling Addeo, *Why Our Children Drink* (Englewood Cliffs, N.J.: Prentice-Hall, 1975), 72-95.

16. Robert Bly, ed. and trans., *The Kabir Book* (Boston: Beacon Press, 1971), 9.

17. James Hillman, *Re-Visioning Psychology* (New York: Harper & Row, 1975), 16.

18. Sherman, "Raging Hormones," 9.

CHAPTER THREE

Men Are Made, Not Born

A man's body is full of undefined energies...
and all these energies need the guidance of culture.
He is therefore deeply dependent on the structure
of society to define his role.[1]

—George Gilder, Men and Marriage

In the days of Theseus of Athens, in Greece,
there were evil-doers and marauders who
oppressed the country by attacking travelers as
they journeyed on the road to Athens. One of these
tyrants was called Procrustes, or the Stretcher.
"He had an iron bedstead, on which he used to
tie all travelers who fell into his hands.
If they were shorter than the bed, he stretched
their limbs to make them fit it; if they were
longer than the bed, he lopped off a portion."[2]

—Thomas Bulfinch, The Age of Fable

Noted anthropologist Margaret Mead observed that the problem any society faces is what to do with the men.[3] All known cultures, except our modern one, marked elaborately the transition of boyhood to manhood. Ancient people knew that the powerful, life-giving male forces must be shaped and channeled, to guarantee the security of the culture and its future survival. They knew that men are made, not born.

Author-poet Robert Bly says, "The young boy cannot grow up to be a male without models to demonstrate the tremendous generosity, the spirit, the willingness to sacrifice for the community that the word male implies in the positive sense."[4] Throughout our cultural history, men have made tremendous sacrifices for the good of their communities. They have been required to conform to Procrustes' bed, as in the previous story, by stretching to fit the cultural need or by being cut down to size. This process has not always been easy for men. In *Gods in Everyman*, Jean Shinoda Bolen, M.D., writes that conforming to society's needs can be "an agonizing process for a man" whose soul calls him to be something different from "what he should be." She continues, "He may appear to fit, but in truth he has managed at great cost to look the part, by cutting off important aspects of himself."[5]

The sacrifices required of men are told in ancient stories that began with the first humans. We parents became important players in this history the moment our sons were conceived. We can trace these dramatic sacrifices in broad, sweeping stages through each chapter of cultural history—the hunting tribes, the agricultural groups, the Industrial Revolution, and today's technological age. To prepare for our modern-day parenting roles in the ongoing story of culture and sons, a historical perspective will help us understand more fully the awesome, ancestral heritage that boys carry, and mothers and fathers inherit. Knowing where we have been as a people will help us chart a future course. It is culture that shapes the male force: the force that has always driven parents crazy.

The Hunting Tribes

A boy is born, and the tribe rejoices. The infant spends his first months wrapped snugly on his mother's body. He has no sense of where he ends and she begins. Mother is his universe. He rides on her back as she works; he sleeps with her; he learns to mimic her daily household tasks; he plays at her feet. He will remain unnamed until the tribe understands his nature, but his mother calls him Solee.

As Solee grows, he explores the boundaries between himself and his mother, and his world expands to perhaps twenty feet from her. He develops relationships with others in the tribe, especially the one called "Father." Father has been nearby since his son's birth and takes an active interest in his development. Although he is involved in tribal business and is often gone on the hunt, he spends as much time as he can with his small son. Under the eyes of his parents Solee grows strong, plays with his friends, and turns mischievous. Soon he grows taller than his mother, and his tricks on friends and adults are more risky and dangerous. He is becoming a problem.

Then one day, there is a different air of activity among the women of the tribe. All day they labor to make new shelters. They work long and hard, uninterrupted because the men are away on a hunt. The children are shooed from underfoot, and the older boys are put to work. That night all go to bed early, exhausted. In the middle of the night, strange shouts and frenzied chants awaken the sleepers. They can see torches lighting the sky, winding their way down the mountain toward the village, borne by wild-looking men. The women and children defend themselves with rocks and spears, but it is useless. The crazy men in masks dripping blood go into each home and take all of the boys who are nine to twelve years old. "Don't take my baby!" the mothers scream, to no avail. The boys, Solee among them, are gone.

They are taken into the hills to a cave where a fierce fire burns. The sounds of drums fill the night and shake the ground. The boys are placed in a circle around the fire. The wild men in the crazy masks dance to the drums. All at once, some mysterious force quiets the drums, and each dancer takes his place in front of one of the boys. Solee is terrified. Knives are pulled. Solee screams with the other boys in panic. Suddenly the masks are removed and the boys scream again, this time in astonishment—"Father!"—as each sees his father's face emerge from behind the monstrous mask.

"Father, why did you do this? Mother's really upset back there. She could have killed you!" The father responds, "Son, I had to steal you away. She is not your real mother." "What do you mean, *not my mother?* Are you drunk or something? Enough of this. Let's go home," says the incredulous Solee. The father replies, "Don't get me wrong. She is a very good woman, but I will introduce you to your true mother in one year."

The boy, who really has no choice in the matter, resigns himself to living for a year with his father and the elders of the tribe, to be counseled about life and what it means to be a man. His strengths and weaknesses are determined, and he receives a new name that reflects his calling in life, Selu, The Wind Runner. He crafts a shield that symbolizes his unique skills and contributions to his tribe. His skin is scored and permanently dyed to indicate that he has become a man. He is carefully taught how to hunt, to fish, to fight, and to love. He learns to seek guidance from the stories of his ancestors and to honor the life-affirming forces that protect him and his tribe.

One day about halfway along, Selu and his father are making arrowheads, and his father says, "Oh, son. There's one more thing I forgot to tell you. I am not your true father." "What? You are not my father? Who are you?" The father replies, "Don't worry. I am a good man, and in a few months, I will introduce you to your true father and your true mother." Again, the boy has no choice but to continue. By now his body has filled out; his muscles are shaped; his skills are more refined. He has passed many of the tests required to be a man in the world of his tribe.

One night the boys are told that the next day they will meet their true mother and true father. They go to sleep anxious and excited. Before the sun rises, the eldest male of the tribe is assisted by the other men to the mountaintop. The boys are roused and told to follow. In this ancient culture the young were protected because they were the hope for the future, and the old were honored because they held the life wisdom from the past. And so it is an elder who says to the boys with the rising of the sun: "It is time to meet your true mother and your true father. Feel the earth beneath you. See the sky and sun above you. These are your true parents. Love them and learn their ways, and they will always support you and guide you. Now go to the village and take your places as warriors and hunters. And from this day, depend only upon your true parents."

A cheer rises as camp is broken, and the boys-made-men go down the mountain to their village. Selu sees his mother by the river. His first thought is, Oh no. She's gonna be mad! She hated me to get dirty, and now look at my skin. He gazes at the permanent stripe of color that marks him a man. When Selu's mother sees her son, she moans hysterically, "My son is dead. My son is dead!" Now the boy thinks, Even my mother doesn't know me. I am no longer her son. I am a man. He takes his place in the tribe and continues to learn while he hunts for, protects, and gives life to his community. Eventually he takes a wife and has children of his own. When his son reaches that difficult age, Selu the father pulls out a mask and heads for the hills in preparation for the making of a man.

—Composite story of a native male initiation

Parenting in the earliest known cultures was shaped by the rituals of The Hunt—the key activity that kept the tribe alive. The people lived from one hunt to the next, sometimes barely surviving between them. Their world was a hostile one, which required that each person fulfill a specific role to ensure that there would be enough food for the tribe's needs.

Masculine roles were very clear in this ancient society. A man's aggressiveness, need to lead, and drive to dominate naturally made him fit as a hunter, decision-maker, and spiritual leader. His urge to wander was satisfied through stalking the herds that fed his tribe. His soul was nurtured by living close to nature and by honoring all of life, especially the spirits of the animals, whom he believed were willing to sacrifice themselves for the survival of his people. His powerful biological force was prized. It assured him a secure and meaningful place in his tribe, and it ensured the continuation of life.

In the above story, the tribe rejoiced when Solee's power and aggressiveness began to push him to be unruly, annoying, and mischievous. The community was patient for they knew that soon he would be initiated into the role of a man: to shoulder the responsibilities of protecting and providing for the good of the whole. The aggressive drives that could have caused Solee and his village much trouble became, properly channeled, his greatest assets. This transition into adult life was abrupt. Solee was literally stolen from his mother to emphasize that he now belonged to another world, the world of men. To acknowledge that he would live in this world for the rest of his life, he was given an adult name and physically marked, changed forever.[6]

If we stop to think about it, the earthquake-like upheaval of living with a teenage boy is similar to the disruptive nature of other cultures' initiation rites. The difference for us today is that we are usually unnerved and controlled by the tremors, rather than being the orchestrators of an accepted, natural, time-honored series of events whose purpose is to help a boy grow into a life-giving, life-protecting man.

The Agricultural Groups

A boy is born, and his parents are happy. He grows fat and contented, snuggled close to his mother's body. She calls him Phormion, and totally envelopes him in her warm, nurturing world. He sleeps on his mother's back as she works in the fields, his chubby cheeks browned by the warm sun. Here in the fields he learns to toddle between the rows, carefully stepping over the tender shoots of new corn. He plays in the dirt, and mimics his mother's chores.

As Phormion grows older, his mother often takes him to the site of the new palace. Here he spends hours watching his father apply bright hues that transform the gray walls into scenes so alive that he thinks he could walk right into one. His favorites are the depictions of the bull dancers, their light, graceful forms in contrast with the dark, powerful fury of the bull. As a fresco painter his father is respected by everyone in the city. He is much in demand, but still finds time to teach his young son how to hold the brush and carefully mix the blues to match the color of the sea.

Gradually, Phormion spends more and more time with Father at his work and less time with his mother in the fields. He has a natural skill with the brush, and tries very hard to please his father.

It is expected that one day he become a fresco painter, too. His training progresses well for several years, and Phormion is content to practice the strokes that bring the activities of his city to life. Then, he begins to feel a restlessness, a yearning for something he cannot name but that haunts his dreams. His father's presence as they work for hours side by side is comforting, but Phormion also senses a discontent within his father, which he had been too young to notice before. He finds his father staring for long moments at the sea, or pacing back and forth before an unfinished fresco, unable to get the colors right. Father spends more time at his lodge in the company of men.

Phormion's own torment stems from his obsession with the bull dancers, those young men and women who challenge death with graceful and daring leaps over a charging bull. He longs for their life of fame, danger, and friendship, for the adoration of the crowds, a place of honor in the city. He acknowledges that Father is esteemed for his skill, but Phormion yearns for the excitement and glamour of the acrobats. He also knows that Mother would never consent to such a life. He is torn between duty to his parents and the path that his male force urges him to follow.

Then one day Phormion disappears. His mother grieves silently, gravely tending the fields. His father spends less time painting and more time walking the beaches, staring for long moments at the ever-changing sea. A year passes, and Phormion's parents attend the ceremonies marking the arrival of spring. The birth of a new year fails to bring the joy that it held for them in the past—until they see Phormion among the bull dancers. Both jump to their feet with the crowd, their cheers ringing out for their son. They hold their breath while he stands facing the charging bull. At the last second Phormion makes a perfectly timed leap to the giant's back. His parents breathe a sigh of relief. He is safe, this time.

—Composite account from the
Great Minoan Culture of Crete, Greece

The shift in civilization from hunting to agriculture initiated profound changes in the definition of male roles. Riane Eisler, in her book *The Chalice and the Blade*, writes, "The agricultural revolution was the single most important breakthrough in the material technology of our species."[7] It required that men sacrifice their natural hunting instincts in order to feed their people. Aggressiveness, the need to dominate, and a drive to stalk and pounce were no longer useful to the survival of societal life. Instead, patience, diligence, plus a careful respect for the slow cycling of the seasons and the powerful forces of nature were required for the culture to prosper. The short-term energies of The Hunt had to be transformed to meet the longer-term requirements of The Fields.

The pulse of life slowed considerably as food became plentiful and the need to follow the herds disappeared. Population increased, and tribal life gave way to city life. Man's impulse to wander became harnessed to a plow. People lived closer together, necessitating that men be more "civilized" toward one another. A man could no longer spend as much time alone in nature to replenish his soul and to match wits with an elusive prey. Time once spent tracking, stalking, and killing was now filled with farming, tending domesticated animals, trade, and such technological endeavors as the crafts of basket making, textile weaving, jewelry making, and woodworking. This change in lifestyle brought a new stability to the world, but from men it required a psychological "lopping off": the powerful, masculine, biological force was no longer a prized asset that assured a man a secure and meaningful role in life.

Simply laying claim to new masculine roles wasn't even an option. Both men and women were capable of working in the fields or perfecting the skills of craftsmanship or trade. Margaret Mead postulated that a new anxiety emerged in men as their roles became less defined and less distinct from women's roles.[8] Aggression, which was previously channeled into The Hunt, now needed a meaningful, new outlet. According to Yale anthropologist David Pilbeam, boys and men are most secure in their life roles when those roles are a refined and constructive extension of the natural, biological, masculine force. A healthy male sexual identity has to involve an affirmative societal role that is a positive outgrowth of a boy's biological drive.[9]

There is evidence to show that the male forces were constructively channeled into astounding technological feats, such as the viaducts, paved roads, and complex palaces with indoor plumbing of Phormion's culture, the Minoans of Crete; and into the advanced understanding of engineering, mathematics, and astronomy, demonstrated by the construction of Stonehenge in England. Although this meant a shift from the natural tendencies of men, it seems that during this developmental phase of culture, masculine energies were used to make life more pleasurable rather than to dominate and destroy. And this was accomplished in partnership with nature.[10]

Not all men welcomed the sacrifice of The Hunt with its rituals and preparations. One African tribe, which had relied on the once-plentiful herds of giraffe for food, successfully changed from hunting to agriculture. The older men of the tribe continued to hunt the few remaining giraffes, even though the meat often went to waste.[11] The men must have felt a tremendous anxiety that they were no longer needed—nor esteemed—in the way they once were. Boys no longer had the unique hunting initiation rituals to teach them their productive roles in life and to provide an outlet for their biological drives. As a result, men developed elaborate, often secret, societies and lodges, where they could be with one another in the woods and pass on the male legacy to their sons. The abrupt events that had transported earlier generations of young boys into the male world gave way to a more gradual transition.

The Industrial Revolution

A boy is born, and his parents, grandparents, aunts, and uncles are proud and happy. They name him Frankie, Jr. He spends his first months in the blissful comfort of his mother's arms, nursed and rocked whenever he cries. Then Mother waits a little before she answers his demands. He is encouraged to try things on his own, to reach the toy by himself, to get up and brush himself off when he falls. He is fascinated by the world and by all it has to offer him. When he feels shy, he can hide behind his mother's skirts, but soon she will push him out to discover that there's nothing there to scare him. Frankie's father works as a salesman for a large manufacturing company and travels away from home during the week. When he returns he always brings Frankie a bat or ball, cars or trucks, but never dolls or other "girl toys." Frankie learns to be tough but obedient and polite. He is his parents' "little man."

Frankie adores his father and tries to please him by excelling in sports. He is especially good at baseball, but his father can't come to many of his Little League games because of his work. They do attend big-league games together twice a year, and his dad occasionally plays catch with him on Saturday mornings, but that doesn't satisfy Frankie's need for male companionship. He begins to hang around the local baseball field where teenage boys play. Their dress, haircuts, language, and playing style fascinate him, and they often invite him to join in their practices. Emulating his new friends, Frankie lets his hair grow long. He practices his ballplaying skills tirelessly, often long after the bigger boys have gone home—a lone figure batting and throwing against the high wooden fence at the back of the playing field.

Frankie's mother complains that he is always gone and doesn't do his chores. His father criticizes his wild hair and sloppy clothes. He also demands that Frankie stay home more with his mother while he is gone during the week, and that he do better at his chores. Frankie withdraws even more from home and family life, spending as much time as he can with his friends. When he is at home, he stays locked in his room.

*—Composite profile of boyhood in urban America
after the Industrial Revolution*

In the hunting and agricultural societies, both mothers and fathers made sure that sons spent long periods of time with their fathers and the elder men of the community. Boys received their first lessons in love, nurturing, and security from their mothers and then learned about themselves, nature, and life from the world of men.

The coming of the machine severely interrupted this parenting partnership. Fathers were permanently absent from the home every day to work in factories, offices, or shops. Boys could no longer work by their fathers' sides to learn a trade or perfect their hunting prowess. Dramatic initiation rites that had once assured an honorable place within the community had completely disappeared. A son now proved himself by getting a good job—usually without the guidance, training, or trials that earlier had served sons by developing strength, honing instincts, and instilling a sense of self-worth.

"Pulling yourself up by your bootstraps" and "rugged individualism" became the creeds of the day. The importance of the tribe now fallen away, people grew isolated from one another. Men stopped talking to other men about the meaning of life and their place in the scheme of things. They stopped meeting in the woods to pass down the wisdom that had long ensured the survival of their people. Men relied more on women to carry the emotions for the family, while they carried the weight of the machine age. They became fascinated and entrapped by their machines. In alcohol and other drugs, men found solace for their souls. The future hope, once held by the son, became secondary to keeping up with the moment in the face of rapid modern change. Change became the new doctrine, youth was worshiped, the wisdom of age was proclaimed outdated, and living for the fleeting moment came to be the standard.

Aggression, dominance, and hunting behaviors were clearly problematic in the home and the workplace. Repetitive work, consistency, initiative, and love and responsibility for a wife and children were now primary for the survival and future of the industrial culture. The masculine force was directed toward building "bigger and better" enterprises; man's powerful sexual drive had to be channeled into stable relationship and work patterns. The industrial culture needed businessmen, factory workers, stable providers, and consumers. Men became lost in the cogs of a giant machine, one which they seldom owned. The sacrifices required by the Industrial Revolution put many men in the bind of no longer being able to meet their requirements for physical, psychological, and spiritual health. Men began to die younger, heart disease and cancer increased, suicide rates multiplied, alcoholism was more prominent, and rates of violent crime soared.[12]

No longer did sons naturally follow their fathers into the adult male world. They became estranged. The "generation gap" developed, in part, because once sons could no longer readily talk to fathers, they had to search for themselves to find a meaning and purpose in life. As a result, boys developed elaborate styles, fads, and rituals, including gangs, long hair, distinctive clothes, and rock and roll. They created their own subculture. Parents were not welcome in this teenage world. In effect, boys sought initiation through their own peer groups. But some boys just couldn't make it, and without the influence of culture to shape their male forces, and without fathers to lead them over the bridge to manhood, many boys became lost, misfits, and threats to society.

The feminist movement in the late 1960s further complicated the picture for men. Hard-won political advances were crucial for the development of women, but a misunderstanding over equality and opportunity left many women, as well as men, wounded, confused, and angry. The struggles of the women's movement during those early years certainly began to expand and deepen opportunities for both men and women. But now, a ghost overshadows the continued movement toward equality. The specter from the sixties and seventies that has followed us into the nineties is the idea of "sameness," that there are basically no differences between men and women. Gender has become "unisex." We focus on being "people," not on being male or female. We have come a long way from the rigid and constricting gender roles that prevailed before the fifties; men and women are now seen to be equally capable of creating successful careers in all work arenas— political, corporate, medical, educational, scientific—and deserving of equal pay and equal opportunities for advancement. But as we have seen, there are basic differences in our biologies that create marked gender differences.

The breakdown of gender roles has left men more confused than ever. Men have been encouraged to rediscover their emotional and nurturing selves, which the Industrial Revolution required them to sacrifice; more fathers now take part in the birth and care of their children and may even choose to work at home. Many men have taken to heart the feminist messages about being more emotionally available, but sometimes at the cost of sacrificing their "oomph"—what Robert Bly in his bestseller, *Iron John*, calls the "wild man"—the drive to create a meaningful career and to be involved in one's community in life-giving and life-affirming ways.

When one of Don's clients entered counseling—we'll call him Jim, aged thirty-three—he was very depressed. His wife was threatening to leave him, and he was out of work. "She said she wanted me to be more sensitive, less aggressive, more thoughtful, and not so forceful. So for two years, I have been trying to be the man she wants me to be." When asked about his male friends, he said, "I gradually quit talking to them, to the point that now I only have my wife and daughter. I also stopped pushing so hard at work, and they fired me. When my wife told me that I wasn't being aggressive enough in looking for another job, I blew up. What the hell does she want, anyway? She said, 'Don't be aggressive.' Now I'm not, and she's still angry with me. I can't please her."

To Jim, being a sensitive man meant becoming more like his wife. Cut off from his male friends, he became disconnected from his own maleness. His buddies weren't ones for deep conversation, but they provided an anchor for him to relax into his masculine self. He soon understood how important such friendships could be in helping him be effective in his marriage.

In truth, Jim's wife liked his forcefulness, but not when it was directed at her. As Jim became more accepting of his powerful drives, he was able to channel them into activities for the benefit of his family, rather than use them as weapons against his wife. His "oomph" for his work returned, and he later said, "It's embarrassing, but I was trying to be sensitive and emotional the way a woman is. I felt guilty about being strong and forceful, but feeling hurt at the same time. My father was such a dry, rigid man. He never showed his feelings. Emotionally, I know I don't ever want to be like him."

Like Jim, most sons still lack the role model of a whole father—emotionally available and self-confident, strong and gentle, aggressive and life-affirming. Many boys are without fathers at all, as evidenced by the skyrocketing incidence of divorce and single parenting.[13] Moreover, welfare laws make it more economical to raise a family without a father in the household.[14] Even when present, fathers, for the most part, are still on the fringes. And men still channel the masculine force into war, crime, and pollution. We are on the brink—financially, ecologically, and socially.

The Technological Age

A son is born, and his parents have mixed emotions. On the one hand, they are thrilled by the birth of a healthy second child, a son. But the mother wonders how this pregnancy will affect her figure, and the financial drain caused by her leave of absence from a stimulating career is stressful for the whole family. She decides not to nurse the baby, so that she can easily return to work in three months.

Josh is a fretful baby who requires constant holding. His mother is alarmed over how much attention he needs, considering how mellow and easy her daughter Jill had been. Although she tries to comfort Josh, nothing seems to make him stop crying. Frustrated, she longs for the day when she can return to work. She spends the three months frantically seeking child-care for Jill (two years, five months old) and the new baby. Her former sitter will not take two children, and Josh's mother wants someone who will come to their home. This would be easier than having to drop the children off at a center so early in the morning before work, and she is concerned that her children get consistent and loving attention while she is on the job.

Josh's father was present at his birth and feels a strong connection to his son. He would like to help his wife more with Josh's care, but he gets home from work after Josh is asleep. His main time with Josh is during the night, when he gives him a bottle and walks the floor for hours to quiet him and to give his wife a break. Each morning he arrives at the office exhausted from the night and from constant worry over how he is going to make ends meet financially for his family.

Josh's mother is unable to find a sitter, so Josh and his sister are left at 7:00 each morning at a day-care center near their home. Josh continues to be colicky and awake much of the time. One care-giver at the center can quiet him, but she is there only a short time. He develops into an uneasy toddler, reserved and shy at the day-care center, demanding and clinging at home. As he grows older, Josh becomes more aggressive at the center and often has trouble playing cooperatively with the other children. Most happy at a solitary activity, such as building with blocks, he is quite adept at creating large, elaborate structures. At home, Josh continues to demand inordinate attention from his parents, and resists doing anything for himself.

When Josh is six, his parents are divorced, with joint custody of their children. Josh and his sister are with each parent for half of every week. Both parents hire live-in people to care for Josh and Jill, so they can continue their hectic work schedules and have some free time to themselves. Outwardly, Josh appears unaffected by these changes. He continues to be aggressive in school and uses jokes and clowning behavior to get attention from his teachers and friends. Disliking the structure and discipline that school demands of him, he waits for Saturdays, when he and his dad spend the day playing football, swimming, or building a project together. Although he seems to prefer to be with his father, Josh is often moody and uncooperative at his dad's house. His father knows he needs to set tighter limits for his son. But because they have such little time together, he hates to be tough with Josh; he thinks this would just cause more problems.

At his mother's house, Josh generally refuses to respond to any request or to take part in any family activities. His mother fears that Josh blames her for the divorce, and that he will use drugs or get into trouble to get back at her. Josh does experiment early with alcohol and other drugs, and gets in deeper and deeper trouble as a teenager. He shows little interest in school, except for his computer and drafting classes, where he excels. He becomes estranged from both parents and spends little time at either home. When he is with his mother, he is belligerent and verbally abusive. Then Josh and some of his friends are arrested for buying and selling grass, and the judge orders that Josh enter counseling.

—Composite sketch of a contemporary American boyhood

...The bombardment of Baghdad seemed like a kind of
video game, at once impersonal and fantastic...[15]

—from an article about the
1990-91 Mideast Gulf War

Jeffrey Zaun, a U.S. prisoner of war who was the bombardier on a fighter jet downed in Iraq during the Gulf War, says that he does not want to kill anymore. He speaks of how he saw mothers and children die after he was grounded in Iraq; his buddies, who returned unharmed, only saw blips on a screen or the flash of a direct hit.16 In many ways, technology puts our lives on screens, a step removed from the human soul—and from the flesh-and-blood issues that are sometimes the casualties of our technological wonders. From warfare to computerized financial transactions and modern medical practices, today's technology makes the inventions of the Industrial Revolution seem clunky and antiquated. We have created an awesome array of power—not only in weapons of destruction, but in household conveniences as well—and we have just begun.

Throughout history, each new leap in technology required that something be sacrificed. Men in the hunting cultures were forced to sacrifice their freedom, and, with the coming of the agrarian age, their partnership with nature as well. Sons lost their connections to fathers as the invention of machines took fathers to workplaces away from home. And today, as never before, our technology distances us from our feelings and our human experiences.

DON | Before our son was born, we had planned a home birth. After thirty hours of labor, and no baby to show for it, we moved to the hospital. At home I had breathed with Jeanne, tended to her needs, and counted every moan, groan, and bead of sweat. At the hospital, a fetal heart monitor was required to ensure that our son was doing fine. His heartbeat pulsed regularly on a screen beside my wife's bed. As if pulled by a magnet, everyone on our birthing team was drawn to the screen, watching the machine's every blip. My wife, still in the throes of labor, was completely ignored. When I realized what had happened, I directed my attention back to my wife, and yet I

> still found myself drawn to the monitor. It was a miracle machine; I knew it could help save my son's life. But I felt pulled away from the human experience of birth—the pain, the joy, and the meaning. I felt pulled away from my life.

Anyone who has recently attended a major-league baseball game has experienced another example of how technology takes us away from our human experiences. We often go to see the Oakland A's play, and are intrigued by the huge TV screen over center field. Most stadiums use these screens throughout the game to show replays, to advertise, and to give players' statistics and other interesting and entertaining data. We have noticed that on many plays, most fans watch the screen for the replay or statistic and ignore what is happening on the field. We, too, feel drawn away from home plate to the big screen over center field. Not only can we watch life go by, but we can see an immediate replay of it!

The ambivalence we parents often feel about raising children in this age of technological "progress" stems from our blaming the technology. We are legitimately concerned that at ever-decreasing ages, our sons are lured into passively watching the action of the TV screen, video arcades, and computer games. But our awesome technological creations are not the problem. The issue is whether we are willing or unwilling to be engaged in our lives and in the lives of others. Men, especially, must be committed to their own lives, or they try to take life from others. To be life-givers, men must directly experience their own source of aliveness. And fathers in the technological age must challenge their sons back into the real life of throwing the football on a Sunday afternoon, making and flying a kite together, or whatever it is that they both truly love doing.

Popular author and lecturer John Bradshaw describes addiction as something that takes the place of legitimate feeling.[17] The dawning of the technological age brings more and more addictive patterns, as we zoom away from our soulful feelings—joy, pain, grief, anger—to seek the quick fix of alcohol, other drugs, food, weekend affairs, and any activity that distracts us from our conscious lives. The stress of growing up in the technological age has driven many of our sons to become early addicts. Even as grade-schoolers, they experiment with drugs and alcohol to cope with the scholastic and psychological pressures of living in the tenuous, fast-paced world of technology.

That scoundrel, Procrustes, is at work again in the modern age. The technological man has chosen to cut off his relationship with his soul in the interest of making ever more sophisticated and intricate machines; in doing so he becomes detached from nature and thus his physical, emotional, mental, and spiritual connections to the natural world.

When a man is forced to fit the Procrustean bed of technological culture, he often becomes dry, angry, and depressed. Because he is cut off from his emotions, he may not realize for a time that he lacks a *joie de vivre*—a delight in being alive. And as the saying goes, like father, like son.

   DON | The following client case history illustrates this point. I first met John, a stockbroker, six months after his divorce. He said he was depressed and wanted to get over it quickly. John was a very ethical and fair person, and his hard-pushing, honest style had taken him to the top of his career. Sensitive to the needs of his employees, he often listened to their personal problems. The divorce had hurt John badly. Yet when he himself was faced with normal, human feelings of grief and loss, he ignored them and became more depressed. The harder he pushed himself, the more despondent he became. He could not allow himself the same compassion and understanding that he gave to his workers. Being a take-charge kind of guy, he tried to delegate his depression to me, his therapist. I told him, "John, you can effectively delegate many things to others in your work life, but you must deal with your loss and grief yourself."

The interesting thing about John's situation is that he learned to ignore his deep feelings from his father's example. John's father, Alfred, had made the Army his lifetime career and had run his family with a hard-line military discipline—always follow the rules, keep a stiff upper lip, and act like a man. To Alfred, "acting like a man" meant that under no circumstances could he let his emotions show. Even when John's mother died, Alfred expected that life would go on as usual. John, at seventeen, was crushed by his loss, and he knew that his father missed his mother deeply. "If only we could have wept together," he says, "I could have experienced my real feelings and worked them through. Instead, Dad went on as though nothing had happened. I knew that he expected me to do the same, because it had always been that way, so I threw myself into basketball and became the star center. I got a girlfriend too, then got married and had my own sons. That was all great, but a part of me felt dead, just like Mom."

The man caught in the technological age follows orders and pushes ahead to reach goals without consulting his inner guidance system, his soul. Like John in the previous story, his Procrustean wound is in his soul. He has had to sacrifice his emotions and concern for others in order to press onward for the sake of progress and economic survival.

A modern Procrustean wound is painful and crushing, but at the same time it offers an opportunity for healing. It is actually an opening to the masculine soul. When John stopped delegating his masculine feelings to his wife and his therapist, he began the inward journey in search of his male, emotional connection to life—his soul. There a man finds not only a way out of his depression, but the way into his life.

Many of us thought that technology would lessen our workload and give us more leisure time to be with our families. We were wrong. If we continue at this pace, families will be a casualty of the technological age. During the Industrial Revolution, sons lost their fathers to the factories. Today, sons are losing their mothers, too. Career opportunities for women and economic pressures have taken mothers out of the home at an alarming rate. Third-party child-care providers, who used to be called "grandparents," "aunts," and "uncles," are now the primary care-givers for our sons. We have used technology to make our lives easier, but at what price to our sons? And at what price to ourselves? Work environments and day-care centers are becoming family substitutes.

But there is no turning back. We are too attached to our conveniences, and technology benefits our lives in so many ways. It is not possible to turn back the clock to the hunting or agricultural periods.

Even the industrial age is far behind us. Like it or not, as the many generations of parents before us dealt with the problems of their times, we must meet the challenge of today: How do we as a modern, soulless culture give life to the sons of this technological age?

End Notes

1. Gilder, *Men and Marriage*, 10.

2. Thomas Bulfinch, *The Age of Fable* (New York: New American Library, 1962), 189.

3. Gilder, *Men and Marriage*, 29.

4. Steve Chapple and David Talbot, *Burning Desires: Sex in America* (New York: Doubleday, 1989), 199.

5. Bolen, *Gods in Everyman*, 4.

6. Michael Mayer, *The Mystery of Personal Identity* (San Diego, Calif.: ACS Publications, 1984), 2-7.

7. Riane Eisler, *The Chalice and the Blade* (San Francisco: Harper & Row, 1987), 10.

8. Gilder, *Men and Marriage*, 32.

9. Ibid., 33-34.

10. Eisler, *Chalice and the Blade*, 32.

11. Gilder, *Men and Marriage*, 31.

12. Shepherd Bliss, interview by Kenneth Guentert, *Special Delivery Newsletter of Informed Homebirth/Informed Birth & Parenting*, Spring 1988.

13. Ronald Kotulak, "Survey Links Youth Problems to One-parent Families," *San Francisco Examiner Chronicle*, Sunday, 9 Dec. 1990, sec. A-5.

14. Gilder, *Men and Marriage*, 87-95.

15. Russell Watson and Gregg Easterbrook, "A New Kind of Warfare," *Newsweek*, 28 Jan. 1991, 15.

16. *San Francisco Chronicle*, "Former POW Doesn't Want to Kill Again," 10 June 1991, sec. A-10.

17. John Bradshaw, *Bradshaw On The Family* (Deerfield Beach, Fla.: Health Communications, 1988), 6.

CHAPTER FOUR

How to Successfully Grow a Boy: The Cultural Force

Dad said, "Take some time, son, hear your child.
Help him find his way.
Quickly open your heart,
And hold him tight.
Next thing you know
Someone will take him away."
—Don Elium, from lyrics,
Working Man album, Unpublished Work © 1992

❦ ❦ *DON* | When our son first came into the world, I was there. After our midwife lifted him up, he crawled up my wife's belly to nurse. I will never forget looking into the eyes of Life itself. My wife and I were giving life to another person! Immediately, I had two of the strongest, most opposite feelings I have ever known: "He's alive" and "Oh, no! He could die." For the first time I experienced life as both soul-stirring and extremely fragile. I was responsible for a life that was not my own. Every birth moment carries the paradox that all parents live with forever: the joy of life and the fear of death. Recently, my father told me that he still worries about my safety—not just that I might do something stupid, but that something beyond his control might come and take my life. It is "life" that we want to give our sons. There is much in the world we parents cannot control, but we can respond to their lives with joy, and to our fear of death, by creating a safe place for them to grow.

The wind said
You know I'm
the result of
forces beyond my control[1]

—A.R. Ammons

Ancient Initiation

Exerting control via the cultural force, humankind has traditionally shaped the powerful biological, psychological, and soulful influences within each generation of sons. Somewhere far back in time, we stopped following our own instincts and experience in determining what our children need to grow strong and healthy. Most recently, we have capitulated to modern medicine, institutionalized education, mass entertainment, and big enterprise. The "experts" know better than we do what our sons need. We feel controlled by the very force—culture— that we need to use to initiate our sons into healthy manhood.

Perhaps we are assuming too much if we say that ancient peoples purposefully used culture to shape their sons into men. However, we know that they followed strict and elaborate rituals that fostered qualities necessary for survival, rituals that were shaped by a shared world view. Common beliefs and values generated clear codes of behavior. Set boundaries prohibited individual behaviors that might erode the rigid control of the culture, and every member subscribed to those accepted ways. For example, hunting tribes needed strong, fierce men to ensure that there would always be enough food; therefore, their manhood initiation rituals were frightening and difficult. To make a boy into a man, these people knew exactly what had to be done and how to do it. Ancient male initiation worked because the tribe was a closed system; everybody lived and died for the sake of the whole.

We citizens of the technological age view ancient initiation cultures with a certain horror. The absence of individual freedoms fills us with indignation and with a self-righteousness that calls such a life unfair, restrictive, tyrannical, even damning. We attach great importance to being able to choose our own marriage partners, free-time activities, and careers—and to change them if and when we have the notion. We abhor the idea that society could be arrogant enough to dictate who we will become, when, and how. And the violence of it all! Young boys being ripped away from their mothers in the night, scared half to death, forced to perform dangerous rituals, their bodies intentionally mutilated, scarred for life. We consider adherence to such ghoulish practices as primitive, superstitious, and addicted to the past.

Modern Violence

Have we really changed all that much? Granted, we insist upon the freedom to speak, act, work, play, treat our neighbors, and parent our children in any way that we choose—adhering, of course, to the laws of our land and our personal codes of behavior. However, the sharp blade of Procrustes slashes the psyches of modern men in much the same way that the glistening knives of the ancient initiators carved the bodies of their young boys. Our men are also acting the parts demanded of them in this age of the computer. And how free are the uneducated, the poor, the sick, and the less able-bodied in our culture to choose how they want to live their lives? The cultural effects of growing up black, of being female, of living in urban slums, of being homosexual, all leave their scars, no matter what our Constitution proclaims about "inalienable rights."

We believe that we long ago shed the brutal lifestyle of ancient peoples, whose violent initiation practices now appear uncivilized and vulgar. Yet the violence directed toward boys in our modern culture seems no less pervasive and toxic. The still-common practice of circumcision after birth gives our sons the message that to be male is to be wounded. Incredibly, this surgical procedure is performed without anesthesia, because we swallow modern medicine's assertion that the infant penis has few nerve endings. Talk to any man about this and watch the unconscious wince in his body. Boys learn from this experience that crying or voicing their pain is futile; and that Mom and Dad really cannot be counted on, because even though they lovingly stand by their son during surgery, they still allow the act to be committed. Through such cultural practices we teach boys that life is dangerous, beyond their control, and that they'd better be on their guard, because someone is out to hurt them.

The second most common type of cultural violence done to boys is the custom of teaching them that it is weak or "sissy" to show feelings when they are hurt, sad, frightened, and so on. Is it any surprise that men have difficulty expressing their emotions in relationships with others? One of the most characteristic complaints wives make is that their husbands do not share their feelings with them. Our society's Procrustean bed demands that boys cut off their feelings to fit the strong, male image. This sacrifice wounds men's souls. The only emotions we customarily allow men in our culture are angry, sexual, and aggressive feelings, and we see their expression everywhere—wife and child abuse, violent crime, and the thirst to go to war, for example.

When men come together in groups to work on their feelings, the emotion beneath all of the anger is grief. The Technological Man carries, for all men through the ages, a grief in his soul—over the sacrifice of his emotional depths, the erosion of his connection to the earth and the forces of nature, and the loss of an intimacy and involvement in family life.

> *Just before he died, my father told me that my grandfather had never held him. My father and I weren't very close either. There were things that I always wished I could talk to him about—how to decide what to do with my life, stuff like that. Now, after my divorce, I don't see my own son as often as I wish I could. Will it ever end?*
>
> *—Paul, a young father*

Also violent is the practice of bending over backward in the other direction—allowing a boy to express himself however, wherever, and whenever he pleases. Humanistic psychology's "let-it-all-hang-out" anthem of the 1970s failed to teach how venting one's feelings can affect others. Many a mother has beheld her teenage son in stunned amazement to hear a torrent of verbal abuse heaped on her in his anger; the boy is often as surprised as his mother. Beginning at birth, the inner training of knowing how and when to express one's feelings calls for firm boundaries on what's okay and what's not okay to do and say. We do our sons, and the community, a grave violence when the lines of authority are not clear and firm.

> *Just in the past ten years I have seen a frightening change in the attitudes of students toward teachers and other authority figures. As a substitute teacher, I always have to deal with rebellious attitudes and trouble-makers. I have learned to use humor mixed with inter-esting assignments and firm limits to keep the class going during my brief stay. On the first day of a recent substitute assignment, as I announced the ground rules, a teenage boy stood up. "We don't work for subs. We will sit and talk. If that's a problem for you, we will leave, and tell the principal that you told us to get out." I chuckled and said, "I know that it's hard having a sub, but that is our situation, and we will work today." I couldn't believe that he stood up again, and said, "Let's go!" All thirty sixteen-year-olds walked out of class, piled in cars, and drove off. I sat in shock for about thirty minutes. To top it off, I was summoned to the principal's office. She had heard from a student that I had told them to get out of class, and that I didn't care where they went. I explained the situation to the principal, but she wouldn't listen. I was written up for the incident; it became part of my permanent records. Not one thing happened to the students.*
>
> *—Gloria, a high-school teacher for twenty-five years, now retired but working as a substitute*

This alarming change in attitude and behavior, which many professionals see in our children, has been facilitated by a square box that sits in the living room of most homes in America. Its power to create violence in our lives is so insidious that some of us take little notice, while many of us have been voicing our concern for years with little effect. Yet the contents of this box have ominous power to shape our culture. There is no greater influence on American lifestyle, eating habits, music, consumer practices, and fashion than television.

Television does violence to our sons by stunting their imaginations, shortening their attention spans, and deadening their empathy for someone else's pain. Proponents of Waldorf education, created by philosopher and educator Rudolf Steiner, believe that imaginative play is the developmental arena for a young boy's emotional and creative growth.[2] Through daydream and fantasy, he adjusts to the difficulties of everyday life by reenacting painful interactions.

> *My son loves to play in the bath long after he has been scrubbed clean. One night he played in the water with his dinosaurs, while I changed his baby sister for bed. I overheard him working out a current problem. His dinosaurs were a family with a father, mother, and two baby dinos. The baby dinos were jumping on each other and crying, "I'm the littlest!" "No, I'm the littlest!" "You always get to be the littlest. It's my turn now," said the boy dino. "Okay, you can be carried and hugged now," said the baby girl dino.*
>
> —*Mother of Jeff, four, and Kris, four months*

Through his imagination, a boy creates a world where he is in charge; his own powerful acts affect people and events. Symbolically, he has created a reversal in the balance of power, which enables him to accept his place in the everyday world. Thus, imagination helps a young boy learn how to relate to the people with whom he comes in contact. Margaret Meyerkort, Waldorf educator, believes it is imagination that gives us the vision to love.[3]

Television crowds out a boy's own images and creative thoughts, and replaces them with adult-created concepts. The characters and scenes he sees on television then become the playactors in his dramas, rather than the soulful images and emotions that are alive within himself. The result is that he begins to rely on what is outside of himself for sources of creativity, ideas, entertainment, and enjoyment. Not only is he deprived of the power to use his imagination, but the impairment of his inward focus causes him to lose contact with his own body. Again, the slash of Procrustes' blade, and a boy is cut off from his imagination and the joys of his own creativity. Maybe worst of all, he is cut off from his personal vision to love.

Most of us watch more television than we read fine literature. Television has not only affected the reading habits of our nation, but has also hindered the ability of our sons to learn to read. Their softly focused gaze as they stare at the set makes the intricate eye movements required for reading difficult and even straining on the eyes. Moreover, watching television programs the mind to expect short, rapid sequences. The speed at which the action is paced allows little time for children to make sense of it. They become easily distracted. As Frances Moore Lappé, noted author and world food activist, mentions in her helpful book, *What to Do After You Turn Off the TV*, librarians have noticed a serious decline in the ability of children to concentrate and use their imaginations to project themselves into a good children's story—one of the pleasures of reading.[4]

> *Ten years ago I could read this beautifully written and illustrated book of Japanese fairy tales to first-graders, and they would sit spellbound until it was over. Now, this pop-up book with twenty to thirty words to a page is about all they can handle.*
>
> —*Jan, a senior librarian*

Another lamentable change in our children, which Lappé discovered when she researched her book on the effects of television, is that they are becoming desensitized to acts of violence and to the pain that others experience.[5]

> *Years ago, when a child would have even a little acci-dent, it was natural for all of the others to gather*

round to see how badly their classmate was hurt and to offer help. Now when someone falls and skins a knee, it's no big deal. It is rare for the rest to even stop in their play to see if he or she is all right.

—Bobbie, a school playground supervisor

On an average there are nine acts of violence during every hour of prime-time viewing and twenty-one violent incidents per hour in children's cartoons.[6] In her book, *Breaking the TV Habit,* Joan Anderson Wilkins cites that the typical American child watches almost six hours of television a day.[7] She calculates that by age fourteen, this child will have witnessed 11,000 murders.[8] He or she will be "programmed" by 350,000 to 640,000 commercials before graduating from high school.[9]

During each developmental stage, a boy's mind, body, and soul are ripe and ready to ingest the information appropriate for that age. The ancient initiation cultures knew that young boys were vulnerable to the fables and stories they heard; legends and tales were carefully chosen and skillfully told.

In the dark of night around a blazing fire, shadows crouched and leapt; the rhythmic throbbing of drums filled one's chest. The storyteller walked among us, and his painted face and wild gestures made the old stories come alive before our eyes. I became one with them, and the images have stayed with me for the rest of my life.

—What storytelling in tribal cultures must have been like

Today, our sons are no longer guided by such powerful, life-directing stories from their elders. Television and movies, programmed by people whose values and standards may differ from our own, provide the images and stories that impress upon our sons the crucial teachings of what it means to be a man. Thus it is easy—and disturbing—to imagine why our children are becoming less empathetic and caring toward others. We could preview the programs that they see, but most of the time we don't. We then spend the rest of our lives dealing with the messages and visions they absorbed during that impressionable time.

Television viewing not only violates our sons; it creates violence within our sons. Numerous studies conducted to uncover the effects of television violence on children underline what psychologists and parents have been saying for years: the continual viewing of television mayhem causes children to be more violent. When the town of Farmington, Connecticut, conducted its "TV Turn Off" for one month, teachers noticed that gradually, less pushing and shoving took place on the playground.[10] Children became more willing to find other solutions to disagreements than hitting and yelling.

Television, according to Frances Moore Lappé, is also one of the three main causes of family arguments in this country.[11]

⊸ ⊸ *Don* | A family—Mom, Dad, Sister, thirteen, and Brother, eleven— came in for counseling. Mom had made the appointment because she was tired of their constant bickering. The family problem manifested itself around TV. Everybody wanted to watch a different program in the evenings; Mom was determined that her family would not be isolated in their own rooms with their own TVs. Voting hadn't worked; rotating choices hadn't worked; Dad laying down the rules hadn't worked. So I made what seemed to me a logical suggestion. "Why don't you try turning off the TV in the evenings?" To this day, I can still see the frightened looks in their eyes. "Are you kidding?" asked the boy. "What would we do with each other?" I brought the question back to the family: "What do you want to do with each other?" Because the session was over, I suggested that they think about this during the week, and we'd talk about it next time. They canceled their next appointment, and never returned. My mistake was not realizing how much they used TV to hold their family together. The arguments were their way of making contact.

TV affects family life, Lappé writes, because we sit passively side by side, watching the same shows without any real interaction with each other.[12] The only contact between family members is to argue about what shows to watch. Consequently, we are isolated within our families, because we do not take the time to learn to know each other. We do violence to one another when we fail to really listen and to see another's viewpoint, experience, or pain.

> *...it (TV) encourages passivity, isolation, confusion, addiction, and alienation; it homogenizes values and shuts out alternative visions.*[13]

> —*Jerry Mander*, In the Absence of the Sacred

In her insightful article, "Human Values, Television, and Our Children," Waldorf educator Karen Rivers writes: "A child's behavior reflects his mental state and his emotional and physical well-being.... The hours that a child spends in a one-way relationship with television people, an involvement that allows for no communication or interaction, affects his relationships with real people. In many families the television has replaced the parents' role in the socialization of the child, the development of human values, family rituals and special events."[14] Have we stopped to look recently at what television is teaching our sons about family relationships, drug and alcohol use, smoking, sexuality, violence, racial prejudices, and values such as honesty, empathy, doing a job well, completing an education, speaking out against injustices?

Television has been a cultural addiction long enough for us to know its effects on our sons. What we do not know is how the next generation of sons will be affected by the growing practice of placing our infants in day-care centers so that mothers may work outside the home. Some boys just one month old are losing Father and Mother to the mysterious work world of the technological age. A reader survey in the May 1991 issue of the magazine *Working Mother* convincingly argues that mothers who work in high-paying corporate careers are happier and better adjusted than mothers who stay home, and that children of these working mothers are better adjusted and happier because they have more positive role models.[15] However, these working mothers are among a minority whose positions offer them more "flextime" and better salaries with which to hire the ideal day-care arrangement. The ones really caught in a bind are single mothers who must work because of financial need; too often they have to settle for day-care situations that do not provide the care their children must have to thrive.

> *Jake's father left me before he was born, so I've always had to put him in day care while I worked. It's been hard enough to have to support both of us, and I had to start leaving Jake when he was so little, besides. It breaks my heart to hear him cry when I leave him, and there he is, still crying, when I pick him up. The lady in charge says that he still won't play with the other kids, and he's such a mess when I come for him—dirty hands and face, even dirty diapers, sometimes, as though they hadn't changed him regularly. On my days off and on weekends, he clings to me and won't play at all. By the time I go back to work on Mondays, I'm exhausted, and so is he.*
>
> *—Jill, a worried single mother*

Even the most attentive and loving day-care provider cannot possibly give the time and energy required to form and maintain the special mother-infant bonding, which Louise J. Kaplan, Ph.D., child psychologist and author, describes as "one of the pinnacle attainments of a human life." As we mentioned in chapter 1, Dr. Kaplan has written a brilliant interpretation of the work of Margaret S. Mahler, world-renowned child psychoanalyst, called Oneness and Separateness: From Infant to Individual. She writes: "Normally an infant learns to use his mother as a beacon of orientation during the first five months of life. The mother's presence is like a fixed light that gives the child the security to move out safely to explore the world and then return safely to harbor. She makes the world of time and space sensible and intelligible."[16] In this age of intangibility, our children deserve the best start they can get, and our world depends on it.

It is time we realized that we must make sacrifices for the sake of our sons. Perhaps mothers must forgo a career for a few years, until their children are ready to extend the mother-child relationship to include teachers and peers, usually around ages five and six. Perhaps we must learn to live more simply on less income. Perhaps fathers must assume more childcare responsibilities. Or perhaps we must be more demanding of our employers to help us create jobs that take families into account.

> *Nancy Bronstein of Belmont is on the "mommy track" at work, which is exactly where she wants to be. "Family comes first," says Bronstein, thirty-four, who has three children at home under the age of five. "We're spending less and saving less," says the mana-ger of human resources systems planning at Bank of America in San Francisco, where she works three days a week. "I didn't want to look back at my life twenty years from now and say I could have spent more time with my family."*[17]

> *—From interview,* San Francisco Chronicle

> *I think we ought to have something called the family job, meaning part-time work, flextime, job sharing. You work part-time for a period of up to ten years, then return to full-time work. I think we have to redesign work to adjust to the needs of parents raising small children.*[18]

> *—Arlie Hochschild, Ph.D.*
> *author of* The Second Shift
> *from interview,* San Francisco Chronicle

Isolated Parenting vs. Cooperative Parenting

Our insistence upon personal freedoms has contributed to the development of the most fragmented and isolated culture in history. In the past, young parents were actively supported by the wisdom and presence of the grandparents. Today, our son's grandparents live more than 3,000 miles away. In the past, friends and neighbors were at the door within minutes of an emergency or need, be it an enemy attack, an illness, or the need to have a barn raised. Today, we are forced to parent in a vacuum; often we have never even met our neighbors. Our walls firmly guard our rights, but leave us single-handedly in charge of the magnificent and awesome masculine forces in our sons.

> *We had lived in the neighborhood for four years when the earthquake hit. Right after the shaking stopped, someone was beating on my door. I grabbed my son's baseball bat, opened the front door slightly, looked at the strange man standing there, and yelled, "Who are you? What do you want?" The man said, "I'm your neighbor. Are you and your children all right?"*
>
> *—Pat, a California mother*

Robert Bly asserts that it takes more than a mom and a dad to bring a son into the adult world as a man. He borrows from the mythology of ancient initiation cultures and modern Jungian psychology to describe one of the stages of male development—finding the "male mentor." To Bly, the mentor is an older man who is nurturing and wise from the experience of having lived fully engaged in his life.[19] Merlin, King Arthur, and Andy Griffith come to mind. This wise, older man serves as teacher and guide to the boy as he winds his sometimes treacherous way into male adulthood. At a recent retreat for Casey Family Foster Parents, a foster father who grew up in the inner city shared, "This may sound odd, but some of my mentors were the winos who hung out on our street. They kept an eye on things and watched out for us kids. When they knew something wasn't right, they told us about it. If one of the kids was in trouble, they told our parents. They were an important part of my survival."

A male mentor becomes especially important in the life of a boy whose father is absent. Single mothers can be relieved of a great burden of pressure when they find an older male to provide guidance and male companionship for their sons. Uncles, friends, teachers, coaches, the Big Brother organization, and religious groups are sources of mentors. We list other possibilities for support in chapter 11 in the "Help!" section.

When our son was born, we were both totally committed to the task of raising him. We strongly believed that two parents were better than one. After a few exhausting weeks of infant care, we realized that at least six more people were necessary to accomplish this consuming job, and the number was growing daily! We envied the Greek and Italian cultures, whose centuries-old emphasis on family closeness assures even today that a myriad of aunts, uncles, cousins, and grandparents are always nearby with eager arms to relieve the tired parents.

Until recently in the history of most cultures, the extended family was the major source of child-care support. There were both positive and negative aspects to what we call a closed family system of raising children. In tribal societies strictly bound by tradition, parents were confident that other tribal members would give their children the same care and discipline that they themselves would. Communities like the Amish, whose religious beliefs provide a continuity and a longevity to parenting practices, instill the same reassurance that children will be safe and treated with the same care and respect that they receive in their own homes. We do not have such confidence today. The search for a babysitter who matches our picture of the person to whom we can entrust our child is sometimes a long process. On the negative side, a closed system of child care, whether in a tribe, a religious community, or a family, can perpetuate unhealthy child-rearing patterns. We see this tendency in the man who was beaten as a child and goes on to physically abuse his wife and children, in the alcoholic whose mother drank herself to death, and in the absent father whose own father left his family when he was young.

Because we live far away from our extended families, we searched for supportive people to help us through our son's infancy. Since he was very small, his favorite babysitter, Nancy, has been so wonderful and important to us that we have always referred to her as a member of our "parenting team." His first teachers, Miss Monika and Miss Mary, have also become loved and valued team members. We only wish that we had ten more like them! Handpicking all of the people who will be involved in our sons' lives is not possible, but we can carefully choose caregivers, day-care centers, and male mentors whose philosophies of child-rearing match our own. Our sons depend on us to find the kind of care we want them to receive in our absence.

Learning the Maze

Our son is fond of drawing mazes. They have definite beginnings—usually involving someone, such as a duckling, who has lost his way—and definite endings, such as the mother duck, very happy to see her little lost one after his great adventure in figuring out the maze. That is what we are trying to do: to figure out the maze of how to use culture to support us in the great adventure of parenting our sons into manhood. There is much that we haven't resolved. How do we take a stand for our sons against the things in our culture that we know are harming them? How do we use culture to shape our sons into healthy, life-giving adults?

One of the best gifts we can give our sons *and* our culture is to teach them how to care for themselves and others—how to live successfully within a group. A commonly heard complaint from women about men is that "all they want is sex, and they only think about themselves." Much of their early training around the house limits males to the stereotypic roles of using tools, knowing about cars, and mowing the lawn. They learn to abide by the absurd cultural law made between men and women during the fifties: "He'll take care of the outside, and she'll take care of the inside." Although more men are taking care of the inside these days, many of us still see it as "helping out around the house." What is missing is a sense of ownership; of being a real member of the family group. As therapist and author of *The Courage to Raise Good Men*, Olga Silverstein points out, "The teaching of the boy starts early and accelerates fast. Much of it takes the form of educating him about the rights and responsibilities accruing to his superior male status (as in "You must never, ever hit a girl!" or "Ladies first").[20]

"Where did my son get the idea that he can ask me to fix him a snack, snarf it down, and leave all the dirty dishes for someone else (the maid?) to clean up?" some mothers ask. Our fast-paced lives in the technological age—where both parents work outside the home, or the head of the household is a single parent—leave little time for the old idea of a son's entitlement to be waited on. Making girls cook and do the dishes while boys study and take out the trash no longer fits anyone's notion of a modern family. How far have we gone, however, in really including our sons in the daily activities of making a house a home?

Teaching boys to ask the question, "What does this group of people need now, including me?" insures their membership in the family, enables them to be aware of the needs and feelings of others, and aides them on their way to the completion of a healthy manhood. Many household activities serve to teach this invaluable lesson, but learning to cook perfectly exemplifies the skill of caring for oneself and others. There are two rooms in the house where the most conflict occurs—the kitchen and the bedroom. Our sons who fare well in the kitchen as boys will succeed in the bedroom as adults. Depending upon a boy's age and maturity level, cooking for the family requires many skills that enhance relationship with others. The list is endless, really.

Cooking requires cooperation. Working with others in the small space of a kitchen takes cooperative choreography. The salad maker needs the cutting board and close proximity to the sink. The baker needs access to various cupboards and drawers, mixing space, and oven mitts. Cooking partners must work out timing to insure that each dish comes out approximately in the right sequence. Being flexible, willing to share, and open to suggestions help enhance the flavor of any person-to-person or group dynamic.

Cooking strengthens a sensitivity to the needs of others. When one is responsible for a family's meal, many needs must be considered. What mealtime is best for all concerned? What foods does everyone like? Must particular foods be avoided because of food allergies or vegetarian preferences? Will personal schedules make the meal quick or more leisurely? Is it a special occasion, such as someone's birthday, Halloween, or Valentine's Day? Cooking for others to celebrate, to lift their spirits, to say thank you, to help out, and so on teaches a boy to tune in to the feelings, ideas, and needs of others. This skill enables him to nurture others according to what they really like, rather than what he wants them to have.

Cooking reinforces forethought. When cooking for his family, a boy must check in beforehand with family members. What time does he need to start preparations? Does he have all the ingredients called for? Has he left himself enough time to do his homework, practice his violin, and pick up his room? Meal preparation pulls a boy out of himself into the larger world of group needs. He has to see a bigger picture, teaching him to know "what comes next," "what happens later," and "How am I doing now?"

Cooking expands attention to detail. Measuring accurately, using the right utensils, and taking care not to make too big of a mess all lead to a successful meal. Remembering that Mom would rather he not bang the spoon on the pot after he stirs its contents teaches a boy how to care for family property. Learning that Dad likes his steak rare and Sis likes hers well-done teaches him to notice individual preferences. Both of these skills are important for relating to others within a group. When others notice and comment upon his care, a boy feels a sense of pride in his accomplishments and a desire to do even better next time.

Cooking encourages creativity. The senses come alive amidst the smells, textures, colors, and tastes of the ingredients used to make a meal. Following a recipe determines certain outcomes, but the flair and style of the individual cook always comes through, leaving a distinctive mark upon the food. As a boy becomes more experienced, cooking is an ideal arena to showcase his talents for presentation, mix of flavors, humor, and even love. As gastronomic author M.F.K. Fisher wrote, "When I write of hunger, I am really writing about love and the hunger for it, and warmth and the love of it and the hunger for it…and then the warmth and richness and fine reality of hunger satisfied…and it is all one."[21]

Cooking challenges sexism. Our children first learn about sex role stereotypes in the home. If Mom does all the cooking and Dad does all the mowing, the boys in the family may be less likely to cook than their sisters. Happily, more men are cooking these days and setting wonderful examples for their children. As boys learn that all family members pitch in to help out with whatever the group needs, they are given more options for belonging. No matter whether they ever get beyond hamburgers or macaroni and cheese, boys who cook have taken another step toward learning to care for themselves and others.

Sam Keen speaks profoundly and personally about what it means to be a man in his book, *Fire in the Belly*. At a San Francisco conference on men's issues, he affirmed that it is time we begin a search for the answer to the question "Can we be kind, again?" "…Kind has 'kin' in it," he explained. Kin, he said, means being connected, being family to other people, to other species, and to all things.

"We are lost," Keen asserted. "When you are lost, first you must drop into feeling, to get back in touch with where you are. Then you must climb the highest tree in the forest, and look far and wide to see where you are going. This is called 'vision.' For the first time in the recorded history of mankind, we humans must fit into a natural world as machine-users. We need incredibly energetic thinkers who can deal with enormous complexity; thinkers who think not just with the intellect, but with head, throat, heart, guts, and balls (or other erogenous parts).

"For the next hundred years, for our culture to survive, we need a new perception, not just of men, not just of women, but of how we need to be in the 'information age.' The hunter archetype is no longer useful. There is nothing left to hunt. The warrior archetype is no longer useful for it has squeezed out of the earth its vital resources and pits the bad against the good. We must be part of a revolution where we are as vigorous toward kindness as we have been about warfare."[22]

As we have seen, certain ancient peoples "used" the hunter archetype to shape their sons into men they needed for their world. Others used the warrior archetype to form their sons into fierce fighters their society needed to survive. We believe that in our wounded world, we can no longer afford to live by archetypes that embody the tenets of domination by the might of the spear or the sword.

Perhaps the archetype of the technological age must be the gardener—the one who follows the seasons; weathers frightful storms; uses the elements of fire, earth, air, and water; cultivates; sows; weeds; prunes; stakes; and reaps.

As mothers and fathers we must be clear about our individual responsibilities as the gardeners of our sons. We must be in tune with the seasons of their lives. We must know how to aim the sun's ferocious light to help them find their inner guidance system of feeling, thinking, and self-direction. We must learn the gentle art of cultivating their souls. We must be explicit and united concerning the ideals and values we sow in their imaginations. We must be free to water and nurture them well with love, and to weed out our own frustrations and anger. We must be strong and kind, committed to staying connected with our sons, no matter what conditions their wild growth might create. We must prune and stake their fragile growth carefully yet firmly, using appropriate fencing. We must be confident, in the face of their fiercest storms and most aggressive outbursts, that deep roots are forming. By following the gardener archetype, we can watch our sons take root, flourish, and bloom into their own lives.

There are two lasting bequests we can hope to give our children...one of these is roots; the other, wings.

—Hodding Carter, Jr.

End Notes

1. A.R. Ammons, "The Wide Land," *Collected Poems 1951-1971* (New York: W.W. Norton & Co., 1972), 48.

2. Karen Rivers, "Human Values, Television, and Our Children," in *Models of Love, The Parent-Child Journey*, Joyce Vissell and Barry Vissell, M.D. (Aptos, Calif.: Ramira Publishing, 1986), 210-16.

3. Ibid., 214.

4. Frances Moore Lappé, *What to Do After You Turn Off the TV* (New York: Ballantine Books, 1985), 7.

5. Ibid., 10.

6. *National Coalition on Television Violence News*, "Violence in Cartoons Increases," June–Aug. 1991, 1.

7. Joan Anderson Wilkins, *Breaking the TV Habit* (New York: Charles Scribner's Sons, 1982), 10.

8. Ibid., 32.

9. Nancy Carlsson-Paige and Diane E. Levine, *Who's Calling the Shots?* (Philadelphia: New Society Publishers, 1990).

10. Lappé, *What to Do After You Turn Off the TV*, 10.

11. Ibid., 13.

12. Ibid., 4.

13. Rivers, "Television," *Models of Love*, 212.

14. Ibid., 212.

15. Carin Rubenstein, "Guilty or Not Guilty," *Working Mother*, May 1991, 55.

16. Kaplan, *Oneness and Separateness*, 16.

17. Sylvia Rubin, "How Parents Change Their Lives to Spend Time at Home," *San Francisco Chronicle*, 25 July 1989, sec. B.

18. Ibid.

19. Chapple, *Burning Desires*, 199.

20. Olga Silverstein and Beth Rashbaum, *The Courage to Raise Good Men* (New York: Penguin Books, 1994), 56.

21. M.F.K. Fisher, *The Gastronomical Me* (New York: The World Publishing Company, 1943), Foreword.

22. Sam Keen in a speech and personal conversation with Don Elium, "Tough Guys, Wounded Hearts" conference, San Francisco, 28 June 1991.

Part II:

The Parenting Team

CHAPTER FIVE

Mom and Dad: The Parenting Partnership

*Just know your lines, and
don't bump into the furniture.*[1]

—Spencer Tracy, advice on acting

❧ *JEANNE*   In the parenting of our son, there have been times when I have wished that I could just do it myself. Wouldn't it be much easier to make my own rules, organize everything myself, and get on with it? Parenting with a father around has sometimes seemed like a lot of unnecessary trouble. When we disagree on parenting styles, boundaries, consequences, or our son's physical care, it can call for a lot of giving and taking to settle our differences. Sometimes we never settle them. Just let me handle it! But I came to understand that I had been wanting my husband to parent our son like I do—to give him the same quality of attention, show the same concern for his safety, and expend the same energy for his comfort as a mother does. Then I realized that, deep down, I am extremely grateful to have a parenting partner who is so dedicated to making this journey together with me and our son. I honor those mothers who courageously parent their sons alone. Today I am thankful that I do not have to make all of the tough decisions alone, be "on duty" as a parent twenty-four hours a day, and be solely accountable for everything that happens to our son. I know that our son does not need two mothers. He needs a father, too.

In our work with the men's movement, we hear men express their feelings of rage or grief toward their mothers and fathers: "He was never there." "He didn't know that I existed." "He never touched me unless he was angry." "She smothered me." "She never let me grow up." "She made me her little lover." What does a son need from his father, and what does he need from his mother? What is a father's unique essence, and what is it that makes a mother?

Mothers: I've Created a Monster!

A mother's job is, after all, to civilize the boy....[2]

—Robert Bly, *Iron John*

George Gilder, an economist and outspoken writer on numerous subjects including men and families, has written that one function crucial to the continuation of culture, which has been accomplished by women, is the civilization of men.[3]

    JEANNE | I must admit that there have been times, when dealing with my son and husband, that I have felt confronted by wild beasts and wondered how I got the job of taming them. I guess it's in my genes. We know that for centuries women have kept the fires of the hearth—the "heart," or center of the family—which is to say the home, from which all activities radiate outward into the world. If we consider the impact of biology on the ways of women, as we have explored its effects on men, we discover why women have been the hearth-tenders, the caretakers of the "heart." Using a woman's body as metaphor for home, which it literally is for the human fetus during the first nine months of life, the womb and the heart make up the hearth, the source of life, sustenance, and love. Women's biology moves us in cycles, in connection with the seasons of nature, our families, and all of life. The extremely rich work of Jean Baker Miller on a new psychology of women illustrates how important "being in relationship" is to the healthy development of women.[4] We, therefore, give most of our attention and energy to fostering connection between ourselves and others. It is through relationship and connection within a family that we all begin life. It is here that we learn, no matter how rudimentary the insight, what it means to be human.

This legacy of "hearth-tender" and "beast-tamer" is not always an easy one to fulfill. Adrienne Rich, in her classic book *Of Woman Born: Motherhood As Experience and Institution*, writes, "To 'mother' a child implies a continuing presence, lasting at least nine months, more often for years. Motherhood is earned, first through an intense physical and psychic rite of passage—pregnancy and childbirth—then through learning to nurture, which does not come by instinct."[5]

My pregnancy was a pleasure—the attention, the planning of a nursery, the anticipation. Then I held this wrinkled, reddened, little alien in my arms, and I thought, "What have I done?"

—Lisa, twenty-six, mother of Jason

I was excited about my pregnancy, until I learned that I was having a boy. I did not want a boy. I didn't want to deal with someone so different from myself and my daughter. What does one do with a creature who gets great amusement from farts and burps, and fashions guns out of anything he gets his hands on?

*—Laura, thirty-seven
mother of Michael and Elizabeth*

Just as mothering comes easier for some women than it does for others, some just naturally know what to do with boys. For other women, being faced with a son's drive, energy, and will is like being asked to put together a jigsaw puzzle in the dark. They realize from the beginning, possibly even during pregnancy, that this baby is different from themselves. Although he is part of them, he belongs to the "other" sex, having a different body composition, differing hormones, and a dissimilar developmental plan.

JEANNE | When I was pregnant, I asked our midwife whether she thought I was having a boy or a girl. She asked, "How do you feel?" I replied that my stomach was constantly queasy, that I had acne for the first time in my life, and that I felt bloated and tired. Immediately she said, "It's a boy!" Of course, my son does not continue to have these physical effects on me, but I sometimes wonder whether boys have a harder time from the very beginning, because they are different from Mother.

Mother Love

If Mother is the primary care-giver during the first year or so of a boy's life, he is deeply immersed in the world of the feminine. Mother is his lifeline, his home base. Nothing lights up his face as much as hearing Mother's voice or seeing her peek at him over the side of his crib. His first gurgles and chirps are primarily for her, and his first attempts at human connection are to elicit her attentions. His first lessons of comfort and pain, fullness and loss come from her. He learns what is Mother and what is not-Mother. If he is lucky, she remains a constant center of his life from which he can venture out to explore his ever-widening world, knowing that she is there to cheer him on, or to which he can come rushing back for reassurance after any too-scary encounter. Dr. Louise J. Kaplan, whose work we introduced in chapter 4, describes this vital, early relationship as the "...elemental dialogue between mother and infant—the dialogue that ensures our humanity."[6]

The mother-infant bond is vital for the healthy growth of a boy, yet Dr. Kaplan asserts that "modern social forces conspire to interrupt the elemental dialogue between mother and infant...."[7] The many cultural constraints concerning the mothering of sons create a constant tug-of-war within mothers.

JEANNE | Very often, I know in my heart what is best for my son, but The Doctor, or The Teacher, or The Therapist, or The Family, says something different. So I go along with them. Then it turns out that I was right all along; I put my son through unnecessary pain, because I didn't listen to my intuition and stand up for him.

When Alan was a baby, he constantly spit up after he nursed. He didn't grow much during his first year, so the pediatrician referred us to an allergist. This doctor insisted on doing skin tests to uncover any allergies he might have. A little alarm went off inside of me, but I figured that the doctor knew best, so we went ahead. The tests were awful. We had to hold Alan down, while he screamed and wriggled to get away from the pain. He was covered with bruises afterward. All the way through, I kept feeling, "This isn't right. This isn't right!" Later, we found a wonderful allergist who said that he never tested anyone so young, because of the trauma and because the tests weren't that accurate in very young children anyway. He gave us a list of the most common allergens; we eliminated them from Alan's diet and environment, and he immediately improved and started growing. He was so little, and I knew that the tests were wrong, but I failed to protect him.

—Jennifer, mother of Alan, six

Another way we betray boy children is to accept our culture's fear of the feminization of its sons. Studies tell us that mothers tend to snuggle and coo less with their boy babies than they do with their girl babies, after they reach six months of age. Mothers tend to wait longer to answer their sons' cries, as well. Megan Rosenfeld, a writer at the *Washington Post*, believes that "we unconsciously begin training boys for independence by not 'babying' them."[8] Olga Silverstein says that the prevailing culture questions a mother's love in the life of boys. "The love of a mother—both the son's love for her and hers for him—is believed to 'feminize' a boy, to make him soft, weak, dependent, homebound."[9] This fear of feminizing our sons creates great conflict within those mothers who naturally hug and caress their children of both sexes.

At the same time that we are unconsciously teaching our sons to be independent by withholding hugs and other "babying" behaviors, we expect them to show affection, learn to share their toys, and cooperate with others. This is a double bind for boys, who are expected to grow up independent and strong, loving to their wives, and affectionate with their children. The mistake we have made is to define "independent and strong" as not needing hugs, kisses, and other signs of affection. Boys need just as much cuddling and touching as girls do.

Findings of a long-term study conducted by Harvard University psychologist Carol Franz and others encourage parents to hug, kiss, and cuddle both girls and boys throughout their childhoods. The study began in 1951 with 379 five-year-olds and followed up on ninety-four of them thirty-six years later. Those children who had been "babied," that is, who had received affection regularly from at least one parent, developed a stronger sense of internal security. This self-confidence enabled them to develop closer marriages and friendships, have better mental health, and enjoy more success in their chosen careers.[10]

Testosterone coursing through their bodies does not preclude hugs, kisses, and cuddling for boys. In fact, many boys are as naturally affectionate as girls are. Their needs and wishes for closeness will vary with age and the developmental stage they happen to be growing through. We have taken our cues for physical holding from our son. Although he is a natural cuddler, and especially loves back rubs, there are moments when he does not want holding; he wants our full attention and understanding. This too is a way of holding him in our affections. We give him the message, "You are important enough for us to respect your changing wants and needs." The Franz study mentioned earlier reminds us that our sons imitate our nurturing behaviors, and will carry this learning with them into adulthood. Regular touching and holding from both parents can help tame the testosterone beast.

Mother Guilt and Overcompensation

We as a society are so concerned that our boys become "Men," that many mothers are afraid of loving them too much. Dr. Kaplan writes, "It is ironic that the vital importance of a human infant's *attachment* to his mother should be subverted by shame and impatience at the very moment in history when the complaints of human *detachment* are loudest."[11]

This was Joy's experience at a family gathering when her son was still nursing. "When Todd was almost two, relatives from out of town came for Sunday dinner. The house was full of family and friends, and Todd was the youngest there. He would play happily, then come to nurse, then toddle off to play again. It was funny to see how the men responded to Todd's nursing. They constantly made comments, such as, 'Here, boy, let's steal you away from your mummy.' 'Come on, you're too big to be wanting to do that.' 'Come with me—I'll teach you to be a man.' I think that they were all jealous of Todd's being able to nurse when he needed to, and it made them uncomfortable to feel whatever it was—sadness, longing, I don't know what.'"

It's not surprising that mothers feel frustrated and confused about how to parent a son. "Mother bashing" (the syndrome of "let's blame everything on Mom" because she was too engulfing) has become as popular as putting all of the blame on fathers for their absence. Part of the truth for many mothers and sons is that, because the father was either absent at work or absent altogether, the mother overcompensated out of necessity—she had to be the parent. Many "single" moms have performed admirably under these circumstances but have failed to provide what their sons needed at certain ages, because mothers make lousy fathers. When mothers must overcompensate for the lack of fathers, sons will be unable to get in touch with their own deep masculinity.

Marcia, single mother of nine-year-old Ben, realized when Ben was young that she needed her brother's help. "I could have explained why girls sit down to pee and boys stand up, but it just seemed better for Ben that someone else with a penis explain it to him, and teach him the finer points of using the toilet. Maybe it was silly, but it appears to have enhanced Ben's good feeling about himself as a boy. Now he and his uncle seem to share a secret understanding, as though they belong to an elite club. It's done wonders for Ben's self-confidence."

The danger in overcompensation, according to Dr. Kaplan, is that a mother may tyrannize her child by possessing his mind and body as though they were extensions of her own self.[12] An invasive mother gives the message, "You cannot be trusted to be in charge of your body or your thoughts. I will do it for you." Self-trust is the foundation upon which a boy develops the skills to be in balanced relationships. The freedom to get dirty, to take risks, to "be a boy," to make his own mistakes, knowing that his mother is there cheering him on, allows a son to learn to trust his ability to "make it" in the world.

Cutting the Apron Strings

Inside every human infant are two forces of equal strength. One is a yearning to merge with the mother, to feel the bliss of oneness; and the other, the urge to move away, to discover and become a separate and individual self. This is the human dilemma: how to be in intimate relationships with others while remaining true to one's self. Perhaps this is one of the most important lessons a boy will learn from his mother. In her insightful book, Dr. Kaplan writes that a baby knows when to begin to separate. Mother just needs to follow his lead. As the dialogue between mother and infant progresses, it changes from one of merging bliss to one that appreciates separateness; that is, it begins to have room for both possibilities at once. "Frequently parents interpret a child's necessary steps to becoming a separate person as signs of rejection and as indications of their own inadequacy and failure," Dr. Kaplan says. "So much of the childhood behavior that engenders self-recrimination in a parent does not really represent failure in the parent but rather the child's need to establish his own sense of identity."[13]

> *Sammy is usually a mellow, easygoing kid. When he started throwing tantrums, I wondered what I was doing wrong. For two weeks, I couldn't ask him to do anything without a fight. It was so awful. Then overnight, he was his cheerful, cooperative self again. The difference was that he was now drawing people and birds, could build a high tower of blocks without knocking it over, and could put his puzzles together by himself. It seemed that he had to struggle against me to push forward into that next stage of development.*
>
> *—Jane, a mother's group member*

The job of loosening the apron strings would be easier if our sons grew developmentally in straight lines; that is, if there were a clear progression from one stage of development to the next. As is the way of human growth, however, our sons will probably be working on several steps at once. This was true for Greg when he was fourteen, and it seemed to his mother that there were two different boys living in the house. Glenda recalls that time: "Greg was already five inches taller than I am, and learning to drive that summer. He was cooperative about curfews and chores at home. It was easy to treat him like an adult. Then he would revert to four-year-old behavior—unable to share with his sister; needing my attention and direction to do the smallest thing, such as opening a can of soup for lunch; stumped by simple problems that came up. When I answered his plea for help, he'd have a tantrum and yell, 'Don't treat me like a kid!' I felt like a crazy person."

The male initiation rites of past cultures took the guesswork out of "cutting the apron strings." It may have been just as hard for ancient mothers to let go of their sons as it is for modern mothers. However, there was no room for choice. When a boy showed certain signs, the men stole him away with the assistance of the mothers. We can imagine them afterward, sitting around the fire, drinking the ancient equivalent of coffee, and talking about what had happened: "Did you see the look on Oog's face when his father grabbed him?" "Oh, my baby boy. It was only yesterday that I carried him everywhere!" "I hope JolOog won't be too hard on him." "Well, he's in his father's hands now." "The men really outdid themselves this year." "I hope we didn't put up too much of a fight against them." Modern mothers too must support fathers to help untie the apron strings, so that sons will be free to follow their fathers across the bridge into manhood.

Although we no longer perform the old, strict rites of passage, the clues signaling the need for passage are still there in our sons. Modern mothers must encourage and trust the fathers, or other men in their sons' lives, to take over the reins of parenting when the time is ripe. The last four chapters of this book will examine a boy's development in detail—what behaviors parents can expect at each age, how to deal with them, and what a boy's soul needs from his parents. We describe specific behaviors that signal the need for passage and offer related suggestions for fathers and mothers in chapter 10, titled "The Tom Sawyer Years: Ages Eight to Twelve."

The Mother Within

By "taking over the reins of parenting," we do not mean that Father completely usurps the job of parenting, and the bonds with Mother are severed. Mother will always remain an important influence in a boy's life, but his relationship with her undergoes a transformation when he approaches adolescence.

What a boy carries with him on this journey in search of the masculine is his "internalized mother," that is, his childhood impressions and experiences of who his mother is as "woman" and as "feminine." In the process of "civilizing the boy," as Robert Bly describes one role of the mother, she indirectly imparts her feminine values to her son by example—the ways she lives in the world—and directly, through how she treats her son and through the teaching stories she tells him.

Mothers use both positive and negative approaches for teaching their sons the ways of culture. Some use shame, some are kind, some moralize, some lecture, some use understanding, some use guilt, some resort to physical abuse, some leave, some are too strict, some ridicule, some are only loving, some trust the inner child. Most of us use a combination of all of these ways. Each approach produces reverberations that will last a lifetime.

What we must understand is this: a boy learns about the world of the Feminine from his mother. We do not mean the Feminine as the stereotypic "sissy" or "prissy" or "weak" or "not logical" or "not good at mathematics," but Feminine as respectful of the earth, nature, and of all life. A boy must internalize the Feminine; it teaches him to value affiliation with others, and how to be in relationship. In this way he masters his first lessons in expressing his emotions, exploring their depths and heights. He begins to learn the art of loving and how to receive affection. He develops a sense of trust in the world, others, and himself. He experiences being held, the bliss of oneness.

A boy's internalization of his relationship with his mother will determine how he later relates to other women in his life. Like most things in life, the Feminine has a dark or sinister side. A client we'll call Kevin, for example, internalized an "engulfing Feminine," which made his relationships with women difficult. Kevin's mother had tried to be both father and mother to him, because his father died when he was young. She protected him from this loss by doing everything for him. Kevin counted on his mother to clean, cook, and to choose, wash, and iron his clothes. Ultimately she made him dependent on her to the nth degree by making all his important decisions—what girls to date, what sports to play, what college to attend, what degree to get. As an adult, Kevin has had numerous relationships with women and two failed marriages. He complains that women treat him like a little boy by mothering him, telling him that he could do better in his career, choosing his clothes, organizing his life. The women in his life are attracted to him because he is sensitive and able to listen to them, but they complain that he doesn't pick up after himself, has trouble making decisions, has no male friends, seems stuck in a job that he doesn't like, won't commit to a relationship, and doesn't think of things until the last minute, making him usually late for a deadline, appointment, or social date.

Kevin's situation is a common one among young males today. They are what many authors have called "puer, the eternal youth," the "flying boy," a "Peter Pan." According to John Lee, author of *The Flying Boy: Healing the Wounded Man*, boys who escape the world of men find "...themselves unable to make commitments, hold down jobs, and have good relationships." They become "flying boys."[14] The lack of connection with their masculine identities and their over-dependence on the feminine, or the internal mother, leaves many modern men without firm ground on which to stand. They either lose themselves in relationships with women, or shy away from relationships because they expect to be engulfed as they were by their mothers.

To some extent, the young man,
each time he leaves a woman, feels it as a victory,
because he has escaped from his mother.[15]

—Robert Bly

Kevin's mother may have done what she thought was best for her son; on the other hand, she may have used her son to help deal with her own grief over the loss of her husband. Either way, the long-term effects of her overcompensation left Kevin with no sense of identity as a man, and with little trust in his own ability to successfully be a separate person in the world. What is best for sons is for mothers to be present in their lives until the sons show that they are ready to begin the transitional walk over the bridge (see chapter 10). Then a mother must take her son's hand, place it in his father's, or in the hand of another committed man, and take one step backward.

No matter what the son's age, Mother will always be an important and necessary home base for him: still setting limits and boundaries; still available for talks, problem solving, political discussions, and advice about love; still nurturing and understanding when life gets hard. But because the mother knows her limits, the son will know where his mother ends and where he begins. Because his father has been part of his growing up, he will stand strong in his sense of himself as a man, one who knows how to give and receive love, who is life-affirming and life-giving.

Fathers and Sons: A Foreign Language

☞ ☞ *DON* | The way my husband and son relate to each other is sometimes a mystery to me. There's all this bumping and pushing and punching each other. My son and I wrestle and tickle and chase each other around, but their play has a different quality, as if they have their own language of grunts, farts, burps, chortles, feints, and holds. The masculine force has a ferociousness that demands, "Ho! Take notice! This is real. This is important. I have a positive and creative purpose." I am learning that my son and his father communicate on a deep level when they engage physically with each other.

Even rough language and threats can be like the chitchat used in social settings to get to know other people. Each family sets its own limits on behavior and language, but fathers and sons will "knock heads," tease, and cajole one another in the way that works best for them.

However, when the teasing or roughhousing is barbed—that is, it comes out of such feelings as anger or resentment, or emerges because father or son is withholding the truth about something important—it poisons the relationship. This is especially true when the barbed arrows come from Dad.

When Barry, age fourteen, was reuniting with his father, their relationship was almost undone before it had a chance to get started again. Barry had been taken out of his home, because of the domestic violence between his mother and father and his own trouble with stealing. After a year of good, difficult personal work, Barry's father was given another chance with his son. Dad now controlled his anger well, began setting appropriate limits for Barry, and was able to really listen to him. One day, Barry came into his joint counseling session feeling hurt and angry. "I'm not talking to Dad ever again," he announced. "He makes fun of my music, like I'm an idiot." His father replied that he had just been kidding, and didn't know that Barry was so angry at him. "Look, Dad, I like it when we kid each other," Barry responded. "Usually you are one of the funniest guys I know, but the way you made fun of me today really hurt." His father said, "I'm sorry, son. I'm trying so hard not to screw this up. I tried not to be angry with you about that music, and I wasn't being straight with you. The truth is that I hate your music, and I love you. How can we work around this?" Barry sighed in relief. The way was cleared to make a compromise. Barry agreed to use headphones and play no music videos when his father was home.

It may seem contradictory, but once boys know what they are truly up against with their fathers, they feel empowered. When communication is "fogged over" with barbed teasing or lying, a boy begins to fall into an "I must be worthless" position. Fathers, after all, are like gods to their sons. Their briefest words and slightest mannerisms fall like thunderbolts from above. A candid, respectful relationship between father and son brings the father down from the mountain and back into the world of humans. When a father can admit to his deeper feelings and concerns with his son, yet stay in his role as father, the son experiences and absorbs a strong, vulnerable masculinity. The message to the son is, "You are worth being honest with." He also learns, first-hand, how relationships are deepened through honesty and the clear sharing of feelings.

Fathers: Who Comes After Oedipus?

...There's a theory in the black community—
mothers raise their daughters and love their sons.
When they overly love their sons they make them babies.
A black man has to teach his son how to be a man.[16]

—John Singleton, filmmaker, *Boyz N The Hood*

A male client of Don's revealed a dream that has haunted him since he was a teenager. "I am making love with my girlfriend. Right at the point of climax, her face becomes my mother's, and my father interrupts us by knocking on the door. I feel guilty, ashamed, and afraid." Dr. Sigmund Freud, the father of modern psychology, would have loved this dream. "Obviously," the doctor might have said, "the son is trying to steal the mother from the father. Son hates Father so much that he would kill him, just as in the story of Oedipus." We have all heard of the "Oedipus complex," but few of us have truly understood its sweeping assumptions. This theory was Freud's attempt to explain psychologically the transition of the son from the mother's world to the father's world. Freud was accurate in describing one of the possible ways for a son to transfer his identification from mother to father: Son wants Mom to himself so much that he is willing to do away with Dad. When he realizes that he cannot have Mom, he bonds with Dad to learn to be like him. Then one day he can attract someone else who is like Mom.

Dr. Freud was inaccurate, however, in assuming that the above simplification is the only way for a son to enter the father's world. Jungian analyst Loren E. Pedersen, Ph.D., challenges Freud's long-accepted explanation of the Oedipus complex in his book about masculine development, *Dark Hearts*. Dr. Pedersen interprets Freud's use of the Oedipus myth to describe the *fall of the relationship* between father and son. Pedersen gives it another meaning. "Freud overemphasized the negative father," he writes. "As the stage of masculine development following separating from the mother, its goal is the *atonement of the father-son relationship*. In order for the father to help his son master this stage successfully he must himself have completed his own emotional separation from the mother. He must also have retained an integrated part of the mother in himself.... Unless he has done so, the relationship with his son will undoubtedly continue to be contaminated, that is, he will abandon his son once again."[17]

When author and researcher Shere Hite interviewed 7,239 men about their relationships with their fathers, almost none of them said that they were or had ever been close to their fathers.[18] Out of 71 male clients studied by psychologist Jack Sternbach, Ph.D., twenty-three percent had fathers who were physically absent; twenty-nine percent had fathers who were too busy with work and uninvolved with their sons at home; fifteen percent had fathers who were frightening, dangerous, and out of control; and eighteen percent of the men had fathers who were severe, judgmental, and emotionally absent. Dr. Sternbach found only fifteen percent who had experienced an appropriate father-son relationship.[19]

Most men are hung up on mother's side of the bridge. Being stuck in this phase of development makes it difficult for a man to parent his own son's crossing. His lack of emotional involvement with his son, according to Dr. Pedersen, is the major factor in creating the Oedipal wound.[20] The son's readiness for the father unconsciously stimulates the father's grief about his own lack of fathering, and instead of grieving his loss, the father covers it with anger and negativity toward his son. When a father reacts to his son's development with rancor and criticism, because he himself has not made the crossing to a positive identification with the father, a boy will naturally seek the comfort and support of his mother. When the psychological force moves the son toward separation from the mother, around ages seven to nine, the father faces a double-edged sword. He himself must leave the world of the mother, cross over the bridge to his father's world, and carry his son along at the same time. This is a Herculean task, which requires assistance from other men.

When I became aware of the new male psychology, I felt defeated and hopeless. I feared that it would take years for me to get strong enough to raise my son, and he was already seven! But I decided to take the first step—to spend lots of time with my son. I was amazed by how quickly we both have taken to really being together. It's embarrassing, but before all this, everything having to do with my son revolved around his mother's wishes. I was more her assistant than a father, always trying to make her happy. Now my son and I go camping alone, regularly. I've found other fathers and sons who go with us sometimes, too. The support of other men has helped me a lot. My wife and I both see how much our son has "bloomed." So many of the discipline problems have quieted down. Just my being home cools the aggressiveness he shows with his mother. My son doesn't have a seasoned elder for a father, who crossed the bridge years ago. I won't be a "wild man" for a while. I guess we'll just have to cross that bridge as far as we can together, father and son.

—*Letter from a father who attended*
a seminar on fathering sons

The hatred, confusion, and guilt that a son feels toward his father, and that a father, in turn, feels toward his own father, derives more from the emotional or physical absence of the father than from the role of "father" itself. As Robert Bly puts it, men today are "father hungry."[21] The lack of a strong, caring, consistent father presence sets the stage for the portrayal of the Oedipus myth. Yet there is reason to hope that father-son roles can be rewritten. Today's new fathers, in partnership with other men and women, are creating a different story.

Fathers and Sons: Reconciliation

...and he told me, he was sorry,
it took seventy long years
for his heart to open.

And I told him, I was thankful,
he fought seventy long years
for his heart to open.

—Don Elium, from lyrics,
Working Man album, Unpublished Work © 1992

The male client mentioned earlier, whose dream suggests the classic Oedipus complex, has told it to many friends, teachers, and therapists, because it haunts him. Don offered him a slightly different interpretation from one Dr. Freud might give. "Father is coming to take you into the world where you belong—his world, the world of men. You are frightened and feel guilty, because you didn't know your father when you were small. His sudden appearance is an interruption and a surprise. It is meant to be a shock, however. He is coming to take you into your manhood." The recurrence of this dream since adolescence demonstrates that the psychological force continues to work within men whether or not they are aware of it. This client had to move from a psychological place where he no longer belonged—an obsessive fascination with the mother, which led to dead-end, dependent relationships with women—to a state of mind, heart, and soul where he does belong—an identification with the father, self-acceptance, self-confidence, and self-awareness as a virile, life-giving man.

This transition will never be smooth and easy. Maturation in males is often slow, painful, and messy. Its onset brings a tumultuous interruption to any young boy's paradise. And the resultant psychological search for balance often continues long after the physical transition from boy to man is complete. In fact, Shepherd Bliss, an international leader in the men's movement, states that many men in this culture do not completely cross over the bridge from the mother's world to the world of men until their middle forties.

Many fathers are taken by surprise when the psychological force begins to push their sons, around the age of nine, to be more like them, to crave more time with them. When this happens, fathers usually have a lot of catching up to do. It is imperative—on the order of an *emergency*—that fathers reach out to other men to deal with their own father-loss. The very future of our sons depends on dads taking the time to deepen talks with male friends, therapists, ministers, other fathers, bartenders, golfing buddies, neighbors, and relatives. When men talk to other men about relationships with their fathers, a door opens between them and their sons.

In the "Men's Forum: A Discussion Group for Men," one man talked about an experience with his father. "He's in his seventies now. Last week I visited him, and asked about his father and their relationship. My old man cried. I did, too, when he told me that he had never sat on his father's lap, nor does he remember ever touching him. In my wallet I carry a picture of my dad holding me on top of a rock in the mountains. I was seven. I look so happy and proud. It looks as though my father were a god holding me to the sky, so strong and proud of his son. And this man who held me never sat on his father's lap! In my eyes that makes him a real hero, to struggle on with his own pain and to father me.

"When I was nine, my father became critical of me; I call it "The Fall" of our close relationship. I'm still hurt and angry and sad all at the same time over that. My son is eight, and it's my turn to carry on the heroic tradition. I want to pick up where my dad left off, and carry my son further, in spite of my hurt, anger, and grief. Better yet, with the help of those old feelings. Our avoiding all of that was what kept my dad and me apart."

Another forum participant shared how a door is opening between himself and his son, after a two-year struggle through an ugly divorce. Both parents had bad-mouthed the other to their son. He stayed with his mother during the proceedings, and the father had not been allowed to see him regularly. The boy was twelve when it all started, and sought father figures elsewhere. William, a bodybuilder who ran drugs in his neighborhood, was the first. Luckily, an uncle started taking him on his boat on the weekends, and then a neighborhood police officer got him involved with wrestling.

"Up until now, I had been pretty passive in this whole mess," the father confided. "I didn't want to disturb my son's life, so I stayed in the background. Then I read about the new male psychology, and I realized that distance wasn't what my son needed from me. I'll never forget when I heard that a father must go get his son, and bring him into the adult male world. I talked to some other fathers, got some counseling, but most important, I went and got my son. We went to the country for the day to ride dirt bikes. We started talking, then arguing, but we didn't let it get too big. We stayed in touch. It was good. Now my ex-wife lets him go with me. I guess she was at her wit's end with his bullying attitude; she felt that I deserved him! When I first saw him after the divorce, he was fourteen, and he looked pretty rough—had gotten big, shaved his head, wore brass chains, and carried a knife. Now, he's a pretty good-looking kid with an earring and an attitude!"

This father's persistence probably saved his son's life. To his counselor, the son talks about his experience this way: "My dad and me have a relationship now. I won't let anything take that away anymore. No one understood that all my rough stuff and drug stuff was 'cause I needed a dad. But I'm still gonna be me. I will still stick up for myself, and I won't let him run over me. I'll be mad when I have to, and we both have the right to our own say. And I'm still gonna be stubborn, just like my dad." The face of this formerly very scary boy breaks into a grin.

The role of the father has changed with each cultural age; he has been, progressively, a hunter, a provider, a worker. There is a call from certain segments in the men's movement to bring back the practice of male initiation in an effort to create a new father-son relationship for the technological age. Interestingly, in most of the hunting cultures the men spent no time with their sons until they reached the age of initiation, usually near puberty.[22] In most cultures, including those of the past to the present day, the father's role has been an external one, working in the outside world and checking in with the family from time to time to see how they were faring.

However, the distant-father model no longer works in the technological age. Unlike the ancient initiation cultures, if today's father doesn't appear on the scene until a son is older and unruly, there is no long-established tradition to bind them together. The modern son can simply walk out. There is no cultural force that compels him to learn to be a man from his father.

I feel ripped off. I thought that once my son got older,
we could be close. But he doesn't want anything to do
with me. I feel tricked.

—Nick, father of a sixteen-year-old son

Moreover, when a formerly "absent" father is pulled by the courts, schools, or social services into the family fracas caused by a frustrated teenager, he enters under a great disadvantage. There are no prior bonds between himself and his son from which to begin to communicate and to understand each other's position.

The new story being written by the technological man involves fathers from the beginning of their sons' lives. Parenting classes, formerly made up entirely of mothers, are increasingly drawing fathers of young children as well.

My father came up from LA last weekend for a visit.
He watched me play with my two boys, ages two and
four. Then we took a walk, just the two of us. We have
never said much to each other, but we do spend time
together in silence. My dad broke the quietness. "Son,
watching you with your kids really taught me some-
thing. I never knew what to do with you when you
were young. Your mother did most of the caretaking,
but I just didn't know how to play with you. You are a
great father to your boys. I'm glad you overcame my
shortcomings." Something inside of me slipped into
place. My father did care about me. He just didn't
know how to share it. Every time, which isn't often, he
tells me his thoughts about me, what he thinks about
life, how he feels about things, I feel myself getting
bigger inside. A son needs to know what his father
thinks about, how he feels, and what his life is really
like. I intend to squeeze as much out of my dad as I can.
My sons will probably have to shut me up!

—James, computer software sales executive
Silicon Valley, California

Unlike the "external" fathers in some nonindustrial cultures, the technological father must begin when his son is born to create personal, internal ties with him. Our society's external ties to its members—the laws and law-enforcement systems, the school system, and the requirements that adults earn a living, provide for a family, participate in jury duty, and such—can never substitute for a father's involvement with his son. These elements of the cultural force are usually without heart and are not concerned with the soul of a boy as he grows into manhood. A son craves—requires—an internal connection with the father to aid him on his long, rocky journey.

Fathers: A Way Back In

Daddy, where did you go?
I was holding your hand,
*   then you let it go.*
Mommy took me by the hand. She said
"Son, your daddy is a working man."

—Don Elium, from lyrics,
Working Man album, Unpublished Work © 1992

The term "corporate father" is an oxymoron. The importance of a father's role in the family has not been a concern of most present-day corporations. "Being a good father who takes time off to be with his family" translates to "He doesn't have what it takes to make it in the corporate structure." The father who is willing to use work time to take his children to a doctor appointment, or to attend that important function at their school, might put his family at risk because most jobs require that he put his work first and his family second. Fathers, whether they work in the corporate world or not, are trapped by our culture into sacrificing their sons to the "gods of the work world." Most modern fathers are looking for a way back into the family.

I leave for work at 5:30 a.m., so that I can quit at 4 p.m. With an hour commute, that means I can be home by 5 p.m., and have the evening at home with my kids. Only trouble is, I'm so tired when I get home that I'm not much good with the kids, or helping my wife with dinner and cleanup.

*—Mitch, exhausted father of
Sara, three, and Joe, five*

Even fathers with more control over their work pace can feel stretched too thin by all the demands on their time. Sam, an insurance broker and manager in Charlotte, North Carolina, reports that the problem isn't confined to bosses who are high achievers. "When I started as the manager of this office, the guy before me hired mostly maniacs. I primarily hire guys like me—stable, work hard, steady, with slow growth over long time periods. I also have a few Type A's, who are up on top one day and down the next. They stir things up a bit, but too many make my family and office life a wreck. Even with having control of my office, it's still a chore to find time for both work and family. I make breakfast for my kids and take them to school. I'm home before bedtime and during most weekends, but my son really needs more of me. It leaves no time at all for me, and I'm really tired. To succeed in one world, it seems that I have to fail in another. Something's got to give."

The technological age has sacrificed its sons to the pursuit of money. We believe that we are working fifty or sixty or even eighty hours per week so our children can have all the benefits and advantages that we can buy them. In reality, all that our sons really need from us is what we seem to be unwilling to give—ourselves and our time. To grow into a healthy man, a boy must develop a close bond with his mother, so he can learn about his own humanity; and then he must be taken by his father to discover what it means to be a man. This takes time and sacrifice. We must be willing to give what it takes to raise our sons healthfully, despite our fear that we will have to sacrifice a successful career or the material possessions that it provides.

What seems to be called for is a change in lifestyle. As was suggested in chapter 4 in the context of infant-care needs, mothers may have to sacrifice a career for *a limited period of time*, or find alternatives to full-time work. Fathers must find ways to give more time to their families by changing the priorities of the work structure. This lifestyle change may mean that families forgo what our culture recognizes as signs of success and power, by spending less money on material possessions and more time together. It may mean that we turn off the TV. Meaningful sacrifice is the solution to our sons' school problems, laziness at home, anger, sexual promiscuity, and violence. These sacrifices give life to our sons and to our future.

Let the hate rescind,
Let this young man's life begin.
Anger and grief work its way on through.
Warrior's sword and heart
can now be handed down,
For the missing piece
Has restored order.

—Don Elium, from lyrics,
Working Man album, Unpublished Work © 1992

End Notes

1. "Sunbeams," *The Sun* magazine, Issue 148, Mar. 1988, 40.

2. Robert Bly, *Iron John* (Reading, Mass.: Addison-Wesley Publishing Co., 1990), 11.

3. Gilder, *Men and Marriage*, 5.

4. Jean Baker Miller, M.D., *Toward a New Psychology of Women* (Boston: Beacon Press, 1976), 83-97.

5. Adrienne Rich, *Of Woman Born* (New York: W.W. Norton & Co., 1976), 12.

6. Kaplan, *Oneness and Separateness*, 27.

7. Ibid.

8. Megan Rosenfeld, "Boys Will Be Boys," *Working Mother*, Mar. 1991, 52.

9. Olga Silverstein and Beth Rashbaum, *The Courage to Raise Good Men* (New York: Penguin Books, 1994), 11.

10. Marilyn Elias, "Parents' Loving Feeling Isn't Lost On Children," *USA Today*, Lifeline, 19 Apr. 1991.

11. Kaplan, *Oneness and Separateness*, 27.

12. Ibid., 218-19.

13. Jerry Mander, *In the Absence of the Sacred: The Failure of Technology and the Survival of the Indian Nations* (San Francisco: Sierra Club Books, 1991), 96.

14. John Lee, *The Flying Boy: Healing the Wounded Man* (Deerfield Beach, Fla.: Health Communications, 1987), xi.

15. Ibid., 41.

16. Gregory Lewis, "Of a Singleton Mind," *San Francisco Examiner*, 8 July 1991, sec. B.

17. Loren E. Pedersen, *Dark Hearts: The Unconscious Forces That Shape Men's Lives* (Boston: Shambhala, 1991), 122.

18. Samuel Osherson, *Finding Our Fathers* (New York: Fawcett Columbine, 1986), 6.

19. Ibid., 7.

20. Pedersen, *Dark Hearts*, 154.

21. Bly, *Iron John*, 92-94.

22. Gilder, *Men and Marriage*, 30.

CHAPTER SIX

Inner Guidance System: Feeling and Thinking

The treasures that lie hidden in the heart of the child spring...from that same heavenly world from which the soul itself originated....[1]

—Daniel Udo De Haes, anthroposophist and Waldorf educator

"**R**ational thinking" is not the first phrase that comes to mind when we discuss parenting. "Out of control," "pulling my hair out," and "driving me crazy" are more commonly used to describe the daily, chaotic experience of parenting. We strive so hard to teach our children to think clearly and to make rational choices in their lives, and yet we frequently feel incapable of achieving this ourselves. There are days when the task seems like walking through a thick, London fog on a dark night. How to teach our sons to listen to feelings, think clearly, and be self-directed—when we ourselves are confused—feels far out of reach.

Parenting and Clear Thinking

❧ ❧ *Don* | My son pushed me over my limit one day. He had agreed to clean up his toys without complaining, if his friend Brandon could come to play. When it was time to end their play and tidy up, my son "went off." As he screamed at me, I lost my calm and said, "That's it! Brandon cannot come to play ever again." Well, my son had been mad at me before; now he collapsed in tears. I stormed out to walk Brandon home. On the way back across the street, my own rage cooled, and I realized that I had said a very stupid thing. To never play with his friend again was a ridiculous consequence, because I could never enforce it. On top of that, the penalty didn't fit the misbehavior. Why was I punishing Brandon, too? So I went back inside, took my son to our bedroom rocking chair, and said, "I made a mistake in saying that you can never play with Brandon. You two can play again. What I need now is for you to apologize to me for not cooperating when you said you would. Then I want you to clean up your room." At this, I could see in his five-year-old face that the unfair weight of the world was lifted from him. He said that he was sorry, and quickly picked up his toys. The following day, he got mad at me about something and raged, "I hate you, Dad!" We solved the problem, and a few minutes later he said, "Dad, I made a mistake when I said that I hate you. I was just mad at you. I really love you."

Most of us think pretty clearly, except when we are angry or sad. During times of intense feeling we may say things that we totally regret later, and we can make some very stupid decisions. We have all been in the grip of feelings so strong that they temporarily blocked our ability to think and act rationally. Most of us took courses on logical thinking in school, or have read books on the laws of logic, but few of us have been educated about the laws of feelings.

The Feeling Curve

Feelings move naturally in one direction, toward completion. They follow a predictable course: they build up slowly or abruptly (see figure 1, A); they peak (see B); and they release (see C). Take anger, for example. When the feeling has been fully released, we feel better, may forget what we said in anger, and can think clearly about what we need to do next. Whether the feeling is happiness, sadness, joy, anger, or grief, our emotional body is stretched and pulled according to the *feeling curve*.

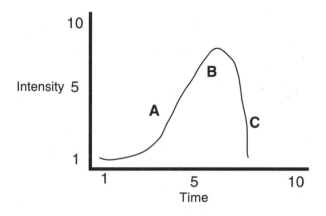

Figure 1. The Feeling Curve

I was nasty to my wife when I left for work this morning. I was so mad at her for something that really wasn't her fault, but she was a convenient target. I spent most of the day criticizing her and making her the "bad guy" in my mind. After lunch I was sitting at my desk, and all of the blaming, nagging, angry thoughts disappeared. I regretted having yelled at her, so I called her and apologized.

—Bob, caught in the feeling curve

Whether we like it or not, a feeling must run its course. Sometimes it takes hours or days for a feeling to pass through its phases. In spite of our efforts to control them, feelings follow a predictable course and an unpredictable timetable.

The Point of No Return and the Non-Thinking Zone

When our son was three, he discovered that he could press the nozzle on the can of shaving cream. To his delight, the white foam created great piles of "snow" on the bathroom floor. When we discovered him, he was frantically trying to put the stuff back into the nozzle. He looked up at us, covered in cream, bewildered. It just wasn't working. Feelings work the same way. Once they start emerging, we can't put them back inside. If we don't understand the laws of feelings, we will end up like our son—with a bigger problem to clean up than the original one. We can let go of the little irritations that sometimes plague us like gnats throughout the day, but once a feeling builds to a certain intensity, it must traverse the entire feeling curve. There is no way to put it back into the "can" or to decrease its intensity. This intensity threshold is called the *point of no return* (see figure 2, D). Everyone's intensity threshold is unique, reflecting differences in temperament, family values concerning the expression of feelings, personal experiences, and such. But once the feeling intensity reaches the point of no return, the feeling must fully travel its course, building to a peak then reaching a point of release.

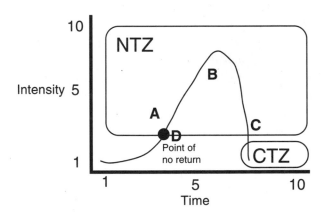

Figure 2. The Feeling Curve with Non-Thinking and Clear Thinking Zones

Once we pass the point of no return, we enter the dreaded *non-thinking zone* (shown as NTZ in figure 2). The non-thinking zone is really the feeling zone. Here, feeling demands our attention, and all thinking and logic falls to the background of our minds. This state has been mistakenly labeled "irrational"; the truth is, this is a time to be "a-rational," or outside of logic. What is solely important here is feeling. It is not an occasion for discussion, thinking things through, fixing, or figuring things out. Just feeling. Traditionally, this is the time when wives complain that their husbands don't listen to their feelings; they just try to fix things. Now is the time to cry, to laugh, to be angry, to experience joy. It is in the non-thinking zone that we feel most alive.

After a feeling peaks, there is a natural release of intensity, the feeling completes its cycle, and we can think clearly once again. The *clear-thinking zone* (noted as CTZ in figure 2) is the source of powerful insights, because here we are most in touch with soulful desires, dreams, and understandings. An insight gained from an experience felt becomes "lived wisdom." Intellectual ideas from books or other outside sources have little true effect on our behavior; the insights we gain from the clear-thinking zone bring the most lasting change. Many couples report that after a "good argument," meaning that both partners have voiced their real feelings and felt heard, they experience closeness and intimacy.

The Vital Difference Between Feeling and Behavior

"So are you saying," a father at a parenting workshop asks, "that I'm supposed to let my son yell, scream, and throw things, so he can think clearly? Excuse me, but that's ridiculous!" That is ridiculous. The key point here is that feeling and behavior are two separate phenomena, which we have confused by linking them together.

Many of us in this culture are afraid of anger, because when we were children we saw someone who was angry behave violently. Consequently, as adults we hear the word *anger* and picture someone hitting, throwing, or breaking something. The truth is that anger can be felt fully, without any movement. Violent acts may not be an expression of anger, but rather, a resistance to feeling the anger. We usually resist feeling angry because we fear the intensity of the feeling, or fear that we might hurt someone.

> *I went to one of those anger classes, and they had a soundproof room, where you could yell without being heard by anyone. I went in with the leader, lay down on a mat, and yelled till I was hoarse. I was exhausted when I opened my eyes. My first thought was amazement that the instructor was still alive. My anger hadn't killed him! Now I know that it's only my behavior that can hurt. Feeling my anger, rage, or any feeling can make me stronger, even if not very comfortable. I've spent most of my life holding down my feelings out of fear of hurting others. What a relief!*
>
> *—Chet, forty-five,*
> *participant in a men's workshop*

Habits and Unexpressed Feelings

No one can control a feeling. Most people *can* learn to control their behavior. Two-year-olds instinctively reach out for a toy and punch another child nearby before they realize what they are doing. As they grow, they learn that hitting hurts; and we teach them how to find other behaviors to resolve a problem. Their feelings will probably remain the same; they will still feel angry when someone grabs away a toy. But they gain more control over their raw behavior. The two-year-old's instinctive behavior to hit develops into a more mature, conscious behavior to see how things can be worked out.

Behaviors that remain immature or unconscious are called habits. We usually label them "good" or "bad," depending on how well they work in our lives. When we drive down the freeway, we regularly but unconsciously look in the rearview mirror to check the traffic flow. We automatically put on the brakes when we see the brake lights of the car in front. These habits help us drive safely. On the other hand, Michael bites his fingernails to the quick when he is nervous. Jordan "blows up" and punches anyone who is close when he gets mad. These habits are immature forms of behavior that may cause problems for those who have them. We give our sons a great gift when we help them learn to allow their feelings, and to consciously manage their behavior with a maturity that fits their age. Understanding the laws of feelings will help them—and us—especially when their testosterone begins to surge during the teenage years.

When Expressing Becomes Threatening

My son just turned sixteen, and he is struggling with lots of difficult feelings. One day I needed to get somewhere quickly, so I told him he couldn't drive. He got so mad that he screamed obscenities at me. I was shocked and hurt. I was even scared when he screamed and waved his fist in my face. I thought that he might attack me. Nothing like this had ever happened to us before. I told him, "That's not okay. You stay here, and we'll talk later." I left the house; I had to get away. When I got back, I told him, "You can feel angry, and tell me, but you will never wave your fist at me or threaten me again. Period." I grounded him for a week, and told him that if he couldn't talk to me without threat, then he could find another place to live. I hated to say that, but I didn't know what else to do. He later apologized. We had a good talk about the difference between expressing feelings and threatening behavior. We also talked about what was really upsetting him. It was a problem with his girlfriend.

—Julie, single mother of two teenage boys

This single mother addresses one of the most difficult situations faced by single mothers of adolescent males. A son doesn't realize that his body is responding to the power of testosterone, and that even though he feels love and connection to his mother, his actions can be threatening to her, to other women, and even to men. Boys may feel safer in expressing their emotions to their mothers, but a mother has to take charge and set firm boundaries about what behavior toward her is allowed.

⋘ ⋘ *DON*   In my counseling practice I see boys and fathers who are shocked to learn that they scare many of the women in their lives when they express their feelings. "I thought that I was doing good," said one husband. "I told her that I was angry as hell with her. She told me to never speak to her that way again. I got madder, then. Before, when I didn't say anything, she got upset that I didn't talk to her. Now, I told her how I felt, and she's furious!" What he didn't realize was that how he expressed his anger frightened his wife.

"The male force is frightening in itself," says counselor Ann Sheridan. "Sometimes it doesn't matter if there are good intentions. The male energy can be frightening to women."[2] Most men do not hit their wives when they are angry. But some do. When a woman hears a man say he would never hit her, it is like hearing the roller-coaster operator say that it hardly ever falls off the track! Violent acts by men are condoned everywhere we look—in the movies, on television, on the streets, sometimes in our own homes. When boys learn that they can allow their feelings and control their behavior, they relax. Learning to navigate the non-thinking zone and reap the benefits of clear thinking are important tasks for both parents and sons.

The Laws of Feelings

1. Feelings follow a definite course called the feeling curve.

2. Feelings move past the *point of no return* into the feeling or *non-thinking zone*. **Warning:** Do *not* try to think rationally or solve problems while in this zone! Just feel.

3. Feelings progress naturally to their peak, at which point they move toward release, then dissolve into the *clear-thinking zone*.

4. The clear-thinking zone provides access to clear insight and to solutions to problems underlying those feelings.

5. Interrupting a feeling by using distraction, fear tactics, or guilt creates emotional and physical problems (see next section).

6. Feelings are an internal activity that requires no movement.

7. Behavior is not directly connected to feeling. Behavior is a choice that is either conscious or unconscious. An unconscious behavior is called a habit.

8. All behavior that occurs in the non-thinking zone is based on habits.

9. Behavioral choices and decisions made while one is in the clear-thinking zone lead to positive resolution of feelings and a willingness to cooperate.

Trusting the Inner Guidance System

Don   When I was six years old, my older cousin, Randy, and I played cowboys down in the cow pasture. We herded the cattle just like Gil Favor and the boys on the TV show "Rawhide." With our BB guns we were serious cowboys. One day we saw a strange sight. My uncle had erected a single-wire fence around a bunch of pigs right in the middle of the cow pasture. My cousin said, "Touch that wire." Of course I grabbed it, and the shock burned a line down the palm of my hand. How I cried and ran back home to be bandaged and to tell about my pain. The next day I was out there again with Randy. This time I was very cautious around that pig fence. Randy said, "Bet you won't touch that wire." I had acted dumb once, and that was enough. As I shook my head, Randy grabbed the wire and held it. No shock! He explained that my uncle had used the electricity the first day to teach the pigs to stay in the pen. They ran away from the fence squealing whenever they had rubbed it with their snouts or backsides. This day he had turned it off, and the pigs still stayed away from the fence. Later, he would take the wire down altogether. What held the pigs in place was the memory of the pain. The same principle works with behavior; it is the core of behavior modification.

Children have been held in place, on an inner level, with a similar technique. Within each of us is a box with a hot wire around it. Inside the box are all of the feelings we were allowed to feel and express when we were children. Outside the box are all of the feelings that our families did not allow, because they were afraid of or uncomfortable with them. When we expressed the not-allowed feelings, such as anger, we were stung with criticism, threats, punishment, or scorn. In time, the memory of that experience caused us to deny our anger. The pain of being stung kept us in line, but it warped our ability to experience and express the full range of our feelings.

If a parent seeks to shape a child's feelings by zapping him whenever he expresses a not-allowed one, the child loses a vital part of himself. This vital part we call the inner guidance system, and it is the source of information that tells us who we are in relationship to the world. This source of wisdom directs our lives at all ages.

We can easily see the inner guidance system operating in our infant sons. When a baby feels hungry, he cries. When he feels cold and wet, he frets. When he feels lonely and wants attention, his howls would melt even the coldest heart. When he's full, warm, dry, and entertained, he smiles and takes delight in his world. We could say that the messages from a baby's inner guidance system are pure, loud, and clear.

As the child grows, however, his experiences may begin to dim or cloud the messages he hears—messages he needs to help him understand how he feels about what happens around him and to him. When the little boy falls and skins his knee, Mother says, "Don't cry. You're okay." At first he is confused. "My knee hurts!" he thinks. Then he sees that Mother wants him to smile instead of cry, and to pretend that he is not hurt. To please Mother, he gets up, smiles, and runs off to play, ignoring the pain in his knee. Repeatedly, the little boy finds that people are more pleased when he is happy and ignores his pain. As he convinces himself that he is really happy, not hurt, his inner guidance system becomes cloudy.

This is what happened to Norman, who appears to be a sweet and agreeable person. He will do anything for others, at work and at home. He has a low opinion of himself, however; he stays at the same level of employment; and, below the surface of his nice manner, he is often depressed. His wife appreciates his helpfulness, but she complains that he isn't really there; his kids wonder why he sometimes seems so sad.

When Norman was a child, his parents punished him and his two brothers whenever they showed anger or dissent, even when they were only expressing their opinions. He discovered that if he said yes even when he felt no, the less hurt and shame he would have to suffer from his parents. As an adult, Norman appears happy but he carries a quiet depression and resentment toward others. Instead of being able to use his feelings of anger as an indication that something is wrong, he becomes compliant and ingratiating, just as he did in his youth. The angrier he gets, the more he tries to please. Although he no longer lives near his parents, the memory of his childhood pain now controls his adult behavior. Deprived of an effective inner guidance system, Norman cannot cope with angry feelings in others, which leaves to his wife such difficult parenting decisions as setting limits and shaping their children's behavior. Norm's *feeling box* looks like this:

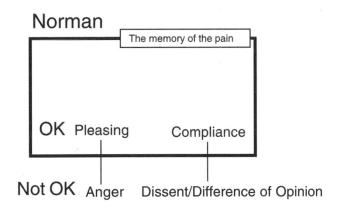

Figure 3. Norman's Feeling Box

Although Norman's aims to please and his compliance were causing him trouble both at home and at work, at least they were socially acceptable behaviors. Fifteen-year-old Jack had responded differently to the severe criticism and sarcasm from his mother. Whenever he got too close to feelings, Jack chose to act silly. He became the class clown, and it was impossible to have a discussion with him. He was disruptive both at school and at home. Jack's father brought him into counseling, afraid that his son was "crazy." The boy said, "I'm not crazy. I just hate being attacked." When Jack understood the feeling box, he could discern who was safe to share his feelings with, and then give up the clownish behavior.

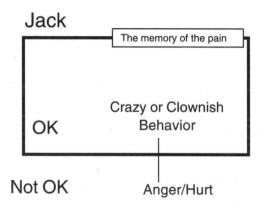

Figure 4. Jack's Feeling Box

Some people use behaviors to cover feelings. Others substitute one feeling for another because their real feeling is not allowed. The most common occurrence is feeling anger but calling it sadness.

   ❧ ❧ *DON* | Elizabeth had been coming to therapy for six months. She seemed fragile and easily devastated. This day, she expressed sadness that her son was disobeying house rules by staying out all night. Whenever he came home he asked her for money, saying he had run out. I pointed out the incongruence between her son's behavior and her "sad" response. "I don't think that you are sad. I think that you are mad." Her shocked look told me that I had hit upon her real feeling. She said, "I've talked to many people, and you are the first one to hit the nail on the head. Yes, I'm mad! The nerve of him!" Inner guidance system now working. Elizabeth's *feeling box* had looked like this:

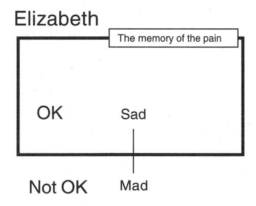

Elizabeth

The memory of the pain

OK Sad

Not OK Mad

Figure 5. Elizabeth's Feeling Box

Elizabeth needed to take strong action with her son, but her sadness had made her unable to act. She hadn't even known that she *should* act. As a child, when Elizabeth felt mad her mother cried—anger made her mother panic. When Elizabeth was sad, however, her mother felt important because she could safely comfort her. To guard against her mother's panic, Elizabeth learned to feel sad instead of mad. This response placed her in situation after situation where she was "ripped off" by others. Her fragile presentation was part of the cover for her anger and resentment, which had kept her in the victim position her whole life.

◁◈◁◈ DON It is acceptable in our culture for men to express angry or sexual feelings. Other feelings are rarely allowed. This was true for Stan, six feet seven inches tall, who came into counseling with his wife, who was five feet four inches tall. They sat on the couch beside each other. She complained that Stan was overly critical of her and always angry about something. As Stan told his side of the marital problems, he spoke loudly and swung his arms in large, wide motions. His wife, who seemed used to these movements, ducked as his gestures barely cleared her head. It was humorous to watch, almost like a dance.

When Stan had finished, I said, "You're a strong man." He looked at me in surprise. "I don't feel that way. I feel so small inside." As we talked, Stan shared that he was the youngest of five children. He was belittled by his parents whenever he showed any sign of personal initiative or strength, because they viewed such behavior as disobedient. His family used anger to communicate with one another, and he inherited this pattern. When he has a personal opinion, he has to get angry to say it. Stan's feeling box looks like this:

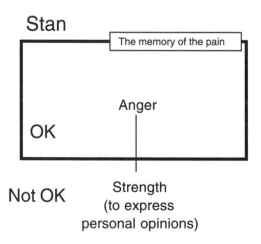

Figure 6. Stan's Feeling Box

⋙ ⋙ *Don* Once Stan realized that his anger was connected to his strong opinions, he was able to touch the deep sadness and depression that he held underneath the anger. In childhood, Procrustes had chopped off his pleasurable and soft, painful feelings and made him a "powder keg" waiting to explode. During individual sessions, Stan learned to let his tears flow when speaking of his past. This released enough pressure to allow him to state his position firmly, without getting angry. He was also able to be in touch with how deeply he cared about people and ideas. I told him, "When you are angry, you are showing how much you care about the person or the issue you are talking about." Stan nodded, "That's what I keep telling my wife. I care. I didn't realize that my size and emotional force made me seem angry all the time. I really do care. I hate it when I am accused of being a bully!" His feeling box grew to hold anger, sadness, caring, and strong opinions.

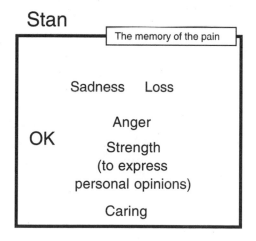

Figure 7. Stan's New Feeling Box

⊲⊱ ⊲⊱ DON | Now Stan's feelings of anger are a cue that he cares about what is going on. His restored inner guidance system enables him to integrate his feelings and his behavior, and to be more aware of the love he has for others.

Restoring the Inner Guidance System

As we have seen, when a boy feels strongly, and he hits the point of no return on the feeling curve, his parents' response has long-term consequences. If they punish or shame him for his feeling, his inner guidance system becomes skewed. He will adapt by having a *cover feeling*, or in psychological terms, a *symptom*. A symptom is a step removed from what he is really feeling. Let's say he is angry, but his parents don't allow this feeling in their home because they believe that people should always be happy. He learns to smile and act agreeable when he is really upset and wants to say no. His original feeling is blocked. Unable to let the feeling flow naturally to its peak and release into clear thinking, the boy flounders in depression, anxiety, or irritating behaviors, until the feeling finds a release. He may turn to sports, exercise, alcohol, other drugs, thrill-seeking, and overeating to help him cope with the blockage of feelings. These are substitutes, however, not solutions.

The memory of pain we felt when our true feelings were blocked holds us in place even as adults, until we venture outside the feeling box, as Stan did, into the forbidden feelings and behaviors. In doing so, we fear the terror we felt as children and resist our true feelings, because of the consequences that *might* come. Instead of annihilation, however, we will rediscover our lives and find new options for facing difficult situations in front of us. And as parents, freeing ourselves from the restrictions of our own feeling boxes is one of the best ways we can help our sons grow to manhood with their own inner guidance systems intact and strong.

Feeling Sticks

Feeling sticks can help us discover what our sons are really feeling and wanting. The original feeling and the cover feeling form two ends of the same stick.

	Not OK	OK
Norm:	Anger	Pleasing Behavior
Jack:	Anger/Hurt	Crazy Behavior
Elizabeth:	Anger	Sadness
Stan:	Caring, Having Opinions	Anger

When a boy continually acts in a problematic way or reports the same feeling over and over with no release or change, he is stuck on the wrong end of the stick. He is presenting a feeling or a behavior that is covering up his real feeling or behavioral desire. When the real feeling —the other end of the stick—is named in a supportive, accepting way, it can peak and release, opening him to clear thinking and a multitude of options. Norm learned that when he was too eager to please, he was really angry at someone. Elizabeth found that when she felt sadness without release, she was probably mad about something. When Jack wanted to act crazy, he knew he felt deeply about the topic or situation and could choose to talk or not talk about it.

There is no absolute list of feeling sticks. People construct their own to deal with the difficulties of growing up. In his book, No Boundary, transpersonal psychologist Ken Wilber writes that to find the shadow (those parts of ourselves that we have lost, i.e., the inner guidance system) is to "translate any symptom [cover feeling or behavior] back to its original form."[3]

In the table that follows,[4] Wilber provides a list of symptoms— what we prefer to call cover feelings or behaviors—and their original shadow forms, or what we term original feelings.

Table 1.

THE COMMON MEANING
OF VARIOUS SHADOW SYMPTOMS

A Dictionary for Translating Symptoms
Back to Their Original Shadow Forms

SYMPTOM translated to	ITS ORIGINAL SHADOW FORM
Pressure	Drive
Rejection ("Nobody likes me")	"I wouldn't give them the time of day!"
Guilt ("You make me feel guilty")	"I resent your demands"
Anxiety	Excitement
Self-consciousness ("Everybody's looking at me")	"I'm more interested in people than I know"
Impotence/Frigidity	"I wouldn't give him/her the satisfaction"
Fear ("They want to hurt me")	Hostility ("I'm angry and attacking without knowing it")
Sad	Mad!
Withdrawn	"I'll push you all away!"
I can't	"I won't, damn it!"
Obligation ("I have to")	Desire ("I want to")
Hatred ("I despise you for X")	Autobiographical gossip ("I dislike X in myself")
Envy ("You're soooo great")	"I'm a bit better than I know"

Keep in mind that we each give unique twists to these cover feelings and behaviors. Wilber further defines a symptom as a signal for an unconscious, or original, feeling. Here is an example: Ed experiences strong pressures at his work. Since the feeling of pressure is a signal for Ed, he may explore the feeling and realize that he has more drive for his job than he knows or is willing to admit. Perhaps he does not wish to admit his real feelings about the job because he likes to give the impression that he has to labor long and hard for the benefit of his superiors, or perhaps he has lost touch with his ambition to do his job well and enthusiastically. "Whatever the reason," Wilber asserts, "the symptom of pressure is a sure sign that you are more eager than you know. Thus, you can translate the symptom back to its original and correct form. 'I have to' becomes 'I want to.'"[5]

Exercises

Most of us don't want to repeat the mistakes that our parents made. Greater understanding of how Procrustes worked in our own early lives will enable us to make conscious parenting choices. Here's a chance for you to discover what your own feeling box contains. Below, in figure 8, are three boxes, labeled **Myself**, **Parenting Partner**, and **Son**. Use another sheet of paper and add more boxes for other children or other important people in your life, if you wish. First, simply list the feelings that were allowed in your family *inside* the box labeled **Myself**. Next, list the feelings that were not allowed in your family *outside* the box. When you have finished your own box, you can speculate about your parenting partner and son. If you can, explain the process to them, and ask them to fill out their own boxes. This makes for quite a discussion.

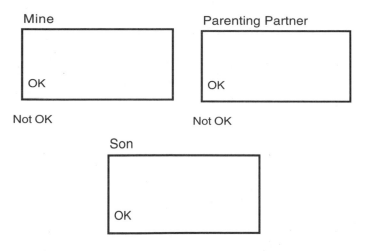

Figure 8.

Now review your family's feeling boxes. You may find that what is inside your box is outside your partner's box. It is amazing how many of us attract partners whose feeling box is the opposite of our own. The feelings outside your box will be the ones over which you most frequently struggle with your son or partner. The feelings outside their boxes will be those over which they struggle with you the most.

Next, by using the feeling stick, see if you can trace the feelings outside your box back to their original form. Sometimes they correspond to feelings inside your box and sometimes they do not. Do the same for your partner and son, or have them do it.

The following part of this exercise asks you to record each cover feeling and/or behavior (feelings/behaviors inside your box, which were "OK" to feel) and what you think your original feeling is (the other, or "Not OK," end of the feeling stick). Then choose a new behavior, to put into practice, that corresponds to your real feeling. See the following example.

MY CHART

Cover Feeling and/or Behavior	Original Feeling	New Behavior
Trying to please	Dissent	Voice my own opinion
1.		
2.		
3.		
4.		

SON'S CHART

Cover Feeling and/or Behavior	Original Feeling	New Behavior
Mad at father for not being home	Grief/sadness	Tell father I missed him
1.		
2.		
3.		
4.		

PARENTING PARTNER'S CHART

Cover Feeling and/or Behavior	Original Feeling	New Behavior
Enraged at son's behavior	Concern about him	Tell son I care
1.		
2.		
3.		
4.		

It takes practice to look beyond our son's behavior and find the feeling underlying it, but the rewards are great. Naming and acknowledging his suppressed feelings brings him relief, joy, intimacy, and the experience of truly being seen and heard. We can all remember times when we felt really understood, and there's nothing like it.

Not always, but sometimes, we will discover that our son's original feeling is one that we have trouble with—a feeling that is outside our own feeling box. Here's an example: Jonathan, age six, cries whenever he is mad. Jonathan uses a "sad behavior" rather than an angry response, because anger is outside his mother's feeling box. Her family did not approve of showing anger. It was okay, however, for her to cry and to feel sadness. Jonathan's mother is able to comfort his sadness, but his anger goes unnoticed. Therefore, Jonathan learns that he cannot trust his inner guidance system to tell him what is going on. The more we allow into our lives those feelings and behaviors from the outside of our "boxes," the more able we will be to cope with them in our sons. And the more able our sons will be to listen to their inner wisdom.

Supporting a Son's Feeling Life

Sex is an experience that follows the path of the feeling curve: beginning interest, slow buildup of excitement (tension), a peak (climax), the rapid decline into relaxation and clear thinking. It is not by accident that feelings, as well as the male and female sexual cycles, follow this path. Such is the way of nature: buildup, release, relaxation. A sure way to prepare our sons to live a loving, sexual life is to fully support their feeling lives, the ups and the downs.

Don Mathews, who works with men in domestic violence cases at the Impulse Treatment Center in Pleasant Hill, California, observes that men act violently out of a rage that covers up vulnerability, which they have never felt allowed to express. A tremendous pressure builds up inside, when one is stuck at the beginning of the feeling curve. Instead of feeling their underlying grief, these men strike out with their fists. According to Mathews, men who batter are often instructed to stomp on long walks or to take up running. This helps the raging feelings to be released downward, instead of toward another person.[6]

> *I snapped, and then it all became a fog. The next thing I remember is being really pissed that someone had ruined my favorite chair and table. My wife and son looked terrified, and then they called the police. Later, they told me that I had destroyed the furniture.*
>
> *—Thomas, member*
> *Violence Abatement Training Group*

After a year of counseling, Thomas is just now putting the pieces of his life back together. He is still aggressive, but he has learned the value of his tears and can comfort other men in emotional pain.

Ted's bottled-up grief took a similar but longer road. As a real estate broker, Ted was aggressive and driven toward success. He was rarely home, except for what he called "guest appearances." "I really went off one night when my wife called me 'the stranger' in front of my twelve-year-old daughter. When I saw the vase in my hand and knew that I intended to throw it, I realized I needed help. My best friend referred me to his counselor, but I couldn't stand for another man to be one-up on me, so I quit after two sessions. Now, two years later, I'm a recovering alcoholic; I go to a meeting a day; and I've just started therapy, again. I've been on the run from my sadness for a long time. It finally caught me, thank God!"

When men don't grieve important losses in their lives, the grief can turn into a powerful cover feeling—a desire for revenge. The movie *Jeremiah Johnson* and the book *Hanta Yo* both tell the story of a man whose wife and children are killed by marauding Indians. Their hunger for vengeance takes contrasting paths to resolution. Jeremiah Johnson seeks to avenge the deaths of his wife and son by killing any Crow Indian he meets. He stays on the move through the Rocky Mountains, never knowing when his sworn enemy will ambush him next. The legends about him travel far, and he is known as a great and cunning adversary of the Crow. What Jeremiah really wants is to live a solitary life in peace. That dream long eludes him while he pursues his private war of retaliation—a classic example of cover behavior.[7]

The lead character in *Hanta Yo* is the tribal chief. After the deaths of his family, he must go into a special tepee, where he is given food and water. He must stay there until he weeps deeply and grieves his loss. This is a traditional ritual of the tribe, because they know the danger of having a leader on a field of battle who has not fully grieved an important loss.[8] He will seek revenge because of his anger, and do something stupid that puts the tribe or himself at risk. We see examples throughout our culture of revenge behavior stemming from unresolved grief—excessive work, excessive play, excessive drugs, excessive sex, excessive material consumption, excessive alcohol, excessive food.

Our homes need to be "special tepees" where our sons and our men are allowed to grieve; to feel all of their emotions fully; to learn to consciously choose behavior that is life-affirming, rather than life-negating; to use the inner guidance system as a source of wisdom, power, and inner nurturing.

We have an important responsibility: to help our sons learn that their feelings reveal truth. A boy must learn that anger is a red flag, signaling that something important is happening; that sadness indicates a loss; that when he feels afraid, he must be vigilant; that his rage warns of an injustice being committed; that discomfort in the face of temptation alerts him to beware, because he is in disagreement with what's happening; and that his happiness signifies that he has been true to himself and all is "A-Okay!"

When a boy trusts his feelings, he is in touch with the reality of his own experience. From this place, he can use his own values to direct his life, rather than being swayed by the thoughts and actions of others. With an inner guidance system that is loud and clear, our sons can form visions that are whole enough to embrace the complexities of living in a technological age. This is the challenge they face as they grow into manhood.

End Notes

1. Daniel Udo De Haes, *The Young Child: Creative Living with Two- to Four-year-olds*, trans. Simon and Paulamaria Blaxland de Lange (Edinburgh: Floris Books, 1986), 15.

2. Ann Sheridan, M.A., conversation with Don Elium, Pleasant Hill, Calif., 23 Apr. 1991.

3. Ken Wilber, *No Boundary* (Boulder, Colo.: Shambhala, 1979), 98.

4. Ibid., 98-99.

5. Ibid., 98.

6. Don Mathews, M.A., M.F.C.C., interview with Don Elium, Pleasant Hill, Calif., 19 May 1989.

7. Joe Wizan, producer, *Jeremiah Johnson*, Warner Brothers & Stanford Productions, 1972.

8. Ruth Beebe Hill, *Hanta Yo* (New York: Doubleday & Co., 1979), 34-35.

CHAPTER SEVEN

Fences:
Making It Safe to Grow

Boys are like cows. The bigger they get, the more pasture they require. But, they still need fences.

—An old grandfather

❧ ❧ *DON* | When I speak to large groups of parents on the topic of "fences," I start with my all-time favorite story about choosing consequences. It was told to me at a parenting workshop by Susan, mother of two boys, Jason, ten, and Michael, eight. This is Susan's story:

"Our family had spent three months planning our first trip to Disneyland. Schedules were rearranged, money saved, and all was looking good as we left on a Monday morning. The boys were especially restless as we set off, visions of Disneyland dancing in their heads. I was tired from our busy schedule during the previous two weeks. Jeff, my husband, wanted a smooth entry into Los Angeles, where we would spend our nights with my sister and family, and our days at Disneyland.

"After two hours on the road, the boys started bouncing in the back seat. This was before the days of seatbelts, and they were trying to hit their heads on the inside roof of the car. In my calmest 'parenting voice' I suggested we stop for a break to let them run around. We took a thirty-minute pit stop, and all looked fine. When they returned to the car, the boys started bouncing again. 'Boys, stop bouncing! It's dangerous.' They didn't stop. I turned around to face them, and said it again. They just kept it up. Then it happened. I can still see the scene in slow motion. I tried to stop my mouth from speaking those dreaded words, but it was too late. The synapses in my brain had already fired; my mouth formed the words, and I angrily said, 'If you bounce one more time, you will not go to Disneyland!' You guessed it. They bounced.

"I remember the look on my husband's face as he slowly pulled the car to the side of the road. We have an agreement to follow through on the consequences we give our boys, so they can depend on us to do what we say. 'Come with me. We have to talk,' he said. We stood with the car idling on the side of Interstate 5. 'You know we have to follow through.' I pleaded with him to make an exception—this one time wouldn't matter. But I knew he was right. We trudged back to the car, and I said, 'Boys, we will continue to LA. But you will be staying with your aunt and uncle, while your dad and I go to Disneyland.' Their faces showed amazement and disbelief. I couldn't believe myself that I was saying it, but that is what we did. Two days at Disneyland for my husband and me, and two days at the relatives for the boys.

"This was one of the most trying experiences of my life. But we never had any serious trouble with our kids after that. When we set limits, they knew we meant business, and we continued to follow through. They are now in their thirties, and they often talk about that fateful trip. They say that they now understand why we did what we did, but they still try to get us to admit we made a mistake. I don't know whether it was a mistake or not, but I do know that I learned to count to fifty before I set any more consequences."

Audiences of parents usually split down the middle over this story. One side agrees with Susan and Jeff: "Follow through, no matter what, so your kids feel they can depend on you to do what you say." The other faction thinks that Susan and Jeff made a terrible decision: they should have forgiven themselves for announcing a stupid consequence, set one that was more appropriate, then all gone to Disneyland. There are always some parents in the crowd who are aghast that Susan and Jeff went to Disneyland without their kids; this was too cruel. Others say they would have resented their children if the family had been forced to sacrifice its first Disneyland trip.

None of their reactions is wrong; a solid case could be made for any of these approaches. Ultimately, the point of this story is that it beautifully underlines the importance of thinking through our own personal approach to parental limit setting and choosing consequences, and the vital need to be in agreement with our parenting partners. There are as many different ways to set limits as there are ways for kids to get into trouble.

Parents As the Good Guys

My son gets so mad when I tell him no.
I often end up giving in, because
it hurts me when he says he hates me.

—Brad, father of a six-year-old

Parents hate to be hated. But the more often children are left to set their own limits regarding their behavior, the crazier family life becomes. And if anarchy is our family's modus operandi, we will never know what to expect from our children when we are with them in public, as well.

DON | One family brought their five-year-old hellion into counseling. They sat together with him on their laps. Suddenly, the boy jumped down and quickly knocked off every book on my bookshelf. The parents just sat, shook their heads, and the father threw up his hands. They did not move from their seats, even when the boy headed for my sculptures. I bolted up, grabbed the kid from behind, picked him up, sat him beside his father, and said to the parents, "I can't believe that you let him run all over you!" To the boy, I said kindly but firmly, "You sit there, until I tell you to move." His eyes widened. No one had ever told him, without malice, what his behavior limits were. The father said to him, "Yes. You sit there," and laughed. The boy sat still for twenty minutes, until he asked to use the bathroom. I told him that he needed to wait one minute until we finished our topic. Then I took him to the bathroom, helped him with the zipper, and gently brought him back into the room. He sat through the rest of the session. Afterward, I took him to my toy room to play, and then we put the toys away together.

What these parents needed—more than empathy for their suffering—was to see how to be caring, yet firm and directive with their son. The boy's father revealed that his own father had been rigid and cruel, and he had feared that he would repeat with his son what his father had done to him. He soon understood that he was repeating the cruelty with his son, by doing the opposite of what his father had done. Without limits, the boy would not learn how to be with other people or himself in positive ways. This five-year-old might take over the home, but he would not be prepared to meet the hard reality of life outside. And this world would treat such a boy harshly.

Boys do not need buddies for parents. Boys need parents who are courageous enough to set firm, appropriate boundaries for their behavior. The male drive to "plunge in" is sometimes stronger than a boy's will to consider the consequences. He needs containment.

I missed doing a lot of fun things when I was young, because after my father left, I worked to help Mom support the family. So I couldn't wait to play with my son. We played baseball with his friends, went swimming in the summer, played ice hockey in winter. It was great, I thought. Then he got real moody. Stayed in his room a lot. Hedged about playing ball, when I'd suggest we go play with his friends. He started getting hard to handle, you know? Talking back, staying out late, not letting us know where he was going. I felt pretty bad. Then one day, after I had suggested we call his friends to get up a game, he said to me, "Dad, it's great you take an interest in my games and all, but I need you to be my dad. Let me go play with my friends alone. Okay?" I guess I was pretty shocked. Well, after that I started laying down the law about getting home on time, and all the rest. We still play catch and stuff on the weekends, but his free time is his own, within reason. I think we're closer now than when we were together so much. It beats me!

—Alberto, father of fourteen-year-old son

To be productive, the piston of a motor needs a strong cylinder to concentrate the energy. Like the piston, a boy needs strong limits to focus his male energies into bold creativity for facing life. Without clear guidelines for his behavior, he will run wild, or he won't run at all. Boys need friendship from their parents, but they need positive limits and fair consequences more. When the lessons of basic, behavioral limit setting are left to others—teachers, the police, the court system, the jails—they will not care as deeply about our sons as we do.

Setting limits alone is not enough. This creates a jail-like atmosphere, which fosters rebellion and revenge. Boys will spend more time plotting a vengeful act than pondering how their behavior affects others. The bond between parents and sons is the key to setting effective limits. Time spent together in fun, listening, learning, and having adventures bonds the hearts of sons and parents.

The balancing of limit setting and parent-son relationships begins at a boy's birth. The father who waits to become alive in the family until his son is a teenager and making trouble puts himself at a great disadvantage; he will have little effect with his son. If he starts "laying down the law," the son can just leave. A thirteen-year-old can live for days by going from one friend's house to another. Equal amounts of quality and quantity time spent with sons when they are young, especially with their fathers, is an investment that pays off royally when the testosterone hits at puberty.

Without a seasoned heart connection between parents and sons, the teenage years feel like wartime. This is how it was for Bobby and his father, a successful corporate executive. Bobby was in counseling because he was cutting classes and flunking out of school. His father had always made his son "toe the line," but was seldom home. In one session, the father said to Bobby, "I only want the best for you." His son yelled, "Since when? You're always gone. All I get are your orders. When have you ever cared enough to be with me? I wasn't convenient. Right, Dad? Sorry, it ain't gonna work, this time. I'll get myself out of this mess. Leave me alone." There are few things more painful than watching a father's face drop in genuine sadness when he realizes that he has failed to be emotionally connected with his son. The person who is a boy's first hero becomes an enemy, and there is no heart connecting them.

Quality time is important, but it never replaces the hours a son needs to absorb his father into his heart and soul. Waldorf educator Rahima Baldwin, in a wonderful book for parents called *You Are Your Child's First Teacher*, writes: "Quality time is not the same as the every-dayness of being together. Let's neither glorify nor undervalue it."[1]

We've seen how counterproductive limit setting can be in the absence of a heart connection. The other extreme, all heart and no boundaries, can create a different kind of chaos and struggle. In our freedom-oriented culture, a boy is sometimes given the controls that belong in the hands of his elders. This is what happened to Mike, whose mother, Jane, came into counseling the day after he ran away from home. Jane explained that Mike had left because she had said he couldn't go to a friend's house at midnight on a school night. He was fifteen. Just before the session, Jane had seen Mike at a hamburger stand and had pleaded with him to come home. He had refused, and asked for money because he was running low. She gave him fifty dollars out of fear that he might not eat.

Counseling helped Jane realize that Mike was using her heartfelt, motherly concern against her. She had to keep her heart connection, while building some strong fences. She decided not to give him any more money and not to look for him. When he did call her to say he was coming home, she countered, "I'm not ready for you to come home yet. I need some more time. And when you do come home, things will be different. I am the boss, and you will have to agree to my rules. I'll be as fair as I can, but the way you have been treating me has ended." Two days later, Mike showed up for his mom's therapy appointment to ask whether she would take him back. "I can't believe I was so stupid," Jane said later. "I was just so scared to see him out alone. The more line I gave him, the more he took. Now there is no line."

Focusing on a son's behavior, like Jane did, usually works if the issue concerns setting better limits. But when problems erupt because of a breakdown in a good relationship between parent and son, bigger power struggles may follow. It is then wise to put the frustrating behavior in the background and concentrate on rebuilding the good connection with each other.

Don | Jake and his mother are a good example. Lisa called for an appointment because of Jake's anger. His father had died three years earlier. Now, at fourteen, he was starting to talk back to his mother and was not cooperating at home. Jake was a tough client; I could tell that he hated therapists. I told them that Jake's anger problem was the least of their worries. I wanted to know, what had happened to their good relationship? This took the focus off Jake and captured his interest. He became a willing participant in sorting out what had caused the loss of connection between him and his mom.

After Jake's dad died, Lisa and Jake had become extremely close. We found that each was worried about how the other would carry on after the death. Jake needed permission to let go of his mom and live his own life. Lisa needed to stop centering her life around Jake and begin building a personal life for herself. Each of them had to trust that the other would be okay without Jake's dad. The anger problem became a side issue as mother and son allowed their relationship to mature.

The parent-son bond, from infancy through the middle years, forms the platform from which the teenage son will explore his uniqueness, his relationship to the world, and the many facets of being male. The absence of this emotional platform leaves a hole in his heart, and he will go looking for something to fill it—drugs, alcohol, obsessive sex, overwork, extreme passive-aggressiveness. The soul force seeks acknowledgment amidst the adolescent male's biological urges. If we focus only on setting limits on our son's behavior, we will continue to create soulless men. We parents must set limits, but they must stand on the foundation of a heart-to-heart relationship with our sons.

Guidelines for Setting
Boundaries and Consequences

"I guess I don't know how to set limits with my son" has become both an admission and a cry for help on the part of many parents. It is hard to set boundaries in a caring, fair way as adults if we never had them set for us as children. There are lots of good how-to parenting books on the market, but the challenge is to stay one chapter ahead of our son as he grows. Those pages dealing with limit setting will be well-worn before he becomes very old. Here are guidelines for boundary making that have helped us.

Setting behavioral boundaries is not a democratic process. There are three styles of parenting. The authoritative parent makes the rules, offers few choices, and expects adherence to family policy. The democratic parent is concerned with the fairness of any situation, considers how everyone feels, offers lots of choices, and makes decisions based on majority rule. The *laissez-faire* parent's children are allowed to behave however and believe whatever they wish.

Adjustment studies of children from these three groups followed them into adulthood, and have astounding outcomes. Children raised in the laissez-faire style grew up to have difficulty cooperating and getting along with others. The democratic style produced adults who found it hard to make decisions. Those raised by authoritarian parents were the most well-adjusted adults, able to make decisions, follow rules, and cooperate with others.[2]

An important distinction must be made between *rigid authoritarianism*, which could be classified as a fourth parenting style, and the authoritative parent. The former, a parent who asserts his or her power through cruelty and abuse, with little regard for the needs, feelings, and well-being of family members, creates children who are less well-adjusted than any of the three other groups. Many of these children become the child abusers, rapists, and mentally insane adults of our society. Again, the most productive parenting style is the benevolent authoritative one; the parent takes charge with kindness, understanding, and empathy for the child's position. This stance assures children that someone is on duty to care for them. They can trust that their parents will follow through on what they say they will do. This relieves children of having to be responsible for situations beyond their ability to handle.

Contrary to popular cultural belief, children are not little adults! Rahima Baldwin reminds us that Jean Piaget, the Swiss psychologist and philosopher, concluded that rational thinking does not develop until ten or eleven years of age. Baldwin writes, "We expect to be able to reason with our children as soon as they are verbal. We reason with them about everything from their behavior and its consequences to why the sea is salty. And indeed, some five-year-olds show great ability to conduct such conversations with their parents—but they have learned it through imitating years of that type of interaction with their parents. Young children do not yet think rationally, and reason has little impact on changing their behavior."3 It takes consistent boundaries and logical consequences to do that.

⊰⊱ *JEANNE*	After setting the consequences for my five-year-old son's misbehavior, I asked him, "Do you know why I give consequences?" In all seriousness, he replied, "To hurt my feelings?"

It bears repeating: set limits kindly and authoritatively. Young sons need brief explanations; older sons need more. But the limits we set are not up for a vote—sometimes negotiation is needed, depending on the age of a son, but not a vote. He can vote when he is eighteen.

Boundaries need to be age-appropriate. A four-year-old son requires tight limits to keep him in a safe and supervised environment. A teenage boy needs more "room"; the safety factor in his case takes the shape of a curfew time, instead of a lock on the backyard gate.

Basic limits are set firmly and with little discussion for a five-year-old. What he needs most is repetition, patience, and the understanding that he is little and will eventually "get it." With a teenager, however, much talk and negotiation may be necessary to keep in contact with his rapid change and maturation. The teenage years require constant evaluation of how loose or tight the rules can be. We can expect to be frequently confused: one moment his conduct is responsible, and in the next, he has "bitten off more than he can chew." If we fail to be open to discussion and negotiation, our sons will revolt. The power struggle will escalate, and our lack of kindness will keep us up late, wondering where they are and when they will come home. The most well-adjusted adults, who can set productive limits for themselves, come from families where the parents are benevolently in charge.

Consequences need to apply directly to the misbehavior. Teenagers usually know what they need from their parents, and they are rougher on themselves than their parents would ordinarily be. One adolescent recalls the time that he brought the car home two hours later than he had promised. "Mom revoked my television privileges for two weeks. That just made me mad! She should have taken away the car for a week, but don't tell her I said that."

⬧ ⬧ *DON* | Sometimes the consequences we set create more frustration for us than for our children. We've all experienced announcing a "Disneyland" boundary out of anger, and having the consequence take up more time and energy than the misbehavior. One beautiful Saturday, my son and his friend were chasing each other through the house, whooping together at a high pitch. In anger I barked, "If you yell once more, you can't play outside!" Of course they yelled again, and instead of a quiet morning spent reading the paper on the couch, I was cooped up all day with two bored boys who begged me to play with them. Consequences are rarely needed immediately. Take time to think things through, instead of impulsively choosing one that everyone will regret later.

Also, beware of setting a consequence too far in the future, such as saying that next Wednesday, when it's time for bedtime stories, your son can't have one. This creates too much anxiety in a younger child. Here's a good guideline for timing: the younger the child, the quicker the consequence. Older boys, whose sense of time and space is more developed, can handle consequences that will go into effect at a later date. The point is to instill responsibility in our sons, not to create emotional disability.

Set boundaries that yield small victories. One of the best-ever bowlers was interviewed after bowling a perfect 300 game. The TV interviewer asked him, "How did you feel as a young boy when you threw your ball down the lane and missed all of the pins?" The bowler replied, "I never missed. I'm not bragging. When I was young, there were "pin boys" who set the pins instead of machines. My father would have me roll the ball down the lane; of course it would hit the gutter, but the pin boy was instructed to put a pin in front of it. As I got older, my balls would roll between gutters, and again, the pin boys put the pin in front of each ball as it came through. I began to hit the pins more and more, until I was throwing strikes most of the time. My father always put the pins where I could hit them."

The key to cooperation and self-motivation is setting realistic goals and behavioral boundaries. Small, attainable successes build confidence and a friendly relationship with discipline and persistence. The following story about Jason, thirteen, illustrates how true this is.

⬨ ⬨ *DON* | I first saw Jason and his parents in therapy just after they had taken away all of his privileges but food, sleep, and school. During my assessment, I learned that because of his high test scores, Jason had been advanced a grade when he was seven. Now, because his body looked sixteen, more was expected of him than he could deliver developmentally. Jason was emotionally behind his peers, he felt left out of the social scene, and could not focus on his studies because of the rejection he experienced at school. Home had also closed in on him, and his depression had reached clinical proportions. His "bowling pins" were not only out of hitting range; when he got close, they were pulled away!

We chose several solutions. First, to loosen the "choke hold" in his social life, Jason was allowed to attend more activities at the family's church, where the age groupings covered several grades. Next, the family hired a tutor to help him catch up on the studies in which he had fallen behind. He was then retested to assess his level of development. His test scores convinced Jason's parents to have his courses changed to match his skill level. This put him a few credits behind, but relieved the tremendous burden of trying to meet impossible standards.

I saw Jason six months later and was amazed at the changes in him. He was animated, excited about his activities, and proud of his achievements. Life came back to him when he was given boundaries that yielded small successes in all areas. His parents' well-intentioned boundaries had been smothering him. Now his parents are his supporters, instead of his taskmasters. "I feel like a fifty-pound weight has been taken off my chest," he said.

Behavioral boundaries are like fences around pastures; they occasionally need to be mended, checked for holes, made stronger, and expanded. Just as "rules are made to be broken," so, paradoxically, we set limits knowing that our sons are inevitably going to test those limits—and push beyond them. A boy crosses a boundary for many reasons and in many ways. If he is pushing on the boundary, like a cow who leans on a fence to reach the greener grass on the other side, he is probably just testing us; he is curious to see how we respond. Will we really follow through? Mending the fence with a short reminder will probably be enough to keep him on the appropriate side. If he is crashing through, like a bull who sees a red shirt, other issues may underlie his refusal to stay inside the pasture.

JEANNE | I always insisted that our young son ride in the cart at the grocery store. He couldn't knock anything off the shelves, he wouldn't get lost or hurt, and our trips took less time. This day he screamed to get out of the cart, and when I refused, he climbed out by himself. He was not distracted by our game of counting all the red boxes, or by my handing him the groceries to put in the basket. Putting him back and firmly telling him to stay put had no effect. Then it hit me that we hadn't eaten since early morning, and this stop was the last in a long list of errands. He had reached his limit, and was telling me in the only way he knew how.

Young children generally crash through boundaries because they are tired, bored, or hungry. A teenager may crash through out of anger or to get revenge. In either case, it is not the boundary that is causing the problem, but an underlying, usually unconscious need that has gone unnoticed or unheeded.

At times boundaries must be made stronger, just as a sturdy corral is needed to hold a stallion new to the farm. His natural orneriness and energy will push him to see if he can get over or through that fence. The same goes for a group of boys in our neighborhood who range in age from three to ten. Habitually, moms and kids gather on one neighbor's lawn in the afternoons, where moms visit while kids play. A certain amount of running and tagging, pushing and shoving, wrestling and tussling is allowed. The line is drawn at hitting and punching, or fighting when angry. One particular afternoon the game got rowdy, and several boys ended up in tears, bruised and slightly battered. Everything was sorted out, and the play continued normally. The next afternoon, the same thing happened, this time resulting in a bloody nose and bleeding knees. The mothers conferred, and decided that some stronger limits were necessary to keep someone from getting seriously hurt.

When a colt becomes just too big for his pasture, the fence needs enlarging to give him more room to run and kick up his heels. We know it is time to make a larger fence when a boy keeps climbing over it.

When Chris was thirteen, he wanted to date. I set his curfew at 9:30 p.m., and decided that until he was older, he must date in a group of friends. He agreed to it, and we didn't have too much trouble, until now. He's sixteen, and I know that he has a steady girlfriend. All seemed fine; he has been pretty good about getting in on time. Then I found the kitchen stool outside his window. He admitted that he had been going to bed around 11, and then sneaking out to meet his girlfriend. She'd been doing the same thing. That night he was so tired when he got home, he forgot about the kitchen stool. I realized then that he was growing up, and it was time to set some new rules.

—Sheila, a wiser single mom

In the following section we will take a brief look at five general types of boundaries, or limits, that we parents can use to structure the lives of our sons. Further age-related detail on when and how to apply these boundaries will follow in chapters 9 through 11, which will explore in depth a boy's development from birth through age seventeen.

Verbal Guidelines

SPOKEN AGREEMENTS KEPT

These spoken agreements between parent and son carry no consequences. Care is shown on both sides that the agreement is kept. Reminders are seldom necessary, and if a mistake is made, the boy voluntarily makes amends. This was the case with John, nine, whose daily chore was to feed and water the cat. When he forgot, he felt remorse for the cat, and worked out a system on his own to help him remember. It was important to him to follow through on his agreement with his parents on behalf of his pet. No consequences were necessary. Rex, sixteen, agreed to do the family grocery shopping. When he forgot three items that were important elements of the family's daily meals, he apologized for the inconvenience and returned to the store without hesitation.

It was a different story for Mary, whose son is one and a half. "I told him not to touch the glass vase, and he went right ahead and knocked it over. I slapped his hand, but the next day, he did it again!" Mary expected her son to follow her verbal boundary, which he was not yet capable of understanding. Before the age of six, most children lack what Piaget called "concrete operational thinking," which enables them to follow instructions and remember them in the future. "Childproofing," putting away all things that are precious or invite danger, is the better solution for small children. Using verbal guidelines is a very mature level of boundary-setting. It is a goal to be reached when our children are ready—usually after the age of nine—and to be celebrated when they reach it.

Picket Fence

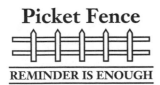

REMINDER IS ENOUGH

This boundary is put in place by parents without negotiation. Its purpose is to promote household functioning, and to teach responsibility for oneself. Five-year-old Matt's chore is to put his dirty clothes in the wash pile. He is usually very good at remembering to do this, but he occasionally needs a reminder. Then he shapes up immediately, and goes for progressively longer periods of time between reminders.

The difference between picket fences and verbal agreements is that a verbal agreement puts parents and older sons on a more equal footing; some negotiation takes place, and the son is self-motivated to stick to the agreement. With a picket fence, the son doesn't take full responsibility for adhering to the limit set. It is still the parent's job to remind him; otherwise, he will hop over the picket fence now and then. Although very cooperative and willing, he isn't fully self-directed. Instead, he is outwardly motivated by others—his parents—to comply with the rules. Therefore, picket fences clearly require more parental guidance, and sometimes need reinforcement through consequences.

In fourteen-year-old Seth's family, the rule is that when food is eaten outside of the kitchen or family room, plates and leftovers are brought back to the kitchen by the eater. Seth likes to eat in his room while he studies, but he often forgets to take the leftovers back to the kitchen. Mom finds them weeks later, smelly and encrusted with mold. Reminders help for a while, but Seth's mom needs a better response to this boundary. Together, she and Seth decide to make a chart that requires him to check his food out of the kitchen, and then back in. If a check is missing, his mother knows to remind him before the plate becomes disgusting.

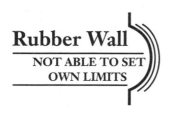

Rubber Wall
NOT ABLE TO SET
OWN LIMITS

Sometimes picket fences aren't enough. Sons feel safer, and more confident in their ability to be responsible, when they know exactly what is expected of them and how much they can get away with. They test their boundaries, by bouncing against them with verbal arguments or by totally disregarding them, to see what the consequences are. Rubber walls are flexible, but the consequences have greater impact than with picket fences.

James, sixteen, missed his midnight curfew by two hours on two consecutive nights, and he failed to call to let his parents know that he'd be late. The first night he was reminded of his curfew. After the second night, his curfew time was changed to 10 p.m. for three weeks, with the understanding that if he honored it, his former curfew would be reinstated.

Rubber walls are most effective if reinforced without parental anger or threats. Respect for the son's occasional need to push against and test boundaries is important, and frequent review by parents keeps limits appropriate and in line with a son's growing maturity. At this stage sons may need more pasture, but they still need fences.

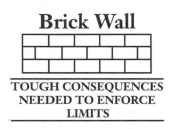

Brick Wall

TOUGH CONSEQUENCES
NEEDED TO ENFORCE
LIMITS

We all know the story about the farmer who hit his donkey with a board every morning before work. A stranger asked him if his donkey was a good worker. "Oh, yes," replied the farmer, "but you have to get his attention first!" Sometimes we need brick walls to get our son's attention. He may be jumping our picket fences, he's unable to keep verbal agreements, and rubber walls invite too much rebellion. Brick walls are used by parents to keep the problem from having to be addressed by the community—school, neighbors, or the police.

Sean, fifteen, was flunking out of school, and he finally admitted to his parents that he was skipping classes. His parents explained the importance of making good grades, finishing school, and going to college. Sean promised that he would stop skipping classes and bring up his grades. He continued to miss class, however, and one day his father caught him in a local restaurant during school hours. Sean proved that he was not able to keep his agreements, so limits involving serious consequences had to be enforced for him.

Before erecting brick walls, parents must seek answers to several questions: When did our son's ability to follow the rules change? How is his relationship with us, with his friends, with teachers? What challenges or problems is he dealing with that might cause his behavior? If authorities outside the family are involved—school officials, in Sean's case—we must take the lead in making sure that family consequences work well with those set by the community.

A brick wall also calls for us to monitor our son's time closely. Sean's school chose to assign him an extra study hall to bring up his grades, and his parents demanded that he come directly home after school to study for an hour. Any outing had to be supervised by an adult. Most important, Sean and his dad would spend more free time together doing projects that they both liked. Sometimes a son's need for brick walls is a call for more time with Dad, although few teenage boys would admit to this.

When the parent-son relationship has been restored, the consequences have been carried out, and the son has shown consistency in abiding by the brick walls, his limits can return to the more flexible, rubber walls. However, this process is not to be hurried; if it is, problems may crop up in other arenas of the boy's life. He may do great in school and never miss a class, but refuse to cooperate with home duties and in family relationships. Each boy and each area of a boy's life requires a customized approach. Parental patience, along with a commitment to give the necessary time, make the development of a self-motivated and responsible son more likely, and the need for brick walls less frequent.

Brick walls are the best limits for very young children where their safety is concerned. A five-year-old, for example, needs many brick walls. He may not play in the front yard without an adult present. He may not play in the street. He may not play with matches. He may not turn on the kitchen stove. He may not get into a stranger's car. Until a child is seven or eight, he does not have the capacity to set such limits for himself, so we must set them for him. With certain children, enforcing these limits will take most of a parent's time. That's what we're here for, but it's reassuring to know that our son will eventually grow up to set his own limits and boundaries.

Iron Bars

AT RISK TO SELF
OR ANOTHER

These are the firmest boundaries, and they require twenty-four-hour supervision by parents or juvenile hall. Iron bars come down when a son breaks the law or the trust of parents or other authority figures. His behavior shows criminal intent, whether the boy sees it that way or not. His free movement must be limited. He may become a ward of the court and be temporarily placed in a group home or other supervised setting for juveniles.

Mitch, fourteen, spent three weeks in juvenile hall, after he was arrested for stealing three thousand dollars to buy rare coins for his collection. Then he spent two months at home on probation, gave three thousand hours of community service, and worked to repay the victim over a two-year period. Failure to follow through on his sentence would entail his return to juvenile hall. Mitch's parents worked conscientiously with the adjunct community services to bring their son back safely to family life. They willingly complied with the court's order for family counseling and personal counseling for their son. There, Mitch underwent psychological testing to determine whether his act stemmed from a deeper psychological disturbance, or whether he had learned a hard lesson and should be given the chance to have his freedom and personal rights returned.

For some families, this process takes anywhere from three months to several years. It is a time of deep soul-searching for parents and for sons, and a time for forgiveness. It is a time for holding steadfastly to the boundaries drawn, and a crucial time to direct the son toward a positive role within the family, as well as in the community.

Setting behavioral limits and consequences is the hardest part of parenting a son. We must give our complete attention to the task. At best, fences are age-appropriate, so we have to be good observers. Our son's behavior will guide us to choose ones that fit his maturity level. The most effective consequences logically fit the misbehavior, so we must think thoroughly before announcing the "sentence." Our sons learn to trust us only when we follow through with what we say, so we must consider the ramifications of choosing "No Disneyland!" Both limits and consequences require diligent monitoring, so we are asked to give our time, often "above and beyond the call of duty." We must hold fast with love and compassion in the face of some of our son's ugliest moments. We must be able to put our mistakes behind us, and be thankful that our sons are so resilient. We will be challenged to look for the positive intention behind their behavior, to hear the voice of their souls.

Fences: A Quick Summary

Verbal Guidelines
SPOKEN AGREEMENTS KEPT

Spoken agreements kept between parent and son that carry no consequences. Reminders are rarely necessary, and there is care shown on both sides to keep the agreement. When the agreement is broken, amends and apologies are made swiftly. The motivation to keep verbal agreements is inner-directed, so they work best with children after age nine.

Picket Fence
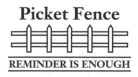
REMINDER IS ENOUGH

Reminder is enough to enforce this limit placed by the parent to promote household functioning. A boy may occasionally hop over it, so minor consequences or negotiation may be necessary.

Rubber Wall
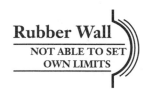
NOT ABLE TO SET OWN LIMITS

Not able to set own limits, so they are set for him. He needs something to bounce off of, to feel safe and to learn responsibility. The consequences have greater impact.

Brick Wall
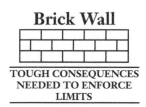
TOUGH CONSEQUENCES NEEDED TO ENFORCE LIMITS

Tough consequences needed to get a son's attention. He needs to "shape up," or he will put himself in trouble or danger. The goal is to take care of the problem within the family lest an outside authority must intervene.

Iron Bars

AT RISK TO SELF OR ANOTHER

At risk to self or another, son requires twenty-four-hour supervision by parents or juvenile hall. Son is in legal trouble. Free movement is limited. He must show serious intent to do good before regaining freedom, privileges, trust, and responsibilities.

End Notes

1. Rahima Baldwin, *You Are Your Child's First Teacher* (Berkeley, CA: Celestial Arts, 1989), 21.

2. Kathleen Stassen Berger, *The Developing Person Through Childhood and Adolescence* (New York: Worth Publishers, 1986), 328-30.

3. Baldwin, *First Teacher*, 10.

CHAPTER EIGHT

The Positive Intent:
Touching His Soul

Be careful when you cast out your demons,
lest ye cast out your best parts.[1]

—Joseph Campbell

It took Betty three years to get a drug treatment center established in the heart of East LA. She was a small-built woman taking on a huge task. The odds against her were great, but in the end, her persistence and keen way of understanding people won out. She worked personally with many of the youths who came through the center, and this is the story of the brother of one of them. Her client was a thirteen-year-old girl who wanted to kick drugs and was working to that end. One day a tall, muscular man with heavy, gold chains around his neck burst into the center looking for the "little woman who is messing with my sister." His wrath set everyone running except Betty. She walked right up to him and said, "You really care about your sister, don't you. So do I. Come in my office, and let's talk about her." The young man immediately calmed down, and followed her into the office.

Betty's work seems magical, and in some ways, its results are, but her method is one that we can all learn. Rather than being put off by the man's threatening presence, Betty listened for the positive message that he was sending to her: "I care about my sister." She didn't judge the brother for being angry. Instead, she assumed that his rage was an immature expression of his feeling of caring. Betty interacted with him on the level of caring for his sister, which they both shared.

Later Betty learned that this man, the local gang leader, kept watch over his neighborhood, especially the kids on the street. At nineteen, he saw himself as their father figure. Soon Betty's treatment center had the protection of his group. He trusted her. Without negative judgment, she spoke to his mature self, addressing his deeper, driving desire, that of caring. Like a seed that gets the proper food, water, and sunshine, his caring sprouted into action.

A boy's soul has a natural urge to grow, but it must have the right conditions to bloom. When our son's difficult emotions and extreme behaviors are viewed as "seeds" that need careful tending, we are better able to let go of our anger, frustration, and judgment, and parent him with love and firmness.

Conditions for Nurturing a Son's Potential

There is a world of difference between the mature mustard plant and the tiny seed from which it started. Betty's method of listening for the positive intent[2] is founded on principles that—like the adequate light, proper soil conditions, sufficient moisture, and protection from pests that a seedling needs to flourish—can provide the conditions under which a boy's soul may thrive, and can lead him down his unique path to maturity.

We need to provide environments where our sons' natural gifts can find mature expression. Most of us would agree that boys need a solid education; social activities; free time; and planned opportunities for growth, such as swim teams, Boy Scouts, church youth groups, and summer jobs. But there is one law that supersedes all parental efforts to put one's son on his unique road: The soul moves when the soul moves. No matter how hard we push, cajole, or pray, his soul will move him onward only when it is ready, and when his, not our, conditions are right. There is no way to calculate when that moment will be, but we will have no doubt that it has happened.

Scott's family had always considered him a "charming but lazy bum," who had "a great gift for gab but no follow-through." His parents spent thousands on his education, but at twenty-two he was barely supporting his meager lifestyle. He had gone from job to job, but nothing suited him. Then he took a job as a janitor at a home for the aging. There, his "gift for gab" made him a favorite among the residents. Not only did he clean; he was also asked to assist with the residents, because he was amazingly able to get them to cooperate in their care.

Scott's gift of giving comfort then led him to accept a janitorial job at a psychiatric hospital. Again, his easy way of relating to patients and gaining their confidence prompted the staff to make him an assistant who helped patients become acclimated to the hospital environment and routine. The doctors, nurses, and psychologists came to value him as a fellow staff member, and Scott was promoted to the intake department. His function was to act like a janitor, but to talk with new patients, to help them feel safe and understood as they were entering the hospital.

Eventually Scott decided to work with people in more dangerous situations. He became a fireman, and was always called upon to calm and comfort people in distress. He is now a qualified paramedic, a scuba diver with a water-rescue team, and may seek police training.

"He's not the brother I grew up with," his sister now says of him. "He works hard, he's well-organized, and he really cares about other people besides himself." Scott is the brother she grew up with. His "gift for gab" was an immature form of his ability to care deeply and to comfort people under stress. Scott was like a seed, who grew from the hibernating "bum" into the effective professional capable of rescuing and comforting those in distress. Within every boy's soul is an urge to ripen his raw beginnings into a productive, life-giving form. As therapist Edith Schutz, Ph.D., says, "You want to help people grow into bigger shoes; not by denying where they are now, but by building upon it."[3]

Listen for the positive intent without denying the immature actions or words. Betty, the drug-center director we spoke of earlier, used the brother's menacing manner and angry words as cues to understanding the positive intent of his visit. If she had ordered him out or called the police because of his behavior, she would have missed a golden opportunity to cultivate an important ally. We parents often miss golden opportunities for deeper connection with our sons, because we are offended or put off by their words and behavior.

I come here to blow out my anger at you, 'cause my mom freaks out. After I get it out, I think more clearly. I can figure out what I need to do or say to her. But if I try to do that before I get out my "beefs," my brain tweaks out, and I just get madder and madder.

—*Fifteen-year-old Bobby to his counselor*

All feelings are the seeds of enormous potential. Denying them either causes our sons to wilt or to overgrow into wild weeds that can take over our homes. Our acceptance and focusing on the positive intent allows them to grow up, mature and healthy.

Son:(loudly) I'm pissed 'cause you won't let me go.

Dad: You really care about this concert.

Son:(calming down) Of course. That's why I'm so upset at you.

Dad: I want you to go, but it's too late for you to be on the road. Too much drinking and driving on Friday nights.

Son: How about if we take the subway with the others?

Dad: I didn't know you could get there by subway.

Son: It's beside the concert hall. I just wanted to drive, because it's more fun.

Dad took his son's anger as a clue that this issue was probably a bigger deal than he had originally thought. Had he focused on his son's anger, their conversation probably would have erupted into a shouting match, with one of them stomping off in a fury. When he focused on his son's burning desire to go to the concert, rather than on his anger, this father cut clear to the heart of the issue. The exchange softened, and each was able to consider other options. The son cared strongly about going to the event. Dad cared strongly about the safety of his son. From the mature place of caring, they found a solution.

Sometimes the movement of a boy's soul will necessarily be bold and audacious. A son's "misbehavior" may be necessary to keep himself awake, or to wake his parents up to a better way to live. We all know the stereotype of "Little Goody-Two-Shoes," who was candy-sweet, obeyed all of the rules, and didn't have a thought in her head. Correct behavior can make everything seem okay on the outside, but can hide an inside that is barren. There's no one home. Denial or neglect of their feelings produces this effect in sons. Even though life may be a little less than calm, we really want our sons to be alive and full of passion, to challenge injustice, to be self-directed, to put their positive, personal stamp on the world. This will take some trial and error, some jumping over picket fences, and some bumping against rubber walls.

Our job in this awakening and maturing of their souls is to keep the boundaries firm, and to cheer on the positive intent behind their "misbehaviors." In other words, we must be there to touch their souls. It helps to think of the people in our lives who have touched us—the ones we remember when we feel down and discouraged. They opened us to the treasure that was inside us, because they recognized that it was there. We can help our sons find the treasure of their fiery natures to enable them to direct their own lives and passions toward meaningful ends.

≪≫ ≪≫ *DON* | Barry, fifteen, was brought to counseling because he spray-painted a huge "Happy Birthday" sign on his teacher's house. His father's major concern was, Is my son a criminal? An incredibly funny young man, yes. A criminal, no. Barry was willing to talk with me, but every few minutes he had to make funny sounds and distract our attention away from the topic. I finally became impatient and said, "I've got it. You're an artist!" He looked quizzically at me. "No, I'm not an artist." I replied, "I don't mean like a Rembrandt. You belong on a stage. I saw a picture of the sign that you painted on your teacher's house, and it was hilarious. The question now is this: How can you be hilarious in a way that doesn't get you in so much trouble?" Barry opened up then, and shared his dreams of having a punk rock band. He brought his lyrics in for me to hear. Some were outrageous; some were very serious. He said, "I don't want to be outrageous just to rebel. I see so much wrong with the world; I want to have a purpose and a point to make."

The Power of Attention

When their babies are small, mothers learn to diffuse their attention. A mother can be involved in small tasks such as washing dishes, ironing, or baking, and still keep ears and eyes attuned to where her toddler is and what he is doing. The child will play for long intervals, perfectly satisfied. However, let mother's attention become focused on a task, such as balancing the checkbook or making a telephone call, and immediately the child needs help with an obstinate puzzle piece, untied shoelace, a lost block, or whatever. The child knows that he has lost his mother's attention.

Our sons crave and deserve our attention at all stages of their growth. We parents serve as mirrors reflecting back to them how their behavior and words affect others. This attention gives them a clear perspective of themselves and nurtures the self-confidence they will need to assume their place in the world.

Listening for and focusing on the positive intent of their behavior does not mean that we let our sons walk all over us.

> *I was livid at my son! He used my car on Friday night, left soda cans and hot dog wrappers in the front seat, used up all the gas, and didn't fill it up. We had agreed that if he takes it out, he cleans it up right afterward, because I leave early most mornings. I roughly shook him awake, and asked, "What's the big deal? The car's a mess!" Groggily, he answered, "Oh, no! I forgot. I was so tired last night that I decided to get up real early this morning to clean it. I guess that was stupid, since I never get up early. I'm sorry, Dad. Can I make it up to you now?" I was torn between giving him "hell" or giving him a break. This was the first time he had screwed up. I said, "Go clean it up, and we'll call it even. You are usually so good at keeping your agreements about the car." I could see how important it was to him that I approve of his efforts to keep his word.*
>
> *—James, a father in a monthly parenting group*

Being able to shift the focus of our attention is crucial in communicating with our sons. Had the father in the story above focused only on the mess his son had left in the car, he would have missed the opportunity to bring attention to his son's efforts at keeping his word. The father would have sabotaged his son's many successes with an overemphasis on this one failure.

⋘ JEANNE   When he was five one of our son's chores after dinner was to bring his plate to the kitchen and put it on the counter by the sink. It was an effort for him to reach the counter top, but he managed his plate very well. One particular night, he also brought his cup from the table, still full of grape juice. In deep concentration, he raised the glass up to the counter, tipped it over, and spilled the juice down his shirt and all over the newly mopped floor.

Past behavior would have had me lecturing him in a loud, hostile voice saying he should have known better than to try to bring his glass in, while I angrily mopped up the mess. This time, I took a deep breath, looked into his eyes, and said, "You really want to help more in clearing the table, don't you?" "Yes," he said, "but I spilled it." I smiled, "Don't worry. You'll get it next time. Here's a cloth. Let's both clean it up." His self-confidence was restored, and I realized what a fine line I had just walked. I saw how easily a triumph can deteriorate into a mess, and a mess can be changed into a triumph.

Exercise:
Learning to Hear the Positive Intent

Finding the positive intent behind a son's angry words or behavior can be quite a challenge for parents. We usually have a lot invested in interactions with our sons, which leaves us too close to the situation to see our way clearly; before we know it, we're knee-deep in mess. To practice hearing the positive intent, we have provided a list of common encounters with sons. Read each one, then write a possible response that recognizes the positive intent behind the words. We've included a sample response to the first statement, to help you get started.

I hate your guts when you always tell me what to do!

Positive intent: You want to have more control over your life.

I don't care if it's safe or not. I want to go!

Positive intent:

I screwed up the lock on your toolbox, when I tried to get a tool to fix the mower when it stopped.

Positive intent:

I will never clean up my room!

Positive intent:

I'm a stupid jerk!

Positive intent:

You blame me for everything.

Positive intent:

You never listen to me.

Positive intent:

How did you do? As with any other skill, learning to find the positive intent calls for practice and patience. To clarify the process, let's continue by looking at the kinds of parental responses that tend to create larger messes, followed by our suggestions for stating the positive intent underlying these responses.

Do These Sound Familiar?

The responses below are ones we may have used in the past, but later regretted because communication either deteriorated or broke down altogether. At times we may have caught ourselves echoing the very same statements our parents made to us. These responses caused us to miss opportunities to connect with our sons and touch their souls. Instead of falling into guilt when responses like these slip out, we can forgive ourselves, look again for the positive intent, and learn a better way to parent.

I hate your guts when you always tell me what to do!

Don't ever talk to me like that again. I'll wash your mouth out with soap!

I don't care if it's safe or not. I want to go!

Well, you're not going, and that's final! Go to your room.

I screwed up the lock on your toolbox, when I tried to get a tool to fix the mower when it stopped.

You what? How many times have I told you to leave your hands off my things! You're grounded for two weeks.

I will never clean up my room.

Oh, yes you will, young man. You march in there right now and don't come out until it's clean.

I'm a stupid jerk!

Don't say things like that about yourself!

You blame me for everything.

Well, look at the messes that you make.

You never listen to me.

If you would talk nicer, maybe I could listen better.

We can all imagine the results we would get by using the above responses. Below are possibilities that we have found to work better in fostering communication and understanding between parents and sons.

I hate your guts when you always tell me what to do!

You want to be more a part of this decision.

Or: *You want me to recognize that you're becoming capable of making more decisions.*

I don't care if it's safe or not. I want to go!

You really care about this.

I screwed up the lock on your toolbox, when I tried to get a tool to fix the mower when it stopped.

You're really brave to tell me the truth.

I will never clean up my room!

You want more say in what happens around here.

I'm a stupid jerk!

You want to be further along than you are.

You blame me for everything.

I'm pushing you too hard.

You never listen to me.

You value my attention.

At this point you may find it helpful to practice applying this process to your own family situation. In the following spaces, we invite you to fill in typical statements your son makes, along with the responses you have used in the past. Finally, fill in new responses for yourself that acknowledge the positive intent behind your son's words.

My son says: _____

I used to respond: _____

My new response: _____

My son says: _____

I used to respond: _____

My new response: _____

My son says: _____

I used to respond: _____

My new response: _____

My son says: _____

I used to respond: _____

My new response: _____

My son says: _____

I used to respond: _____

My new response: _____

My son says: _____

I used to respond: _____

My new response: _____

My son says: _____

I used to respond: _____

My new response: _____

In the midst of pain, depression, confusion, or loss, we may have difficulty seeing anything but the negative. It is sad that many parents and sons have fallen into the habit of seeing only the negative in each other. Our sons suffer from it, and so do we.

But when we look deeply enough, we will find a positive intent behind most things that happen in our lives. The same is true when we look deeply into our son's life. In fact, we can develop the habit of seeing the positive intent behind our son's words and deeds. And, in the long run, he may even follow our example and return the favor. After years of being blamed for every upset in his life, and of having our caring stance met with resistance, the day may come when he listens for the positive intent behind words of upset that we ourselves speak. What greater reward do we parents receive than to have forged a soulful connection with our son, and then to feel him touch our soul in return?

End Notes

1. Joseph Campbell with Bill Moyers, "The Power of Myth," Apostrophe S Productions with Public Affairs Television and Alvin H. Perlmutten, 1988.

2. Positive Intent is a phrase used by Vernon Woolf, Ph.D., in his "Unfolding Potential" seminar, San Rafael, Calif., 17-19 Aug. 1990.

3. Edith Schutz, Ph.D., M.F.C.C., interview with Don Elium, Pleasant Hill, Calif., 27 May 1989.

CHAPTER NINE

When Love and Limits Aren't Enough: Attention Deficit Disorder

I didn't belong as a kid, and that always bothered me. If only I'd known that one day my differences would be an asset, then my earlier life would have been much easier.[1]

—Bette Midler

❧ ❧ *DON* | In my therapy practice over the years I have met boys and parents of all types and temperaments. Two situations stand out as significantly different from the rest. Both sets of parents tried all the right parenting tools, pursued their own psychotherapy, and had their sons in therapy. Harold and Zeke's extreme behaviors left their parents feeling perplexed and hopeless.

Harold (14)

By the time Harold's family came in to see me, his parents had tried everything. They were firm but kind leaders, setting consistent and fair boundaries, following through on consequences, and looking at their own mistakes and personality flaws. Nothing they did seemed to have any effect on Harold's behavior. He had no respect for house rules or curfews, frequently skipped school, talked endlessly, had difficulty listening to others, refused to do any chores at home, and felt entitled to be left alone to live his life the way he saw fit. He wanted to quit school, get a job, and pay rent for his room. His parents had tried everything to deal with Harold's out-of-control behavior. He had nothing left in his bedroom except for his bed, a light, and his clothes. He had no free time in the evenings, and he was grounded socially. Nothing worked to bring him into line with family limits. A desire for self-reliance is characteristic of many normal adolescents, but Harold's demands were extreme; he wavered between violent, angry outbursts and boredom, constantly demanding more and more, and getting no satisfaction.

Zeke (15)

Zeke's parents had also tried everything and were "worried sick" about his behavior. Unlike Harold, Zeke was quiet and complacent, always nice and willing to cooperate. Unfortunately, he acted as if no one was home in his body. Dreamy and spaced, he spent most of his time in his room, continually lost things, had few friends, and did minimal school work. His parents were at a loss as to how to help him, because Zeke was unable to describe what was bothering him. He readily agreed to see me for counseling.

Here were two very different boys whose families had tried everything to help them, and nothing seemed to make any difference. Some piece of the puzzle that would reach these boys was missing.

The Missing Piece

When good parenting and psycho-emotional therapeutic practices are of no lasting benefit to a boy, his therapist must look elsewhere for clues to healing. The missing piece may be biological. There is a wide body of research comparing the causes of behaviors common to people who suffered frontal head injuries and children who were labeled as "hyper." These shared behaviors include the inability to sit still for long, impulsive actions, inability to sustain a focus of attention, and forgetfulness. These commonalties prompted researchers to further investigate the orbital-frontal cortex of the brain (located directly behind the forehead) in non-injured but hyper children. Results led researchers to believe that non-injured children and adults who are less able to inhibit behaviors (act before they think), prone to hyperactivity (can't sit still, can't concentrate, mind runs "a mile a minute"), and have a short attention span have a bio-chemical disorder in the orbital-frontal cortex of their brains. This area controls the inhibiting, prioritizing, and organizing functions of behavior. Researchers believe that when this area of the brain is underactive, the symptoms of Attention Deficit Disorder (ADD) and Attention Deficit Hyperactive Disorder (ADHD) occur.[2]

ADD and ADHD

His room is always a mess.

He gets so distracted. He can't remember that he went outside to empty the trash, even when he has the wastebasket right there in his hands.

He's lost three coats in the last six months.

He talks constantly. No one can get a word in about anything!

He goes off on tangents. A new fad comes around, and he's onto it.

He has two or three projects going at once and never finishes any of them.

He always leaps before he looks, acts before he thinks.

He's always late.

You never know what stunt he's going to pull. He's always being funny and embarrassing everyone.

I'm afraid to trust him with the car keys.

He can't sit still and finish even one page of math homework.

Most of the time when I call on him in class, he's not there. He's staring off into space, lost to the world.

He works on his computer, and I can't get him to stop.

It's as though he's gotten lost in there.

These comments are often used to describe an adult or child with Attention Deficit Disorder (ADD)—Inattentive Type, where inattention and impulsivity are dominant features, and Attention Deficit Hyperactive Disorder (ADHD), where the person is also hyperactive—constantly moving, constantly talking, constantly worrying, and so on. As adults, these people continue to exhibit out-of-control behaviors, often full of shame, because they believe they lack the strength of character or willpower to change. Evidence shows they are fighting a biological battle.[3]

> *More than once I've gone to a fast food drive-in for a quick burger, paid at the window, and driven off without my food. My wife has fits every time I leave my bank card in the automatic teller machine, and I've lost my razor three times in the last six months. I've done things like this all my life, and my dad always called me "stupid" and "irresponsible." I shrugged it off by saying I had more important things to think about, but I always felt a little bit ashamed. After I tested positive for ADHD, everything began to make sense. I felt sad at first that my brain was "broken," but then I was relieved that it wasn't willpower I needed to sustain my promised changes. I needed something to help my underactive brain!*
>
> *—Jeb, twenty-eight*

Harold and Zeke

With boys like Harold and Zeke, standard parenting and therapeutic interventions alone do not work well, or sometimes do not work at all. With most children, we assume that once they have a chance to sort things out after getting a consequence for their misbehaviors, they will stop repeating what got them into trouble. This is a big assumption, however; that they can sort things out in a normal way; that they can sustain attention on the event and consequences long enough to think it through; that they can connect past actions and consequences; and that they can remember to choose better options in the future. Harold and Zeke, with an underactive part of the brain in charge of sorting, connecting, and inhibiting, cannot consistently react normally. They are struggling with a biological disability. Unless we understand the intricacies of Attention Deficit Disorder-Inattentive Type and Attention Deficit Hyperactive Disorder, these disabilities will become liabilities in the future.

Distraction

To understand ADD/ADHD, we must take the following word very seriously: *overwhelmed.* That is what people with ADD/ADHD feel much of the time. The orbital-frontal cortex of the brain that we will call the "executive sorter," does not have the biochemistry available to do its job at a normal level. Like a company executive, the executive sorter of the brain handles the job of prioritizing, ordering, and regulating the incoming sensory information. In those whose brain is working normally, the executive sorter takes in the information, synthesizes it, and delivers it to the appropriate center, all in a matter of milliseconds. The amount of sensory information processed by the human brain in each moment is incredible—outside noise, a brilliant idea, old hurt from the past, worry about an exam, expectations from someone we care about, hunger pangs, and so on. It all passes through the executive sorter. According to Russell Barkley, Ph.D., director of Psychology and Psychiatry at the University of Massachusetts Medical Center, the presence of the orbital-frontal cortex is what distinguishes humans from other animals.[4] Our ability to (1) separate thoughts from feelings, (2) inhibit our reactions, (3) think of a plan, and then (4) act in line with our long-range goals makes us distinctly human.

When the executive sorter is underactive, the brain's normal prioritizing, sorting, connecting, inhibiting, and focusing skills are not consistently available. Only brief focus is possible, leaving piles and piles of sensory messages unsorted. The person feels caught in an overwhelming, raging flood. Based on outward appearances, parents might conclude that their son is choosing to distract himself; when they talk with him about a problem, he changes the subject. He does this because his ability to sustain attention is weak. That this distraction is not a conscious choice is more easily seen when he is young. As he grows older, he can gain more control, but it is inconsistent and significantly impaired. These distractions may be intellectual, emotional, or physical—fantasizing, sleeping, taking drugs, constantly playing video games, lost in watching TV, obsessive use of computers, endless listening to music, continual talking or busyness, squirming, fighting, risk taking, thrill seeking, gambling, or over-working. His inability to maintain sustained focus forces parents to structure a boy's life to help him learn ways of staying focused, and creating and learning how to make good choices.

According to Robert McEleese, Ph.D., director of the Attention Deficit Disorder Institute, many researchers think that Attention *Inconsistency* Disorder or *Selected-Attention* Disorder may more accurately describe what we call ADD/ADHD.[5] Under certain situations and in certain environments the executive sorter is able to manage better and the person is able to follow through. This inconsistency confuses and frustrates parents, the family, and co-workers, as well as the person afflicted, because they think, "If he can do it once, why can't he do it more of the time?" However, the executive sorter cannot biologically rise to the occasion consistently and, therefore, cannot manage the normal flow of sensory stimuli over the course of a person's day. When called upon to sustain focus on an activity from beginning to middle to end, a boy with ADD or ADHD feels overwhelmed and struggles unsuccessfully with something he cannot alone control. His distraction or inattention is due to internal, biological underactivity. Physical exertion can sometimes interrupt these chaotic, mental reactions. James, fifteen with ADHD, says, "After an intensive karate workout, my mind is calm for a good two to three hours. Then it starts up again, and I go two directions at once. Caffeine helped me focus better for awhile, but I felt so jittery I had to stop."

Impulsivity

People with ADD or ADHD tend to be impulsive—they act before they think. Their brains seem to have less space between thought and action. That is, the underactive part of the brain is less capable of inhibiting an action following a thought or feeling impulse. When the biochemistry is firing properly, action is inhibited after a thought or feeling long enough for reflection on the consequences of that behavior. The person separates his feelings from his actions and then has a choice in his responses. When ADD or ADHD gets in the way, the person responds automatically, before any thinking process has a chance to happen. The following is an example of how the two brains work:

Situation: Reaction to a friend's hurtful behavior

Boy Without ADD	Boy With ADD
1. I feel angry at you.	1. I feel angry at you.
2. Inner pause to reflect on bigger picture: "But you are my friend, and I want to keep it that way. I wonder why you did that?"	2. Little to no inner pause to reflect on bigger picture.
3. Action toward friend: "Hey, that hurt! Why are trying to hurt me?"	3. Action toward friend: Hits or yells and walks away, or withdraws and avoids him whenever possible.

The boy without ADD or ADHD is able to verbally work out the difficulty without resorting to acting out his initial hurt. The boy with ADD or ADHD faces several options because of his impulsive actions: Later, he may regret hitting his friend and feel he is a horrible person; he may defend his actions to himself and others by making a case that the guy deserved it; or he may withdraw into fantasy where he either feels worthless or plots revenge. Rarely is he able to talk with anyone about the incident or his feelings.

The crucial difference between the behaviors of the two boys above is *choice*. The aggressive (hitting, yelling) or passive aggressive (withdrawal, avoidance) reactions of the boy with ADD or ADHD are biologically-triggered, knee jerk responses. Without room for choice in his actions, this boy will continually struggle to learn and follow healthy protocols of relationship. Because his mind moves rapidly from one thing to the next, he develops the habit of letting things go unresolved. His attention never stays in one place for long, so he is often unaware of how his aggressive and passive aggressive reactions affect others. He cannot understand why the other person doesn't just "move on and forget about it," because he has.

Impulsivity inhibits the ability to prioritize and order things within the context of a bigger understanding of a situation. Impulsive actions are re-actions lacking thought, evaluation, choice, planning, and appropriate follow-through. To the brain with ADD or ADHD, the bigger picture is just another overwhelming piece of sensory data that aggravates a fight (aggressive) or flight (passive-aggressive) response, and this behavior becomes the familiar pattern of social interactions.

> *I have always prided myself on being spontaneous and finding unconventional ways to do things. After learning I had ADHD, however, I began to understand the difference between spontaneity and impulsiveness. Now I define my behavior as spontaneous when I do something unexpected that brings delight to me as well as anyone else involved. When I do something impulsive, the unexpected brings delight to me, but not to the others.*
>
> —*Don, forty-two*

Hyperactivity

Hyperactive means having a heightened state of activity. Early research focused mainly on the physical symptoms of this behavior—boys not being able to sit still in school, facial and body tics, fighting, being always on the go, and so on. Recent research, however, broadens the scope of symptoms to include not only the physical, but the emotional and intellectual realms, as well.[6] Emotionally, a boy with ADHD gets stuck in strong feelings, cannot stop talking about them, cannot complete them, and cannot make the transition to the next emotion. Verbally, he chatters constantly, interrupts others, fails to listen, and generally monopolizes conversations. Intellectually, a boy with ADHD gets lost in an idea or fantasy, incessantly working it over and over in his mind, unable to let it go by himself.

Like ADD Inattentive Type, the hyperactive component of ADHD is also caused by the brain's inability to sort, prioritize, and execute according to a plan. We can compare what happens in an underactive brain to the behavior of the people in charge of a computerized mailing list program that crashes at deadline time. Everyone speeds up to handle the crisis when the prioritizing and ordering system breaks down. The over-action is not caused by the speedy behavior of the people involved. The over-action is caused by the under-activity of the machine. So it is for a boy with ADHD. The ordering part of his brain is sluggish, so his biology compensates by becoming impulsive, distracted, and hyperactive to wake his brain up. His underactive brain leaves a boy fighting to say afloat in a sea of unsorted and unprioritized thoughts, emotions, memories, and reactions. He is unable to respond in the moment to the world around him. Experiencing a continuous cycle between boredom and powerlessness, boys face uncompleted tasks and difficult personal relationships. Eventually, these contradictory states of being feel normal.

Is It ADD? How Can We Tell?

With any new understanding of human biology and associated behavior, premature diagnosis, and misdiagnoses are common. Everyone wants to understand why they do the things they do. Be aware of this important fact about ADD and ADHD: *ADD/ADHD is not a character defect.* Evidence shows that it is a biological disability. We caution parents to have boys tested by a trained professional before making the diagnosis of ADD or ADHD. One of the most-asked questions in our seminars on raising sons is, "Isn't ADD just a pathological name for being male?" We answer with an emphatic "No!" The individual symptoms—inattention, distractibility, impulsiveness, hyperactivity—are common to all of us, both male and female, at one time or another. How is ADD or ADHD different from having these occasional symptoms? The answer is in two words: *intensity* and *duration.*[7]

Most boys exhibit impulsive behaviors, such as thrill-seeking and risk-taking activities that engage them physically, emotionally, and intellectually. Most boys also have the capacity to think, reason, and learn from the consequences of their actions. They are able to form relationships with others in responsible ways. Boys with ADD and ADHD, however, behave impulsively with an *intensity* that leaves no time for reflection or change. They have difficulty at work, with personal relationships, and with introspection. They learn to take short cuts, act as if they understand when they don't, hide from routine aspects of life they can't handle, and feel like impostors.

Boys do not develop ADD or ADHD. Evidence shows they are born with it. The severity of the symptoms may vary over time—they may appear stronger and harder to deal with at certain ages—but it is something these boys will deal with over the *duration* of their lives. We must guard against labeling our sons as good or bad according to their behaviors. They need us on their side. Have a trained professional rule out everything before making a diagnosis. If the cause of a boy's troubles is ADD or ADHD, there is effective treatment available.

What Parents Can Do: Structure, Structure, Structure

The first step is to discuss our son's problematic behavior with the family doctor. He or she will want to rule out other possible causes, such as thyroid disease, hearing problems, allergies, upper respiratory illnesses, and neurological problems.[8] If the above conditions are not the cause, the next step is testing by the doctor or a psychologist. With a positive diagnosis of ADD or ADHD, there are many helpful ideas, treatments, and tools for parents and other members of our son's parenting team.

Education about the disorder is vital for parents, grandparents, siblings, teachers, and friends of a son with ADD or ADHD. Learn about the symptoms and share this information with our parenting team. The more people we involve, the more we have to take time out to regroup, to see to our own needs, or to attend to other children. Be specific in our son's needs and our own needs. Share specific ways we work with him in short lists and reminders. Don't try to deal with the problems alone. Join a support group, write letters, communicate on the Internet in chat groups with other parents, and build a community that understands our situation. (See resource section at the end of this chapter for more ideas.)

Make a parenting "attitude adjustment" about our sons. We have to look at him with new eyes to see the special needs he has. The important word here is *structure*. Giving our son more structure than usual will help boost the weak "executive sorter" in his brain. Russell Barkley, Ph.D., author of *Taking Charge of ADHD*, suggests a list on the bathroom mirror, refrigerator door, and a bulletin board at work to remind us about structure:

- Give immediate, frequent, powerful feedback and consequences.

- Act, don't yak. Keep it simple, short, and clear. Remember, our son is not stupid. He just has trouble remembering, following sequences, and completing a task. Telling him something over and over will do no good. Kind, firm action with small steps, rewards, and consequences work wonders.

- Keep a disability perspective. Do not personalize a son's problems. Remember we are dealing with a biological disorder, not a personality flaw.

- Use incentives before punishment. Make physical contact often. Use five genuine praises to one negative correction.

- Structure and strive for consistency. Be consistent in what we expect of him while working, playing, and relating to others. He learns from our example rather than from lectures.

- Plan ahead for problem situations. Keep to a familiar structure for trips, evenings, and weekends.

- Practice forgiveness of self and child. Most people with ADD/ADHD have average to above average intelligence. Most are extremely creative, resourceful, and refreshing individuals. Relating to them is easier when we practice seeing the positive intent behind their actions, in spite of the results.

- Delay responses and practice relaxation. We do not have to respond immediately to a problem with our son. Disengaging for a few minutes allows us time to think and shows our "speeded up" son how to slow down.[9]

Construct and follow parenting and school plans for behavior issues, chores, homework, and family/social activities. Written plans including all aspects of a son's life are a must. Resources at the end of this chapter contain detailed, ready-to-use charts and ideas.

Use counseling for the child, parents, and other family members when needed. The long-term effects of undiagnosed ADD/ADHD can wreak havoc on a family, a marriage relationship, and on all individuals involved. Dr. Susan Campbell's study at the University of Pittsburgh of mothers whose children had ADHD indicated that these mothers were required to give more suggestions, approval, disapproval, and directions to their impulsive children than did other mothers.[10]

Similar studies by Dr. Russell Barkley found that children with ADHD were much more likely to wander off task, be more negative, were much less compliant, and had more difficulty following their mothers' commands. He also noted that the mothers gave more commands, were more negative, and were less responsive to their children with ADHD. Over time, of course, these mothers became exhausted and stressed. But the symptoms diminished, the mothers returned to less commanding, more positive, and more responsive behaviors.[11]

During Dr. Barkley's study, many mothers indicated that the fathers were more successful in working with their children with ADHD. Though unsure of the reasons for this, Dr. Barkley suggests that when mothers are the primary caretakers, fathers often have more influence; that fathers are usually larger and stronger; and that mothers tend to use more reasoning and affection to get the child to follow directions, whereas fathers resort more quickly to repeated commands and discipline when the child did not cooperate in the completion of a task. The observed style of the fathers seemed to be more aligned with the needs of a boy with ADHD—more immediate, less verbal, and more powerful consequences.[12]

Regardless of the differences noted, a child with ADD or ADHD brings stress to the adult relationships in a two-parent family, step-family, single-parent family, or grandparent family. Counseling can help parents stabilize relationships by learning compassion, under-standing, and joint responsibilities. Parents begin to work as a team, learning from each other and giving relief. After treatment structures are in place, couples may want to check in with their therapist several times a month to stay consistent, maintain perspective, and keep unaddressed frustrations from building up. Counseling for the family group may be helpful to sort out which problems are related to the child with ADD or ADHD and which problems result from other issues, thus avoiding labeling the child as the cause of all family difficulties.

Counseling for the boy with ADD or ADHD depends on his age and current needs. Beginning counseling includes the planning of structures, choosing reward systems, and coaching. Older boys may need time to talk about learning the social skills they lack or how to deal with any emotional delays they have because of the ADD/ADHD. It is vital to understand that verbal psychotherapy alone for a child with ADD or ADHD will not be effective. Psychotherapy must be directly linked to the plans engaged at home and at school. As part of the overall plan of coping with ADD and ADHD, psychotherapy can be helpful in making family relationships healthier and more meaningful.

The Effects of Undiagnosed/Untreated ADD/ADHD Over Time

Boys with ADD and ADHD often do not feel good about themselves. Their early experiences may be something like the following: while playing at daycare, a boy becomes bored with a toy and tosses it over his shoulder. The toy hits a child behind him, and she starts to cry. The teacher, who saw the boy toss the toy, admonishes him for his behavior, and he gets labeled as aggressive. This scenario usually repeats itself many times. Over time, he is seen as a behavioral problem—a trouble maker and a bully. What began as a natural—although impulsive—response to feeling bored with a toy becomes a power struggle between the boy and his teachers, the boy and himself. The teacher mistakenly believes that discipline will help him remember not to throw the toy next time. Because the boy is unable to control his short attention span and his impulses, he is disciplined again and again. As the discipline becomes stronger, and the boy continues to fail, he begins to feel ashamed of his failures, and angry at himself and others.

Boys like this one, who are labeled as trouble makers and bullies, may develop severe problems at school or in the workplace and land up in juvenile or family court. This is what happened to Harold, whose case we mentioned earlier. Because of his troubled relationships at home and at school, he learned to see himself as a "bad guy." Harold could not find a way to work successfully within the system, so to preserve some sense of self-esteem, he lashed out to destroy the "evil system." When Harold was finally tested for ADHD, he scored high in hyperactivity. This component made him strike out physically and verbally in response to feeling overwhelmed. His art ("The one thing I do well.") and smoking marijuana gave him some relief from his inner clatter.

Zeke, however, tested low in physical hyperactivity, but high in distraction, impulsivity, and mental hyperactivity. He was the child in the daycare who would sit for long moments looking out the window or playing alone, lost in fantasy. Many children learn to play quietly by themselves, but Zeke's behavior was extreme and constant.

Don Zeke told me one day, "My mind is always busy, and I always fail with things outside of me, because I can't stay with them. The only time I don't feel bad about myself is in role-playing games or when using my imagination to create a story about finding life on another planet." Zeke was not in therapy with me because he hurt someone or broke the law. He was here because a friend told his father that Zeke was talking about not wanting to live. At school, Zeke was one of those "good kids" who get missed, because he didn't disturb the class. Although passing, his grades were always low C's. "I never said anything in class, even when I knew the answer," he reported. "I could never control what came out of my mouth. One day a teacher asked me what I thought of the homework assignment. I told her I thought it was stupid. The class laughed, but she didn't. After that I just started shutting up."

Harold and Zeke had many ADD/ADHD symptoms in common: they both could not "not react" impulsively to others; and they both frequently felt overwhelmed, lost, and frustrated when given detailed instructions. Zeke said, "I loved baseball, and I couldn't wait until I was old enough to play on a team. When I finally made it, the coach told me to do so many things at once that I froze up. He made fun of me in front of the team when he caught me staring off into space. I never went back, even though my mother threatened to ground me. My mind just couldn't stay on the coach's track." Harold reported similar experiences. "When my mom tells me to do *this*, *this*, and *this*, and then when you're done, do *this*, I freak out! I'd try to remember it all, or start doing the first thing, but then worry about forgetting the next thing. I'd end up throwing garbage cans across the fence, or smashing a dish from the dishwasher on the floor. At first, I was shocked at what I did. Then I got used to it, and I figured it just must be how I am. I stopped trying to do it all. The consequences were better than the agony of staying with something where I felt lost and helpless."

Another thing Harold and Zeke have in common is educational struggle. Both boys suffered in school—one because he spaced out, the other because he acted out. Reading was a challenge for both boys. Harold was overwhelmed by too many words and thoughts on a page. By the time he finished reading, the rest of the class was way beyond him, and he failed to remember much of what he read. Cliff Notes were helpful because of their short, to-the-point, digestible format. Zeke could read anything that he was passionate about, such as science fiction. Other kinds of books were difficult to complete. He constantly struggled to finish assignments and usually put projects off until the very last minute.

A boy with ADD or ADHD can occasionally override the symptoms for a time when he has a very strong passion for something. Zeke's passion was computers. For hours and hours he invented new games. Art was Harold's love. He poured his heart and soul into his paintings, so different from the persona he created to deal with his feelings of being overwhelmed and impulsive. Many people with ADD or ADHD—lawyers, physicians, psychologists, MBA's—complete complex courses of study and become successful in their careers. It is in their private lives where the powerlessness and struggles with failure show through. Why do boys like Harold and Zeke have so much trouble in others areas of their lives? With ADD and ADHD, boys need more than passion to help them through the regular routines of living. Reducing or eliminating television, caffeine, and sugar, getting regular exercise, being in nature, and adequate sleep are beneficial. They need outward structure, understanding, and, when necessary, medication.

Medications

The most commonly prescribed medications for ADD and ADHD are Ritalin, Dexedrine, and Cylert. We may wonder why stimulants are used for people who seem over-active already. As we discussed earlier, hyperactivity, impulsivity, and distractibility are caused by an *under-active* orbital-frontal cortex of the brain that we call the "executive sorter." The treatment plans for ADD and ADHD all involve building outer structures, because the inner self-control is weak. Ritalin, Dexedrine, and Cylert are extremely helpful in making the orbital-frontal cortex more active. Strengthening the executive sorter enables a boy to think, pause, reflect, and then choose an action, rather than impulsively act on a thought or feeling before thinking about the consequences. These medications help him sustain focus and attention, fidget less, feel more connected to other people, choose actions that lead to future goals, and act from the storehouse of information he has stored in his head—information that he was never able to access before taking medication. With a treatment plan that included medication, Zeke reported, "I joined a softball team, and I'm doing really good! I still get confused some, but I don't get overwhelmed like I did before."

We suggest that parents read about the medications used for ADD and ADHD, taking note of the side-effects, expected reactions, and so on. Some of these drugs have received bad publicity over the last few years, and it is important to separate propaganda from fact. Deciding to have your son take medication is not a small matter. Read carefully, talk to other parents, ask others who take the medication, and confer with a knowledgeable doctor about what is best for a son's unique situation.

The correct medication gives a boy the experience of what it is like to be able to focus, choose, and complete things. This awareness often helps make the home plan and the school plan successful. Medication does not cure ADD/ADHD, but it makes life more livable and successful for a boy and his family. No longer engaged in an over-whelming fight against a biological weakness, a boy on medication now has room to live from his quieter, deeper self without the interfering noise of distraction.

Listening for the Positive Intent

This chapter has targeted the basic symptoms and troubles of ADD and ADHD to help us understand the complexities and be better able to parent our sons. Their difficult and unpredictable behaviors have perhaps led us to see them at times as weak in character, will power, and ambition. When we look deeper, we know that the direct opposite is more often true. We all deal with biological and psychological challenges, but a boy with ADD or ADHD has special difficulties over which he has little control—without our help and understanding, treatment plans, and, if necessary, medications. With a strong support system in place, our son can take more direct control of his destiny and develop meaningful relationships and careers. And he wants to do just that. All his behavior, no matter how frustrating to us, is motivated by his desire to cope, to do good, to keep himself awake. Without denying how hard our son is to live with, looking for the positive intent behind his actions calls forth a more positive self-image in him. When a boy with ADD or ADHD feels better about himself, he has more access to those greater qualities that lie hidden beneath all the turmoil.

Mary Sheedy Kurcinka, licensed teacher and founder of the "Spirited Child" workshops, offers parents new ways to see their difficult children in her reassuring book, *Raising Your Spirited Child.* Rather than seeing him as demanding, see the son with ADD or ADHD as holding high standards; rather than unpredictable, see him as flexible, a creative problem-solver. He is not loud, but enthusiastic and zestful; not argumentative, but opinionated and strongly com-mitted to his goals; not stubborn, but assertive with a willingness to persist in the face of difficulties; not nosy, but curious; not wild, but energetic; not extreme, but tenderhearted; not inflexible, but traditional; not manipulative, but charismatic; not impatient, but compelling; not anxious, but cautious; not explosive, but dramatic; not picky, but selective; not whiny, but analytic; not distractible, but perceptive.[13] Thinking of our sons in more positive ways with a solid parenting structure empowers them to grow into the truly wonderful people they are.

Resources For Children With ADD/ADHD

Organizations:

CHADD (Children With Attention Deficit Disorder)
499 Northwest 70th. Avenue, Suite 109
Plantation, FL 33317, (800) 233-4050

Books:

Taking Charge of ADHD, by Russell Barkley, New York: Guilford Press, 1995. From an expert in the field of ADD/ADHD, a factual and practical manual. Local bookstores.

Maybe You Know My Kid, by Mary Fowler, New York: Carol Publishing Group, 1995. Describes by age groupings what to expect and how to help a child with ADHD. Local bookstores.

Raising Your Spirited Child, by Mary Sheedy Kurcinka, New York: Harper Perennial, 1992. Gives specific guidelines for developing structured home and school plans. Local bookstores.

A Parent's Guide to Attention Deficit Disorders, by Lisa J. Bain, New York: Dell, 1991. Covers the cause of ADD, diagnosis, treatment, therapy, living with ADD, and resources available from experts in the field working at the Children's Hospital of Philadelphia. Local bookstores.

Is Your Child Hyperactive? Inattentive? Impulsive? Distractible?: A Practical Program for Changing Your Child's Behavior With and

Without Medication, by Stephen Garber, Marianne Daniels Garber, and Robyn Freedman Spizman, New York: Villard Books, 1995. A step-by-step program to help parents change their children's difficult behaviors at home. Local bookstores.

ADD Success Stories: A Guide to Fulfillment for Families with Attention Deficit Disorder, by Thom Hartmann, Grass Valley, CA: Underwood Books, 1995. A great book of hope with practical guides and references. Local bookstores.

Computer Internet Bulletin Board:

For on-line discussions and information: http://www.chadd.org

Catalogs:

ADD Warehouse, (800) 233-9273. Offers books, tapes, videos, and other information about ADD/ADHD.

For Adults With ADD/ADHD

Organizations:

AADF (Adult Attention Deficit Foundation)
132 North Woodward Avenue
Birmingham, MI 48009

Books:

Driven to Distraction, by E. Hallowell and J. Ratey, New York: Pantheon, 1994. Personal insights into the symptoms and treatment by two experts in the field of ADD/ADHD who have the disorder themselves. Local bookstores.

You Mean I'm Not Lazy, Stupid, or Crazy?!, by K. Kelly and P. Ramundo, Cincinnati, OH: Tyrell and Jerem Press, 1993. Offers hope and boosts the self-esteem of adults afflicted with ADD and ADHD. Local bookstores.

Other Special Needs

Organizations:

LDAA (Learning Disabilities Association of America)
4156 Library Road
Pittsburgh, PA 15234
(412) 341-1515

National Center for Youth With Disabilities
University of Minnesota
P.O. BOX 721
UMHC/Harvard Street at East River Road
Minneapolis, MN 55455
(800) 333-NCYC

Tourette Syndrome Association
(800) 237-0717

Support Group for Parents of Autistic Children
(800) 3AUTISM

Books:

Raising a Child Who Has a Physical Disability, by Donna Albrecht, New York: John Wiley and Sons, 1995. Offers excellent information and exhaustive lists about support organizations and hospitals for many physical disabilities in children. Local bookstores.

Books for Children:

Josh: A Boy with Dyslexia, by Caroline Janover, Burlington, VT: Waterfront Books, 1988. Ages 8-12. A learning-disabled fifth-grader braves a storm to get help for an injured friend.

Welcome Home, Jellybean, by Marlene Fanta Shyer, New York: Macmillan, 1978. Ages 9-13. Neil's older sister is coming home after spending most of her life in an institution for mentally handicapped children.

The Man Who Loved Clowns, by June Rae Wood, New York: Putnam, 1992. Ages 11-15. A friend helps Deirita see that her beloved uncle's Down syndrome is nothing to be ashamed of.

The Snow Goose, by Paul Gallico, New York: Random House, 1992. All ages. A respected classic about a painter with a disability who rescues a World War II soldier.

Barry's Sister, by Lois Metzger, New York: Macmillan, 1992. Ages 10 and up. Ellen learns to live with and love a brother with cerebral palsy.

Endnotes

1. *The Quotable Woman* (Philadelphia: Running Press, 1991), 39.

2. Lisa J. Bain, *A Parent's Guide to Attention Deficit Disorders* (New York: Dell Publishing, 1991), 42-43.

3. Russell A. Barkley, *Taking Charge of ADHD* (New York: Guilford Press, 1995), 56.

4. Ibid., 44-45.

5. Robert McEleese, Ph.D., Director of the Attention Deficit Disorder Institute, in a consultation with Don Elium, Walnut Creek, CA, 17 Feb. 1996.

6. Bain, *A Parent's Guide*, 22.

7. McEleese, 17 Feb. 1996.

8. Stephen W. Garber, Marianne Daniels Garber, and Robyn Freedman Spizman, *Is Your Child Hyperactive? Inattentive? Impulsive? Distractible?* (New York: Villard Books, 1995), 23-24.

9. Barkley, 130-135.

10. Ibid., 94.

11. Ibid.

12. Ibid., 25.

13. Mary Sheedy Kurcinka, *Raising Your Spirited Child* (New York: Harper Perennial, 1991), 21.

Part III:

From Cradle
to Career

CHAPTER TEN

The Catch-Me-If-You-Can Years: From Birth to Seven

Babies are such a nice way to start people.[1]

—Don Herold, author and humorist

Developmental Tasks

The focus of a boy's growth between birth and age seven is the development of his body—especially his arms and legs—and the engagement of the will. We call these the willing years. Through touching, grasping, sucking, sitting, crawling, creeping, walking, climbing, running, watching, and listening, a boy uses his body to learn about and to influence the world around him. This is the age of discovery, imitation, and repetition. From the first moment that he finds his fingers and toes, even the tiniest speck comes under his intense scrutiny. The world will never again hold such great delights. He performs amazing feats for the first time—grasping the rattle, throwing the ball, hopping on one foot, whistling—and he will repeat them over and over until they are part of him.

> **JEANNE** | One day I thought that I would scream if I had to read "Chicken Little" one more time!

A son's every waking moment is spent in rapt examination of himself and everything else that comes within range of his voracious appetite to explore. These early sensory messages leave their permanent impressions upon a boy's physical and emotional development, like a potter's thumbprint in the clay. The boy in these first years does not yet discriminate between good and bad, so, to him, everything seems appropriate to take in and imitate.

When he begins to learn the names for the things he is discovering, memory, language, and thinking start to develop. Now he has an even greater capacity to explore, by taking in the images he sees and putting them back out again in fantasy and imaginative play. His play is his "life's work"; it must be given respect and allowed uninterrupted time. This is vitally important, because it is during play that a boy works out all of the confusion, disappointment, and strong feelings experienced in daily living with his family. So often, well-meaning parents interrupt necessary play with suggestions that fulfill an adult need for variety, not understanding that their son's repetitive and familiar games and fantasies are nurturing and satisfying in themselves.

Fundamental emotional lessons are also learned during these early years. Infants and toddlers learn the beginnings of trust, guilt, and autonomy. According to child development theorist and psychologist Erik Erikson, Ph.D., a basic conflict during infancy involves trust versus mistrust.[2] If babies are consistently kept warm, dry, and well-fed, they learn to trust their world and the people around them. When care-givers are withholding or inconsistent in their nurturing, babies develop mistrust in themselves or others.

Between the ages of one-and-a-half to three, according to Dr. Erikson, the toddler faces the conflict of autonomy versus shame and doubt.[3] His fledgling attempts to try new tasks on his own can be trying for parents, but how we acknowledge these attempts affects his development of confidence in his ability to achieve what he sets out to accomplish. When parents are encouraging and understanding, a boy confidently attempts new experiences on his own. When parents are too restrictive or disapproving, he feels shame and doubt in his abilities.

Another emotional lesson in these early years is whether or not a boy is allowed to show his feelings, and in what ways. The feeling boxes discussed in chapter 6 illustrate how powerful and long-lasting these basic learnings are. If a boy learns that sadness is not allowed in his family, as a man he will cover his grief with anger, overwork, or whatever emotion was okay to express at home.

Boys from four to seven also learn how to share and cooperate. Babies are social creatures from the beginning, but our sons cannot truly understand the concepts of sharing and cooperative play until around the age of five.[4] It is important for parents to encourage their sons to share at all ages, but until five, they do not have sufficient social maturity to be able to share and cooperate on their own without gentle reminders.

Progression through the developmental tasks of these years is seldom smooth. Before our son accomplishes a new level in development, such as increasing his vocabulary, conquering a new motor skill, or handling stronger feelings, he tends to revert a little. He may need help in dressing when he had been doing it quite well on his own; he may want more hugging or need assistance in getting along with a friend. Then he suddenly leaps ahead in maturity. One mother aptly described this growth pattern as the "slingshot phenomenon." A boy pulls back to a previous stage, then ping! He lets go and shoots forward with new skills and abilities. Rather than labeling our son's pulling backward as "being a baby" or a "sissy," we recognize it as a signal for a new growth spurt. It is a boy's nature to pull back and spring forward. Parenting this little Christopher Columbus requires the diligence to provide healthy and appropriate learning experiences, bushels of patience, the willingness to make mistakes and go on, strong fences, age-appropriate consequences, and being there.

Needs

In the beginning, boys need closeness. There is no truth to the old belief that we might spoil the baby if we answer every cry, carry him about, and let him sleep with us. We recommend exactly that—answer his every cry, carry him constantly about, and sleep with him, too. We call the first twelve to fourteen months of life the time for "wearing the baby." Ideally, during these early months the infant exists in a warm field of bliss, comforted by constant contact with his mother's or father's body. As he grows, he will learn to break the physical contact by exploring the world around him, knowing that he can return to comforting arms whenever he needs reassurance.

Picture two tall, slender, brown women walking down a dusty road. Each woman balances a huge, clay pot

full of water on her head. Under one arm, each carries
a large bundle, and on the other hip sits a naked baby.
They are animatedly talking with each other about
village life. In a graceful motion, one mother performs
what to us would be an astounding feat. She swings
her body to the left and holds her baby over the side of
the road, where he has a quick bowel movement. The
child is then deftly returned to her hip. All of this is
accomplished without spilling one drop of water,
without dropping her bundle, and without missing a
word in the conversation with her friend. Contentedly,
the baby nestles into the crook of his mother's arm and
goes to sleep.

—A composite of contemporary African village life

The bond described above between mother and infant is so strong
that the baby has only to move or grunt in a specific way, and his
mother knows what he needs. This scenario describes a connectedness
that seems hard for "modern" parents to believe. Yet it is this degree of
closeness that a boy needs with his mother or father to thrive. This
parent-infant bond is the foundation of a boy's positive sense of himself
and his place in the world.

The remarkable findings of author and therapist Jean Liedloff,
described in *The Continuum Concept: Allowing Human Nature to Work
Successfully*, emphasize the importance of physical closeness to a child's
development. Her experiences among the Yequana and Sanema peoples
of the South American jungles underline the natural, instinctive habit
of native mothers to carry their babies constantly until the babies begin
to crawl, and the natural need of human babies to be constantly
carried. She writes, "I would be ashamed to admit to the Indians that
where I come from the women do not feel themselves capable of
raising children until they read the instructions written in a book by a
strange man.... A look at other millions of parents in Third World
countries—who have not had the 'privilege' of being taught to stop
understanding and trusting their children, reveals families living in
peace, and with an eager and useful addition to the family labor force

in every child over the age of four."[5] Many of us would give everything we have for family peace and for children who cooperate willingly in family chores.

The idea that a baby might be spoiled if his natural need for closeness is met—what Liedloff calls being "in-arms"—would be utterly absurd to these gentle jungle-dwellers. In fact, the reverse is true. The baby is spoiled, that is, wounded, if he is not constantly carried in-arms by mother, father, or older child.

The symptoms of modern "in-arms deprivation" are many and varied, and they are absent from the jungle cultures that Liedloff studied. She writes, "In-arms deprivation expresses itself perhaps most commonly as an underlying feeling of unease in the here and now. One feels off center, as though something is missing; there is a vague sense of loss, of wanting something one cannot define. The wanting often attaches itself to an object or event in the middle distance; put into words, it would be 'I'd be all right if only...' followed by some proposed change, like having a new suit, a new car, a promotion or raise in salary, a different job, a chance to go away either for a vacation or permanently, or a wife or husband or child to love if one does not already have one."[6] Besides our attachment to materialism, other symptoms of in-arms deprivation that are easily seen in our culture are the high incidences of drug addiction, suicide, child abuse, violent crime, and divorce.

A boy needs to be in the arms of his mother or father until he is old enough to begin to explore the world through crawling, creeping, and then walking. It is in his parents' embrace that a boy learns to trust himself and the outside world. He develops a sense of rightness about his being, a feeling that he has a place in the scheme of things that will be with him for the rest of his life. These early learnings determine his capacity to give and receive love, to form relationships with others, to commit to the demands of work and community service.

The demands on parents during this time are tremendous; and if our focus is on how hard this stage is, they may seem unendurable. Mothers and fathers must find ways to include in-arms time with their sons in their work schedules. This may mean that one parent stays home while the other works outside the home; that one or both parents take the baby to work; or that parents create a home business, do shift work, participate in job-sharing, etc. As we look back on our son's first years, we wonder how time went by so fast. We sacrificed sleep, career, time alone, sex, evenings out together, and luxuries that a second income would have allowed. It was awful, yet empowering and wonderful at the same time.

A boy needs protection from negative cultural influences. The first protective act required of parents in our culture is to choose a good birthing environment, one with attendants who will honor the parent-infant bond. Parents must insist that the baby be allowed to stay in contact with his mother's skin after birth, to nurse; to become accustomed to the changes in temperature, sounds, and lighting of this new world; and to continue the bonding that began during his growth within his mother's womb. The baby who is left in his mother's arms, rather than being snatched away to be weighed and measured and tested and stabbed and wrapped, will lie quietly and look deeply in her eyes, as though to say, "Ahh, here you are at last."

The second protective act parents must consider is whether circumcision is necessary for their son. There are differing medical and religious motivations for this procedure (see "Help! Is Out There" at the end of this chapter), but as we stated in chapter 4, we strongly feel that this early wounding of boys is barbaric and sets a precedent for violence. We advocate the use of soap and water instead of a surgeon's knife.

Stress is the third negative cultural influence from which a son needs protection. It is customary these days to take the new baby everywhere, and indeed, infants were included in most activities of tribal life. However, the jungle and fields were nothing like the shopping mall, the movie theater, Marine World, or the supermarket. The bombardment of neon and fluorescent lighting; garish colors; artificial noises; stale and polluted air from dyes, perfumes, chemicals, plastics, cleaning supplies, etc. overstimulates an infant's sensitive nervous system. Even the nursery may be overwhelming to him with its bright colors, busy pictures, plastics, and polyester fabrics. Some babies react to technological assault by simply going to sleep. Others quietly bear the attack until they are home again, and then release the tension with a good cry. Our son reacted by crying long and loudly, and it was difficult to think of it as a "good" cry, since his response created stress and guilt for us, his well-meaning parents. We learned to avoid over-stimulating events and places until he was old enough to handle the stress or to release it through active or creative play.

Suggestions on how to create peaceful and healthy home environments for children can be found in several books listed in the "Help!" section at the end of the chapter. We have observed that most children function best in rooms with soft lighting, pastels, natural fabrics, and limited pictures or other ornaments. It is also better to have a few, simple toys of natural materials—wooden rattles, soft balls, and so on— and they play more comfortably in a room where all the toys have a place and are regularly put back. Children, like adults, need order and beauty in their lives.

In chapter 4 we examined the most pervasive negative cultural influence to come out of our technological age—television. Boys from birth to age seven and, it could be argued, through the "Tom Sawyer" years from ages eight to twelve, must be protected from its damaging influence. Young children usually respond to TV viewing in two ways, passiveness or hyperactivity. Don't be fooled by the appearance of relaxation in your son—glazed eyes, slightly open mouth, immobile body. His senses may seem dulled while he watches, but every detail is being imprinted upon his whole being. The images he sees—bad guys shooting the good guys; Bugs Bunny hitting Elmer Fudd over the head with a mallet; the Ninja Turtles blasting Rock Steady and BeBop; Power Rangers facing off; subtle put-downs of race, gender, religion, or philosophical ideas; commercials selling happiness through toys, cereal, fast cars, fashion clothes—all contribute to the values by which he will live his life. Laura Kennedy, therapist and mother of three, notes that parents used to be held responsible by society to teach cultural values, so that their children would grow up respectful of cultural norms and mores. "Now," she says, "culture has gotten so out of hand that we must protect our children *from* those values."[7]

Studies of early hunting cultures found few differences between how boys and girls were raised until puberty, when they were separated to learn specific gender roles. The distinctive manhood initiation rites that shaped boys into men allowed boys a freer childhood than they have today. The roles for adult males in our culture are so ambiguous and undefined, and the passage from boyhood into manhood so undistinguished, that our culture expects parents to pressure boys into their male roles from the beginning. Boy babies are dressed in blue—not pink!—and are given balls to play with—not dolls! This early push into male stereotypes erodes a boy's tender emotional side and his creative imagination, both vital to his ability to love. Boys need to unfold as children within a structure that will guide their male forces, not imprison them.

> *I was shocked when my three-year-old son asked for a kitchen for Christmas. He wanted all the plastic food, dishes, sink, everything. I thought, "Oh, no! He's gonna be a sissy." He got the kitchen for Christmas anyway, and the first thing he did was to create a restaurant. For a year, we've been served plastic eggs and rubber toast! I know now that he is imitating our family eating out in restaurants and eating at home. That makes perfect sense to me.*
>
> *—Jonathan, father of Chris, four*

Imitation of events in the world around him is the key play activity for the two- to seven-year-old. Through imitative tasks a boy develops creative imagination, motor skills, and the basis for forming relationships. We must protect our sons from cultural gender stereotyping that dictates how our sons must play and what toys they may have.

Perhaps the most wounding cultural prohibition for boys is the denial of feeling. "Big boys don't cry." "You're ok. Get up quick. You didn't fall that hard." "Don't be mad." "Be a big boy." "Here's a cookie." "It's no big deal." Bob, a bachelor businessman, was amazed when his friend Rich held his young son after he had hammered his finger. Later he confided to Rich, "I couldn't help noticing that while we were talking about football, your boy naturally came over to you when he hurt himself. He hopped in your lap, you moved to hold him, you rubbed his back, you let him cry it out, then he was ready to go back to his play. You did all of this without missing a beat of our conversation. You didn't say a word to him, and he was comforted. That is foreign to me. My parents taught me to be smart, but they never comforted me like that. To this day, when I hurt, I distract myself with some intellectual endeavor."

Until recently, there was no room for feelings on the cultural Procrustean bed. Men are now recovering those lost parts of themselves by telling their stories of pain, by weeping, and by grieving their losses. Emotions are part of a boy's birthright—the salve that soothes his deepest grief, the spark that ignites his creative fires, the balancer of his intellect, his barometer for injustice, and a doorway to connection with others.

Inner Guidance System

From birth to three years of age, a boy is all feeling. An infant's hunger pangs or a toddler's stubbed toe are felt all through the body, and his entire body cries with the pain. In the next instant, he may be wiggling all over with giggles from the joy of seeing his mother's face. The young boy reacts to emotion without considering the consequences: he hits without thinking and is then surprised at the effect, as though his arm moved by itself. Rarely does he direct his energy at someone out of a deep personal motive. There is no need for him intellectually to understand his feelings and reactions. He is not developmentally able to do this, anyway. His feelings merely need to be acknowledged, and his behavior managed, in age-appropriate ways. We offer suggestions in the section on Fences later in this chapter.

From four to seven years of age, feelings become more event-specific. Anger can mean, "This is very important to me." Tears can mean, "I want to do more than I am able to do." Sadness can mean, "I don't want to let go of you." Rage can mean, "I need you to protect me from myself."

The home environment shapes the effectiveness of a boy's inner guidance system. Whatever feelings his parents allow, along with the feelings that they either consciously or unconsciously deny, will form his feeling box. In the beginning, Kenny's inner guidance system was working properly. When he was angry at his mother, he told her that he was mad. His first feeling box looked like this:

Kenny

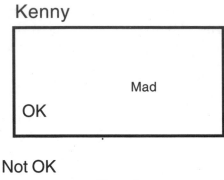

Figure 1.

When Kenny got a little older, his anger began to make his mother uncomfortable. His mother's response, "You don't really feel that way," made Kenny madder, so she would put him in his room for a "time out." Eventually, Kenny learned that if he wanted to have his play time, he had to pretend he wasn't mad. He realized that his mother could handle sadness, so over time, he learned to appear sad whenever he felt mad. Anger is usually a signal that something is wrong, but because anger was outside his mother's own feeling box, he lost this important clue from his inner guidance system. Now when something is wrong, Kenny feels sad and gets comfort from his mother, but he is unaware that anything needs to change. His box became compatible with his mother's and now looks like this:

Kenny

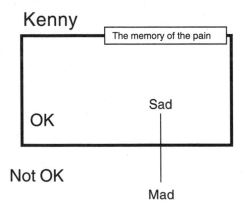

Figure 2.

Below is a feeling box for your son. Put his feelings that you are comfortable with on the inside of his box. The ones that make you uncomfortable go on the outside.

Your Son

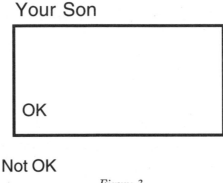

OK

Not OK

Figure 3.

We are often unaware of how the conditions of our own inner natures, that is, our inner guidance systems, feeling boxes, and such, affect our sons. Certain life experiences have left us wounded and incapable of relating clearly to our sons, in ways that support and enhance their healthy development. Bob, a therapist and valued friend of ours, shared that his mother had done everything for him and had provided what she believed was the best mothering possible. The effects of his mother's oversolicitous care, however, left him unable to take a stand on his convictions, unsure of his abilities, incapable of choosing compatible life-mates, and with an overwhelming sense of inadequacy. Her unconscious fear of the world and low self-esteem were inherited by her son.

Our first parenting responsibility to our sons is to become engaged in a genuine personal search of our own inner natures. In his helpful book, *Inner Work*, noted author and Jungian analyst Robert A. Johnson writes, "Every person must live the inner life in one form or another. Consciously or unconsciously, voluntarily or involuntarily, the inner world will claim us and exact its dues. If we go to that realm consciously, it is by our inner work: our prayers, meditations, dream work, ceremonies, and Active Imagination. If we try to ignore the inner world, as most of us do, the unconscious will find its way into our lives through pathology: our psychosomatic symptoms, compulsions, depressions, and neuroses."[8] We would add that our unconscious will find its way into our lives *through our sons*, because they often "act out" for us the very thing that we have been ignoring or are unaware of within ourselves. The more able we are to open to our own traumas, losses, feelings, joys, and achievements, the more able our sons will be to grow into full, loving human beings.

Fences

A boy is not a little adult. The most common error parents make with their children between infancy and seven years is to treat them like tiny adults. As soon as our sons learn to speak, we begin explaining why they may or may not do something, giving them choices, logically admonishing them to change their behavior, and overwhelming them with rational, spatial, time-related reasoning. The young child views time and space much differently from the way an adult does. This is why a four-year-old can spend so much time brushing his teeth—he gets lost in the wonderful feeling of water running between his fingers. And it's why he has so much trouble understanding how long it will be before Daddy comes home from work. Two hours seems just as long as two days, to his understanding. Telling him, "As long as it takes to drive to Grandma's house," may send him into fits of crying, because the half-hour drive to Grandma's house may seem much longer than that. It is far better for a boy of this age to become involved with us in a game, story, or household task, to help the time pass for him, than for us to try to explain how long it will be before Daddy finally walks through the front door.

The young boy needs guidance, not choices. We are all familiar with the following scenario: Mother is in the kitchen, where her three-year-old son is playing with clay. She asks, "Do you want cereal or pancakes for breakfast? What kind of cereal—Cheerios, Corn Flakes, Oatios, or granola? Do you want yogurt, milk, or Half and Half on your cereal? How do you want it sweetened—honey or sugar? Do you want white or brown sugar?" and on and on. Waldorf educator and internationally known lecturer Eugene Schwartz asserts that "a child who lacks the living example of a self-assured and guiding adult will have to struggle, in a later life, to attain inner assurance and inner guidance…a child who is given too many choices will become an adult who has difficulty making decisions."[9]

The boy in the first seven years of life is dependent upon his parents to create a space for him to grow, to set the rhythms of his day, and to create rituals that give distinct shape and secure continuity to his existence. It is important for him to know that after he awakens in the morning, he takes his bath with Daddy, he finds his clothes laid out for him and gets dressed, the family begins breakfast together by holding hands and giving thanks for the food, he is responsible for bringing his cereal bowl to the kitchen when he has finished eating, he brushes his teeth and washes his hands, and then it's play time.

These simple routines are established through the parent's lead. That is, we take the boy by the hand, say "Now it's time to take our bath," and bring him into the tub with us. Or, "Now it's time to pick up toys. These blocks are lost cars. Let's (let *us*) find the garage (the box they belong in)." Power struggles over getting things done, such as dressing, brushing teeth, and putting toys away, could be diminished by setting firm routines and being there to help the child follow through. During the willing years, we must appeal to his will. He is proud to imitate us in any task required. It is vital, however, that we not expect him to assume self-motivated responsibility for doing what we ask. This is the age of repetition, and he will require patient and persistent modeling before he is able to follow the routine on his own initiative.

The young boy needs brick walls. The boy from birth to four or five, depending on the individual, needs brick walls to keep him physically safe and emotionally secure. Young boys look to their parents to order their lives, so that they may be free to follow their Christopher Columbus instincts with a natural zest and lack of inhibition. They should not be allowed to play in the street, near rushing water, and on the kitchen stove. These are absolutes with no room for discussion. Until they are five, boys play most safely in large, fenced yards with securely locked gates. In our part of the country, our son had to learn that he was not allowed to play in the front yard without an adult present.

He still lives by this inflexible rule, but other walls have softened. He may now cross the street alone. He helps cook at the kitchen stove with our supervision. Picket fences are beginning to be appropriate for him, indicated by his willingness to assume responsibility for feeding the cat and setting the table for dinner. He often forgets, but usually does the job when he is reminded.

Consequences must fit the situation and the boy. Nothing in his world will go untouched, untasted, undiscovered. This means that Great-grandmother's crystal vase and the matches on the hearth must be moved out of his reach. "Yes! I slapped his hand," said a distraught mother, who was feeling out of control with her two-year-old son. "He has to learn not to touch my things!" The trouble with this picture is that her son simply felt hurt and shocked when his mother hit him. The pain in his fingers bore no relationship to the beautiful, shiny thing he had been enjoying. No harsh words, explanation, or hand slapping work as well as putting the breakable or dangerous object out of reach until the boy is old enough to handle it carefully, or to understand that it is to be admired but not touched.

Pavlov proved that we can condition animals to do as we wish by using reward and punishment. We could achieve this with a son, as well, but at great cost to his, and our, emotional well-being. He is on a mission of discovery, and we are the guides who make his journey as smooth-sailing as possible.

We have provided space for you to take a close look at the fences you are using for your son. Think of three areas where he needs fencing. Choose a fence that is appropriate to his age and developmental needs. Describe how you can set up this fence, so that he is safe and can be at his optimum learning level, without pushing him beyond his abilities.

Age	Problem	Fence	Describe the Fence
2	*Running into street*	*Brick wall*	*Constant adult supervision the when in unfenced areas*

It is important to note that if your fences are not working, they may be too tight or too loose, too small or too large. Adjust them until you find a pattern that works for you and your son. He will continually grow and need more room to roam. Frequent review of how his developmental needs match the strength of your fences will guide his growth and save your sanity.

Sexuality

Parents must be clear about their own sexual values. What is it that scares us so much about our son's sexuality? Mention the subject in any group of parents, and we squirm in our seats, groan, roll our eyes heavenward, and grin foolishly. The answer is that few of us escaped the guilt and embarrassment of growing up sexually in America. It is difficult to separate our son's sexuality from our own; and of course, we want somehow to spare him the humiliation, abuse, or guilt that we experienced.

Sex in this culture is too often linked with violence, which is confusing and frightening. Often, billboards, music lyrics, magazine ads, TV, and the movies sell sex as a way to be "cool," powerful, loved, and successful. The words and pictures say, "Do it. Do it. Do it." Churches, some teachers, and many parents say, "Don't. Don't. Don't!" How can we raise sexually responsible, healthy sons in the midst of ambiguous cultural values?

The AIDS epidemic has brought out most everything about sexuality into the open. Perhaps a positive result is that we now have permission to talk more freely about all aspects of sexuality—our fears, needs, desires, prejudices, fantasies, and hang-ups. AIDS has given parents an opening to talk with their children about sex.

The place to start talking about our son's sexuality is with our parenting partner. It is helpful to explore these important questions with each other:

How do we feel about our own sexual relationship?

What are our own sexual values?

How do we feel about masturbation?

What about nudity and privacy in our home?

How do we talk to our son about sex?

Who should talk to him—mother or father?

When do we talk to him?

How do we feel about our son's sexual play with other children?

How will we handle it when it happens?

How do we protect our son from sexual abuse?

What if he tells us he is gay?

His parents' sexual relationship speaks louder to a son than any words can. The foundation for a boy's healthy sexuality lies in how his parents relate to each other—touching, making time for each other, showing concern for each other's feelings, honoring each other's needs, sharing household chores, showing respect for each other's ideas, laughing together, and working together on family projects. The time to start dealing with our son's sexuality is before he is born, or right now.

From birth, our sons are sexual beings. A baby delights in the sensuous feelings of sucking, being held, tiny fingers clutching soft blanket bindings, being tickled, the warm feeling in his diaper after urination. Parents also delight in this delicious, soft, little, cuddly being. Through physical contact we teach our sons about love and affection, preparing them for their future sexual relationships. Well-known authors and sex educators Sol Gordon, Ph.D., and Judith Gordon, M.S.W., assert in their helpful book, *Raising a Child Conservatively in a Sexually Permissive World*, that our sexual feelings and attitudes are formed by the time we reach the age of five.[10] How a young boy learns to feel about his body will positively or negatively influence his sexual development. Toilet training, for example, if pushed too early or harshly instituted, can cause feelings of guilt, self-doubt, and shame about his body and his ability for self-control. A boy will learn to feel pride in his body, rather than shame, when parents follow his lead, meeting his questions and natural curiosity about sexual issues with acceptance and an easy readiness to explain.

Young sons are curious about everything they see in their homes and naturally, they want to experiment. Some behaviors may worry parents who are concerned their sons might become gay or bisexual. Little boys are often fascinated by their mother's makeup, jewelry, and clothes, wanting to try it all on and gaze at their reflections in the mirror. Many boys love to play with dolls, dressing and undressing them, cradling them lovingly, singing and talking softly to them. Whether they are gay, bisexual, or heterosexual, they will more than likely go on to other activities as they grow older. The point we want to stress is that our son's sexual orientation is not determined by whether he likes pink, wears Mother's lipstick, or plays with dolls. Many of us fear that our parenting may be the cause of our son's sexual identity, and experience unnecessary guilt or shame. The truth is that no one knows the origins of homosexuality or bisexuality. It is important for parents during the willing years to examine our fears about our own sexuality and learn to accept the many degrees of difference along the scale of human sexual response.

Because boys in the first seven years of life are body-oriented, their perhaps not-so-simple questions about sex require simple answers. They are not yet ready for technical information about where they came from and how they got here. However, it is vital to try to ascertain what they really want to know, and to use the correct terminology in our answers. When a boy of three or four asks how the baby got inside his mommy, our answer will differ from the explanation we would give if he were six or seven. It is appropriate and important to respond to both age groups in the most direct way we can. The Gordons assure us that "parents are far less likely to go 'wrong' by responding to children's questions with perhaps a little more sophistication than they believe the child can handle, than they are by underestimating the child's capabilities."[11] To the three-year-old, we might say, "The daddy put a sperm cell inside of the mommy's body, where it will meet an egg. When the sperm and egg meet, a baby will grow." The seven-year-old may require more information, such as, "Daddy puts a sperm cell into Mommy's vagina with his penis. The sperm swims to meet an egg inside of Mommy's body, and when they meet a baby will grow in Mommy's uterus."

As we have seen, during the willing years the body is a boy's vehicle for exploring the world; and because his body is part of the world, it will also come under close investigation. Mothers often become troubled that their sons constantly pull and rub their penises.

> *In the bathtub, especially, I'm afraid he'll pull it off! And then I was so embarrassed when Aunt Mary visited yesterday, and Jeff wouldn't keep his hands out of his pants. Is it normal? I don't want to shame him and make him feel bad about his body, but I can't handle this. Does this early fascination mean that he's oversexed?*
>
> —*Susan, mother of Jeff, aged two*

Privacy is an important aspect of sexual development. Early fascination with his own and others' bodies is totally normal in the young boy. Pulling, poking, and rubbing his penis and scrotum are sources of pleasure and comfort. When we treat his behavior as normal, rather than as a cause for alarm or shame, he is less likely to become what we all fear he will become—obsessed with masturbation, perverted, or oversexed. A good guideline for all of this is to let our sons know that we know that rubbing his penis feels good, that it is okay for him to do it, and that it is something he does in private—in his bed, in his room by himself, but not in front of Aunt Mary or his friends. The Gordons assure us that "masturbation is a normal sexual expression for all people, no matter at what age or stage in life they happen to be—child, teenager, young adult, middle-aged, elderly, single or married."[12]

Teaching our boys about privacy and "private parts" will also help when we must deal with the inevitable sexual explorations between our sons and their friends. Rare is the parent who doesn't stumble in on a game of "Doctor" or "I'll show you mine, if you show me yours." A helpful response is offered by child care expert Eda LeShan, in *When Your Child Drives You Crazy*. "I know that you want to learn about your bodies, but you know when grown-ups go to visit each other, they don't take off their clothes."[13] Letting your son know that you understand his interest, that you will be glad to answer any questions he has, but that undressing is done in private, sets the rules firmly and creates an opportunity to talk about sexual matters that may be puzzling him.

֍ *JEANNE* | A young boy's request for privacy clues us that he is entering a new level of sexual understanding and development. When our son was four, he asked that I not look while he undressed for bed, and he no longer wanted my help in the bathroom. He was no longer comfortably nude in front of me. My initial feelings were of being shut out, and I thought, Hey! I cleaned and diapered your bottom. I know every inch of your body. What do you mean, don't look at me? But this was an important signal that he was developing a clear sense of being himself, a person separate from me, in charge of his own body. My respecting his request conveys to him that I value his needs, that he is important, that it is okay for him to ask me for what he wants regarding his personal needs. In this way, he learns to respect his own and his future partner's needs and preferences, which is paramount for developing a healthy sexuality.

The Positive Intent

A boy is not his bad behavior. It is crucial to make a distinction in our minds between our sons and their misbehaviors. LeShan makes an important declaration about children of this age group: "Kids are not bad. They are only young."[14] The positive intent behind much of our sons' naughtiness is the hunger to explore and to learn firsthand about life (to review how to listen for a son's positive intent, see chapter 8). Most of us have forgotten how tempting and exciting any new experience can be, and we take too much for granted. Our son will literally stop and smell the roses, the grass, the rocks, the caterpillar, and anything else on his path, every chance he gets. His apparent misconduct is often his way of telling us, "I am alive!" "I want to know!" "I need your help!"

Giving attention to bad behavior reinforces it. The best response to some behaviors is ignoring them. Hurtful phrases and "dirty" words are good examples. When we wash out a boy's mouth with real or figurative soap, we draw undue attention to the once-meaningless phrase and give it meaning. He now knows how to get our attention and direct our behavior. The positive intent of his statement may be just that—he needs our attention, or our attention is important to him. The positive intent behind his use of a vulgar word might be a call for our help in understanding a missing piece in his sexual education. This may be a perfect opening to initiate that conversation about sex that we had been putting off. Before reacting to a misbehavior with a consequence we may later regret, we need to listen for his positive intent and respond to him on that level.

Following are statements and actions common to boys between birth and age seven. Before reading our suggestions of their positive intent, decide what you think it is.

Infants (birth to walking)

Behavior: Cries when you lay him in his crib or put him in the plastic carrier. There doesn't seem to be anything wrong (diaper is dry, he just nursed, he's already had his nap, and so on).

Positive intent: To thrive, I need to be carried around, to be part of the excitement of your daily activities. I need contact with you. You are important to my well-being.

Behavior: Refuses to lie or stand still while his diaper is being changed.

Positive intent: I don't have time for this nonsense anymore. There is too much world waiting for me to explore!

Toddlers (walking to four years)

Behavior: Takes the clean, folded clothes out of the laundry basket, drags them across the sticky kitchen floor, and stuffs them into the dryer.

Positive intent: I want to be just like you. I want to help.

Statement: "No!" to everything you request of him.

Positive intent: I am practicing becoming a person.

Little Boys (four to seven years)

Behavior: Pees in the backyard instead of coming inside to use the bathroom.

Positive intent: My play is too important to interrupt right now.

Statement: "I hate my sister Kate. I wish she never came to live with us."

Positive intent: I need your love, too. I'm unsure of my importance to you. Where do I belong in this family?

Taking Action

The job of parenting can be tiring and lonely, and sometimes the effort needed to reach out to others or to create new family habits seems difficult, if not impossible. The frightened look that crosses parents' faces at our suggestion to turn off the TV or limit its use could be comical if it did not reflect genuine fear and panic at the thought of cutting off what has become to many families the lifeline through which they connect with one another. After the frightened look passes, the first question is, "But what would we do?" Here are some of our suggestions. As you get more practice, you may be surprised by your own ideas. We encourage you to take back the control of your family's attention and time, and explore these suggestions together.

Learn the art of storytelling. Throughout history, storytelling was a highly valued art form, and the storyteller was always a welcome guest. Carefully selected tales were used to teach children the rules and values of their culture, and to educate them in the mythological and spiritual traditions by which the people lived. Stories were used to mark and to remember important events, to honor great achievements, to amuse and to entertain, and to move the people to action.

To get you started, read *I'll Tell You a Story, I'll Sing You a Song*, by Christine Allison (New York: Dell Publishing, 1987). This is a delightful parents' guide to the fairy tales, fables, songs, and rhymes that we all heard in childhood but no doubt have partially forgotten. It will be just the inspiration needed to get you started. Then, to perfect your skills and to learn new stories, you might want to join a storytelling club or start one of your own. Even the youngest children can participate in the telling, besides being spellbound listeners. Other book suggestions are:

Catch Me & Kiss Me & Say It Again, by Clyde Watson, New York: Philomel Books, 1978. Filled with delightful verses and rhymes. Local bookstores.

The Family Storytelling Handbook, by Anne Pellowski, New York: Macmillan, 1987. A complete guide to telling well-known stories, made-up stories, and personal anecdotes, which children love so much to hear. Gives suggestions for using story props. Loads of fun! Try local stores with a good selection of children's books, or order from: *Music for Little People* catalog, P.O. Box 1460, Redway, CA 95560, (707) 923-3991.

The Three Bears & 15 Other Stories, by Anne Rockwell, New York: Harper and Row Junior Books, 1975. All of the old favorites in versions short enough to learn to tell. Local bookstores with good children's selections.

Learn to play together. Frances Moore Lappé's book, *What to Do After You Turn Off the TV* (see the following Help! section under Needs), has enough ideas for family fun to fill several childhoods. Your family will quickly find their favorites and ask to play them together again and again.

Read aloud together. We have long known the importance of regularly reading aloud to children, beginning as young as six months of age. The joy and excitement of experiencing the drama of great literature will fire even the youngest of imaginations. Being read to helps develop an ability to concentrate and the disciplines of listening, paying attention, and focusing, and it aids in the development of proper language skills. Plus, we can't imagine a nicer way to enhance family bonding than by cuddling up together to enjoy a good "read." For age-appropriate book suggestions, try:

The Chinaberry Book Service, a wonderfully annotated catalog of books and music for children and families written by a mother who has tried the selections out on her own family. Write: 2780 Via Orange Way, Suite B, Spring Valley, CA 91978, (619) 670-5200.

The New York Times Parent's Guide to the Best Books for Children, by Eden Ross Lipson, New York: Random House, 1988. Check local bookstores.

Cook together. The toddler loves to do anything Mom or Dad is doing in the kitchen, glorying in the smells, textures, tastes, and pure delight of being part of what's going on. Cracking eggs, whipping cream, putting in the nuts, setting the timer, and playing in the soap-suds all nurture a young boy's sense of discovery and accomplishment. He is interested in the outcome, because he feels included. Because of his age, he sees the needs of others through his own needs, but giving him a place in the kitchen now assures his interest and participation later. Our favorite cookbook for preschoolers and up is *Pretend Soup*, by Molly Katzen (Berkeley, CA: Tricycle Press, 1994). The delightful illustrations, good recipes most children love, insightful notes to adults, cooking hints, safety tips, and simple, pictorial instructions for children to follow make *Pretend Soup* a delicious guide.

The Uses of Enchantment, by Bruno Bettelheim, New York: Random House, 1977. Explains the importance of fairy tales in children's development. Local bookstores.

Create music together. Children are naturally musical, and even the youngest love singing and banging to simple rhythms. First music makers can be percussion instruments that the family creates together, such as simple drums from oatmeal boxes, sticks that are tapped together, spoons, bells, and rattles made from toilet paper tubes filled with beans or corn. You can start a family band, which some evening might extend into an entire neighborhood jam session. Numerous books are available on how to make simple musical instruments. Here are recommended resources:

Sound Designs: A Handbook of Musical Instrument Building, by Reinhold Banek and Jon Scoville, Berkeley, CA: Ten Speed Press, 1995. Pretty sophisticated but great ideas. Local bookstores.

Folk Song Encyclopedia, by Jerry Silverman, Milwaukee, Wis.: Hal Leonard Music Publishing, 1975. A super collection of more than one thousand folk songs from our American heritage of song. Available from the Music for Little People catalog (see listing below for address).

I'll Tell You a Story, I'll Sing You a Song, by Christine Allison, New York: Dell Publishing, 1987. (Previously listed.)

Kids Songs, by Nancy and John Cassidy, Palo Alto, Calif.: Klutz Press, 1986. These songs will tickle everyone's funny bone. Check local toy stores and children's music catalogs.

The Laughing Baby, by Anne Scott, South Hadley, Mass.: Bergin & Garvey, 1987. Full of well-loved songs and nursery rhymes. Local bookstores.

Music for Little People catalog. Full of marvelous recordings from around the world; offers a large selection of books, gifts from many cultures, and musical instruments. Our son loves his child-sized guitar. Choices for all ages. Their staff is especially helpful with gift suggestions and any questions you have about their merchandise. Write: P.O. Box 1460, 1144 Redway Drive, Redway, CA 95560, (707) 923-3991.

The Reader's Digest Children's Songbook, Pleasantville, N.Y.: Reader's Digest Association, 1985. A collection of 131 songs adapted from show tunes, movie classics, and folk and American favorites. Includes simple piano arrangements and guitar chords. Available from the Music for Little People catalog.

Create a family masterpiece. Who knows? There may be a budding Picasso or Renoir hiding behind the T-shirt and jeans of your young son. He's made great pictures out of his chocolate pudding, hasn't he?

A great way to develop hidden talent is to have the whole family join in the fun of playing with clay, painting, papier-mâché, simple weaving, sewing, and knitting. Many great surgeons have kept their fingers nimble by tailoring their own suits, the ex-football great Rosey Greer loves to needlepoint, and knitting was invented by early sailors. The following great guides to arts and crafts will help you get started:

The Ark catalog. Crayons, beeswax, and painting supplies, as well as books and toys in the Waldorf educational tradition. Write: 3845 24th Street, San Francisco, CA 94114, (415) 821-1257.

The Children's Year, by Stephanie Cooper, Gloucester, U.K.: Hawthorn Press, 1988. Simple toys, dolls, and animals. Available from HearthSong catalog (see below).

Face Painting, by the editors of Klutz Press, Palo Alto, Calif.: Klutz Press, 1990. Local toy outlets and children's bookstores.

Festivals, Family and Food, by Diane Carey and Judy Large, Gloucester, U.K.: Hawthorn Press, 1987. Order from HearthSong catalog (see below).

Hanky Panky, by Elizabeth Burns, self-published, 1973. Comes with white handkerchief and directions for making clever, magical creations with folds and knots. Available from: Informed Birth & Parenting Books, P.O. Box 3675, Ann Arbor, MI 48106, (313) 662-6857.

HearthSong catalog. A resource for art supplies and wonderful children's books, toys, and musical instruments. Write: P.O. Box B, Sebastopol, CA 95473, (707) 829-0944.

Making Soft Toys, by Freya Jaffke, Millbrae, Calif.: Celestial Arts, 1981. Gives directions for making simple toys, such as knot dolls, for young children. Local bookstores.

The Natural Way to Draw, by Kimon Nicolaides, Boston: Houghton Mifflin, 1969. A great guide to freedom from the fear of drawing. Local bookstores.

Painting with Children, by Brunhild Muller, Edinburgh, U.K.: Floris Books, 1987. Available from HearthSong catalog (see above).

365 Days of Creative Play for Children, by Sheila Ellison and Judith Gray, Foster City, Calif.: Fantashe Publications, 1987. Local bookstores.

Help! Is Out There—Where to Find It

The following books, magazines, and organizations have been useful to us in our search for parenting support. They are listed according to what was most helpful, rather than in alphabetical order. We pass them on to you in hopes they will make your challenging job as parents a little easier.

Developmental Tasks

Books

You Are Your Child's First Teacher, by Rahima Baldwin, Berkeley, Calif.: Celestial Arts, 1989. This book has just about everything! See your local bookseller. If they don't have it, they can special-order it.

Oneness & Separateness: From Infant to Individual, by Louise J. Kaplan, Ph.D., New York: Simon & Schuster, 1978. Provides fascinating insights into the development of newborns to three-year-olds. Local bookstores.

Miseducation: Preschoolers at Risk, by David Elkind, New York: Alfred A. Knopf, 1987. Discusses what young children need educationally, and why parents and preschools are "miseducating" them. Available from Informed Birth & Parenting Books. (See previous listing.)

Children at Play: Preparation for Life, by Heidi Britz-Crecelius, New York: Inner Traditions International, 1972. A beautiful, sensitive book that offers practical guidance for parents in a technological age. Available from Informed Birth & Parenting Books (see above).

The Young Child: Creative Living with Two- to Four-Year-Olds, by Daniel Udo De Haes, New York: Anthroposophic Press, 1986. Emphasis on language development and appropriate teaching stories for young children. Available through the Anthroposophic Press, R.R. 4, Box 94A1, Hudson, NY 12534, (518) 851-2054.

The Radiant Child, by Thomas Armstrong, Wheaton, Ill.: The Theosophical Publishing House, 1985. Chronicles the spiritual as well as the psychological development of young children. Offers heaps of resources and recommended reading for parents and children. Published by the Theosophical Publishing House, 306 West Geneva Road, Wheaton, IL 60189, (708) 665-0130.

Your Baby & Child: From Birth to Age Five, by Penelope Leach, New York: Alfred A. Knopf, 1977. A practical guide to everything. Local bookstores.

Needs

Books

The Continuum Concept, by Jean Liedloff, Reading, Mass.: Addison-Wesley, 1975. An amazing theory of child development. Try local new or used bookstores.

Born Dancing, by Evelyn B. Thoman and Sue Browder, New York: Harper and Row, 1987. Helps parents trust themselves as parents. Check local bookseller.

Special Delivery, by Rahima Baldwin, Berkeley, Calif.: Celestial Arts, 1986. A helpful guide for expectant parents including pregnancy, birth, and the postpartum period. Available from Informed Birth & Parenting Books.

Birth Without Violence, by Frederick Leboyer, New York: Alfred A. Knopf, 1975. A beautiful guide to birth without the fear, pain, and confusion. Local bookstores.

Models of Love, The Parent-Child Journey, by Joyce Vissell, R.N., M.S., and Barry Vissell, M.D., Aptos, Calif.: Ramira Publishing, 1986. Includes the spiritual side of parenting. Local bookstores.

Big Spirits, Little Bodies: Parenting Your Way to Wholeness, by Linda Crispell Aronson, Virginia Beach: A.R.E. Press, 1995. Full of wisdoms such as, "The differences between ourselves and our children are the catalysts for growth spurts of the spirit. They hint at what we will teach each other." Local bookstores can order it if not on hand.

Pretend Soup and Other Real Recipes, by Mollie Katzen and Ann Henderson, Berkeley, CA: Tricycle Press, 1994. A feast for the eyes as well as the palate. A cookbook for preschoolers and up. Highly recommended for the beginning cook. Local bookstores.

What to Do After You Turn Off the TV, by Frances Moore Lappé, New York: Ballantine Books, 1985. Full of wonderful ideas for the whole family to enjoy together. Check local bookstores.

Four Arguments for the Elimination of Television, by Jerry Mander, New York: Morrow, 1978. Gives a provocative account of the whys of TV program content and its effects on viewers. Local bookstores.

Breaking the TV Habit, by Joan Anderson Wilkins, New York: Charles Scribner's, 1982. Offers insights and suggestions for dealing with family television viewing habits. Local booksellers.

Growing a Business, by Paul Hawken, New York: Simon and Schuster, 1987. An insightful guide to starting your own business. Local booksellers will have it or order it for you.

Do What You Love, the Money Will Follow: Discovering Your Right Livelihood, by Marsha Sinetar, New York: Paulist Press, 1987. Our work can support our families and ourselves financially and emotionally, too. Check local bookstores.

Growing a Business/Raising a Family, edited by Jan and Charlie Fletcher, Fayetteville, N.C.: NextStep Publications, 1988. A collection of essays by "homeworking" parents. Local bookstores.

Magazines, Booklets, and Newsletters

Mothering, a quarterly journal filled with wise and wonderful parenting support. Order by writing: P.O. Box 1690, Santa Fe, NM 87504, or calling (505) 984-8116.

Circumcision Booklet, includes reprints of selected articles from Mothering. Order from *Mothering*. (See previous listing.)

Welcome Home, a publication in support of mothers who choose to stay at home. Write: 8310 "A" Old Courthouse Road, Vienna, VA 22182, (800) 733-4MOM.

Journal of Family Life, a quarterly for empowering families. Offers insights from both laypersons and experts in the parenting and birthing fields. For subscriptions: 72 Philip Street, Albany, NY 12202, (518) 432-15578.

The Whole Work Catalog, a catalog with options for more rewarding work, including self-employment and home business opportunities. Write: The New Careers Center, P.O. Box 297, Boulder, CO 80306, (303) 447-1087.

Networks

The Liedloff Continuum Network
P.O. Box 1634
Sausalito, CA 94965

A worldwide network of parents who want to bring the Continuum Concept into their family lives. For a membership list and newsletter, send SASE to the above address.

Mothers Home Business Network
P.O. Box 423
East Meadow, NY 11554

Write for their Homeworking Mothers Newsletter.

National Organization of Circumcision
Information Resource Centers (NOCIRC)
P.O. Box 2512
San Anselmo, CA 94979
(415) 488-9883

Write for information about the practice of circumcision, and to receive their newsletter.

Inner Guidance System

Books

Inner Work, by Robert A. Johnson, San Francisco: Harper and Row, 1986. A practical guide to using dreams and active imagination for personal growth. Local bookstores will have it or can special-order it.

The Drama of the Gifted Child, by Alice Miller, New York: Basic Books, 1981. Rare insights into our experiences as children. Local bookstores can order it, if they do not have it in stock.

Lifeways, edited by Gudrun Davy and Bons Voors, Gloucestershire, U.K.: Hawthorn Press, 1983. A collection of wonderfully insightful essays by parents about family questions. Local bookstores.

Ourselves and Our Children, by The Boston Women's Health Book Collective, New York: Random House, 1978. Written by parents about everything having to do with parenting. See local bookstores.

The Wounded Woman, by Linda Leonard, Athens, Ohio: Swallow Press, 1982. Personal insights into healing the father-daughter relationship. Local bookstores.

The Girl Within, by Emily Hancock, New York: Ballantine Books, 1989. A helpful guide to understanding feminine psychology. Local bookstores.

Goddesses In Everywoman, by Jean Shinoda Bolen, M.D., New York: Harper and Row, 1984. Weaves the ancient goddess myths to create a new understanding of modern woman. Local bookstores.

Fire in the Belly, by Sam Keen, New York: Bantam Books, 1991. A practical and personal new look at how men are changing. Local bookstores.

Iron John, by Robert Bly, Reading, Mass.: Addison-Wesley, 1990. A mythopoetic book about men by the leader of the men's movement. Local bookstores.

Gods in Everyman, by Jean Shinoda Bolen, M.D., New York: Harper and Row, 1989. Gives insights into modern men through the ancient myths about the gods. Local bookstores.

Self-Esteem: A Family Affair, by Jean Illsley Clarke, San Francisco: Harper & Row, 1978. A practical workbook for nurturing self-esteem among all family members. Local bookstores.

Focusing, by Eugene Gendlin, New York: Bantam, 1981. A guide for learning how to understand and follow the wisdom of your feelings. Local bookstores in the psychology section.

Fences

Books

You Are Your Child's First Teacher, by Rahima Baldwin, Berkeley, Calif.: Celestial Arts, 1989. Can't say enough about this book! See listing above, under Developmental Tasks, for information on where to get it.

When Your Child Drives You Crazy, by Eda LeShan, New York: St. Martin's Press, 1985. A wonderfully supportive book for parents, with practical suggestions on what to do during those difficult moments of childhood by someone who's been there. Local bookstores.

Children: The Challenge, by Rudolf Dreikurs, M.D., New York: E.P. Dutton, 1964. Helpful guide to finding the balance between letting children run wild and stifling them. Local booksellers.

Sexuality

Books

Raising a Child Conservatively in a Sexually Permissive World, by Sol Gordon, Ph.D., and Judith Gordon, M.S.W., New York: Simon and Schuster, 1983. A clear, outspoken guide for talking to our children about sexual issues. Check local bookstores.

Did the sun shine before you were born? by Sol and Judith Gordon, New York: The Third Press, 1974. A beautifully illustrated first book about sexuality for children. Ask local bookstores to order it for you, or try the Planned Parenthood chapter in your area.

New Our Bodies, Ourselves, by The Boston Women's Health Book Collective, New York: Simon and Schuster, 1992. A perceptive, comprehensive guidebook for women. Check local bookstores.

For Yourself: The Fulfillment of Female Sexuality, by Lonnie Barbach, Garden City, N.Y.: Anchor Press, 1975. A sensitive, personal exploration of female sexuality. Local booksellers carry it or will order it for you.

Male Sexuality, by B. Zilbergeld, New York: Bantam, 1988. A very practical and human book that dispels the myths about male sexuality. Local bookstores.

The Joy of Sex, edited by Alex Comfort, M.B., Ph.D., New York: Simon & Schuster, 1972. An adult guide to lovemaking. Local bookstores.

The Berenstain Bears Learn about Strangers, by Stan and Jan Berenstain, New York: Random House, 1985. Books by the Berenstains are the kind many children love and most parents hate, so you may want to think twice before introducing these books to your home. We find them tiresome reading, but our son loves them. Some sex-role stereotyping in the characters, so you may want to edit as you read aloud. The books deal with important topics about growing up. Children's bookstores.

The Courage to Heal, by Ellen Bass and Laura Davis, New York: Harper & Row, 1988. This guide for women survivors of child sexual abuse has an extensive bibliography with suggestions for parenting couples, children, lesbians, single parents, sexual abuse survivors, and more. Local bookstores.

It's MY Body, by Lory Freeman, Seattle, WA: Parenting Press, 1983. For children ages 4-6. Teaches children how to say "No!" to unwanted touching. Local bookstores.

Beyond Acceptance, by Carolyn Griffin, Marian Wirth, and Arthur Wirth, New York: St. Martin's Press, 1990. Parents of gay children talk about their experiences from the initial shock to increased understanding and closeness. Local bookstores.

Loving Someone Gay, Don Clark, Ph.D., Berkeley, CA: Celestial Arts, 1987. Help for families and friends with their prejudices and confusion about homosexuality. Local bookstores can order it.

Networks

Your local Planned Parenthood chapter has written materials for parents and children of all ages on all aspects of sexuality. You can also write or call: Planned Parenthood Federation of America, 810 Seventh Avenue, New York, NY 10019, (212) 541-7800.

Positive Intent

Books

When Your Child Drives You Crazy, by Eda LeShan. See previous listing.

How to Talk So Kids Will Listen and Listen So Kids Will Talk, by Adele Faber and Elaine Mazlish, New York: Avon Books, 1980. Offers practical how-to's for listening to and talking with your children. Local booksellers will have it.

End Notes

1. *A Mother's Journal* (Philadelphia, Pa.: Running Press, 1985), first page.

2. Berger, *The Developing Person*, 221-22.

3. Ibid., 222-23.

4. Ibid., 322-23.

5. Jean Liedloff, *The Continuum Concept: Allowing Human Nature to Work Successfully*, rev. ed. (Reading, Mass.: Addison-Wesley Publishing Co., 1985), 18, xvi.

6. Ibid., 110.

7. Laura Kennedy, M.A., conversation with Jeanne Elium, Berkeley, Calif., 14 May 1991.

8. Robert A. Johnson, *Inner Work* (San Francisco: Harper & Row, 1986), 10-11.

9. Eugene Schwartz, "Education Towards Freedom: Teaching Self-Discipline and Decision-Making," *The Peridot*, Fall/Winter 1990, Vol. 3, No. 2.

10. Sol Gordon and Judith Gordon, *Raising a Child Conservatively in a Sexually Permissive World*, rev. ed. (New York: Simon & Schuster, 1989), 72.

11. Ibid., 46.

12. Ibid., 34.

13. Eda LeShan, *When Your Child Drives You Crazy* (New York: St. Martin's Press, 1985), 348.

14. Ibid., 4.

CHAPTER ELEVEN

The I'm-On-My-Way-But-I-Don't-Know-Where-I'm-Going Years:
Eight to Twelve

I hear,
and I forget.
I see,
and I remember.
I do,
and I understand.

—Ancient Chinese proverb

Developmental Tasks

The years between eight and twelve are the feeling years. The focus of development is in the heart and lungs. A boy's budding capacity for understanding the feelings of others begins to influence his behavior. According to renowned researcher and psychologist Erik Erikson, Ph.D., these years are spent in a struggle between industry and inferiority.[1] A boy wavers between being attentive, hard-working, diligent, and industrious, and feeling slothful, worthless, and destructive, as though he can do nothing right. The male force begins to push him powerfully in both directions, and everything is either black or white. There are no "maybes" during this stage. He wonders, "Am I important and productive to my family?" and, alternately, "Am I worthless and destructive?"

The development of self-esteem now centers on doing. How he meets the challenges that he creates for himself will determine a boy's self-esteem and his hands-on style in the world of home and work. Explains Dr. Erikson, "As children busily try to master whatever skills are valued in their culture, they develop views of themselves as competent or incompetent...as either industrious and productive or inferior and inadequate."[2] Unlike a five-year-old, who can be motivated with the promise of a new toy, the eight- to twelve-year-old experiences the pleasure of successfully accomplishing a task. Often this is all the reward he needs. His psychological force pushes for a job well done.

We have watched our young neighbor, Sean, work with his father in the yard. His father's praise of his efforts encourages him not only to mow the lawn, but to clean the mower when he's finished and put it away without being asked. The key to understanding a boy of nine is written on Sean's face—a determination to learn it well and do it well, and to please the father.

Like Tom Sawyer, though, he'll connive to find ways to get the job done easier and faster. Remember that Tom not only figures out a way to get his friends to paint the picket fence, but he gets them to enjoy doing it. Ned, a single father, witnessed both this need for action and a budding ability to scheme in his nine-year-old son, Franklin. Ned works as a night chef, and before his habitual afternoon nap, his son asked him for five dollars. "I said that if he washed my car, he could have the money," Ned recalls. "I drove the car into the yard; set up the hoses; got buckets, soap, and rags; and told him that he needed to finish by the time I woke up. When I checked on him later, I got a big surprise. The car was washed, but Franklin had recruited three of his neighborhood buddies to help him. To make the job more fun, they had piled bikes and lawn chairs next to the car to make a wall for a water fight. My car wasn't damaged, but the scraping of metal on metal sent chills down my spine. To top it off, Franklin had raided the kitchen for snacks as an additional incentive for his friends' help. The big feed was all laid out under a shade tree, where he was concocting giant sandwiches for all. I ran out and grabbed Snickers, sodas, boxes of crackers, everything you can imagine out of the boys' hands, and sent them all home. After I cooled down, I was able to tell Franklin that I respected his initiative and that he had done a good job. Then we talked about the rules that he had unknowingly broken. I gave him the five dollars. Next time I'll give him a lot more supervision, too!"

Child-development expert Jean Piaget calls these the years of "concrete operational thinking."[3] Although the boy still has difficulty with abstract and hypothetical thought, he begins to understand and apply simple, logical thinking to concrete situations and problems in his life. He now understands more about the needs and values of the people he is trying to persuade or help, and he is interested in their opinions. A boy in the middle years also develops skills in negotiation, using what he observes about others. He can present counter-arguments to deflect a parent's objections before they can be given.

> *When my son Nathan was five, he would simply ask for permission to do something, such as, "Mom, can I paint?" Now he's eight, and he says, "Mom, I've cleaned up the toys in the kitchen. Can I paint?" He also responds differently to my saying no. When he was younger and I would say, "No, you may not paint, because your toys are all over the kitchen," he would cry and yell at me. Now, he persuades me with something that he knows I will like or praise him for.*
>
> —*Jill, mother of Nathan, eight*

Needs

Sons need their parents' supervision and involvement. The eight-to-twelve years present special challenges for parents, because the boy is no longer satisfied with free play. He wants to go further, to master physical challenges, make things, and build with a goal in mind. He requires more parental involvement in planning, supervising, and providing opportunities at home and in the world that help him develop the skills he craves. Parents will be drafted as a taxi service to shuttle sons to and from music lessons, aikido lessons, ballgames, and on and on. They will find themselves serving as Little League coaches, soccer officials, assistant builders of model cars and airplanes, and in whatever capacity the current interest requires.

Boys seek role models and leaders. It can drive parents nuts when their boy models himself after the worst character he knows. One of Don's young clients was asked why he was talking hatefully to his mother. "Hey! I'm practicing to be a teenager," he proudly replied. "Bobby next door (who is sixteen) talks to his mom like that all the time." Boys in the middle years mimic behavior that contributes to self-image and the development of moral values. Therefore, they are heavily influenced by playmates, parental actions, and the stories they hear and see in movies, videos, and on TV.

> *When my son James plays with our neighbor, Timmy, he is a handful for the rest of the day. He's "mouthy," uncooperative, and out-of-sorts. For now, I let James play with Timmy for only two hours a week, until his behavior toward me improves. James is doing better at not following Timmy's lead when he knows it's something he shouldn't do. Last month James couldn't play with Timmy for three weeks when Timmy got the idea to throw bricks through our garage windows. They now know that I mean business, and that kind of stuff hasn't happened since then. But James gravitates toward male energy; and with his dad gone and school out, Timmy is it, even if he acts like a hooligan sometimes. I know I need to find other male role models for my son to be around.*
>
> *—Carol, mother of James, nine*

Parents are a boy's first models. Our actions always create a deeper impression than the verbal lessons we give. This was true for Marty, now eleven, who no longer has the true "Tom Sawyer" drive "to do."

He spends his free time watching television and eating donuts. He wasn't always this way. Both of Marty's parents work, and when he was eight, he would eagerly greet them after work with a new model car to construct or a game to play. Unfortunately, Marty's parents were usually too tired to spend much time with him, and his parents mostly watched TV in the evenings. Marty's mother remembers when he made a model airplane by himself and showed it to his father as he watched TV. "I'll never forget the look on Marty's face when his father glanced at the plane, grunted approval, and went back to his program. I think Marty lost a part of himself that night. I feel guilty that I didn't do something then. It was so clear that he needed us—his dad, especially. Now he looks so depressed, and his teachers are asking us what the problem is at home. The problem is that we work, watch TV, and eat. Now Marty is just like us."

Boys need encouragement to find their unique talents. Sons between eight and twelve need a broad smorgasbord of projects, games, chores, lessons, and art forms to meet their ravenous appetite for accomplishment. Sampling can help a son find what he does best, for every boy has his own particular gift. Our modern culture gives conflicting messages to boys as to what values and skills they must master. At this age, it is vital to see what each boy himself values as success. It is easy to make the mistake of focusing on what he does well, rather than on what really excites him.

For example, everyone knew that Manley, aged ten, loved baseball. He collected cards, knew the players' stats, and was a top-notch pitcher for his Little League team. He was such a good pitcher, everyone overlooked the fact that he couldn't hit—everyone except Manley. He often put himself down because of his poor hitting. Manley's uncle, a retired semi-pro ballplayer, immediately saw his trouble when he came to one of his games. "He struck out three times that night, and even though he pitched a no-hitter, Manley felt bad," says his uncle. After two days on the ball field with his uncle and a bucket of baseballs, Manley got his first hit of the season. After the game, he jumped into his uncle's arms with tears of joy in his eyes. That uncle's picture sits on his bedside table, a little altar to the man who saw deeply into a young boy's feelings.

We parents know we must accept the task of guiding our sons to learn responsibility through doing household chores, and to learn the social graces of communication by treating family with respect and courtesy. Just as important, we must foster self-esteem and confidence in our sons by encouraging them to discover their unique, soulful interests—where their passion for life lies.

Boys need to experience success. Boy Scouts, swim team, Indian Guides, 4-H, vacation Bible school, Campfire Rangers, and organized sports all survive on the eight- to twelve-year-old's readiness to work hard, to achieve, and to succeed. We don't mean the kind of success that must win the championship, nor the success of the adult world, but the success that comes when a boy masters the use of his hands, his mind, and his body.

The four-year-old tries again and again when he fails to stack the blocks as he wants them. The ten-year-old will more likely become discouraged and stop trying, if he fails repeatedly at a task. This is the age group known for getting stuck in what Dr. Erikson called "learned helplessness."4 When a boy has few successes, he develops a sense of inferiority and holds a dim picture of himself.

> *Robbie always picked himself back up and cheerfully tried again whenever he learned something new. When he started to walk, to slide, to ride a tricycle, he'd try over and over again before he got it right. Now he's nine, and even the smallest setback seems to get to him. I watched him begin to draw a picture for his dad. He made a few lines with red, scratched them out, then wadded up the paper, and started another one. He did the same thing three times; in frustration he gave up on the drawing. He then constructed a very complicated paper airplane. He was very proud when his father praised him.*
>
> *—Maria, mother of Robbie, nine*

A boy at this age can be extremely competitive or not wish to compete at all. The best sort of competition has a boy striving to better his own performance, rather than trying to match or better someone else's. Parents can help by structuring experiences at which their son can succeed. Pushing him to take up a sport before his eye-hand coordination is well-developed, for example, could contribute to unnecessary failure. Certainly, a boy can learn from a setback or defeat. But repeated failures due to challenges that are too great for his abilities and age can be devastating now. Abe, a young friend of ours, went backpacking with his father into high country when he was eleven. His father was well-known as a competitive hiker, one who could go on for miles without a rest, never slowing his brisk pace. Abe was thrilled to be going with his father, and was proud of his new hiking gear. After they returned, Abe refused to go anywhere with his father again. We learned years later that his father had been unwilling to slow his pace or to allow Abe to rest, leaving him alone on the trail for hours with the fear that his father had abandoned him. The agony of failing in his father's eyes was too great for Abe, and he refused to ever let himself be in a position like that again. Because of his insistence on a performance beyond his son's capabilities, Abe's father essentially lost him. At nineteen Abe is extremely critical of himself and his achievements, although he is a bright and capable young man.

Sometimes parents must be selective by channeling their sons into activities that minimize the possibility of serious injury. One issue that came up in Chuck's family was what kind of sport his parents would allow him to undertake. Chuck was always naturally athletic; his family even thought he'd grow up to be a ballet dancer because he loved to leap over the furniture! He had a medium frame and was average height. His parents vetoed football because they feared injury during Chuck's growing years. Chuck was very upset for a while, but his parents encouraged any other athletic interests he had, buying him ice hockey equipment, paying for swimming lessons, and so on. As a result, Chuck, now in his early 30s, remains very physically active. He works out regularly at a gym, enjoys archery and other sports, and is in great shape.

Boys crave time with their fathers. As a son grows, no longer is he so easily cuddled, or moved when his mother needs him to move. Usually in his ninth or tenth year, a boy begins to become less identified with

Mother. The world of the fathers is calling him, and he is difficult for Mom to handle. He signals this change by becoming uncooperative in tasks that are mother-supervised. When fathers are absent during these transition years, a tough job falls on mothers to hold a firm line.

> *My boys fight like cats and dogs. Their father lives close by, but he says he doesn't know what to do with them, so he dumps them back on me. In a parenting class I learned a lesson that saved my life. Instead of being soft with them, like "What's the problem with you two. Let's work it out," I learned to take charge by setting clear limits and tough consequences. I don't have to be mean, or anything—just make rules that I can enforce. It's not easy. I don't naturally get into my "mother-with-a-mission" role. But it has brought manageable chaos to our house.*
>
> —*Sheila, mother of Ryan, eight,*
> *and Shawn, eleven*

Fathers are especially vital during this transition time. When they are involved with their sons, cheering their successes without exaggerating them, and holding limits and boundaries firmly, boys bloom like well-watered flowers. Our young neighbor, Jason, who is ten, loves to spend time with his father. They camp and fish and play together, and Jason's father loves it, too. The key to their successful relationship is that both Jason and his father like what they do together.

That wasn't always the case for Gilberto, a divorced father, who sees his eight-year-old son Jamie every other weekend for four days and occasionally for a night or two during the week. The rest of the time Gilberto travels for his business firm. Jamie was always glad to see his father, but usually became sullen and hostile before their visit was over. His mother complained that he was withdrawn and angry most of the time at home, too. He yelled at her and refused to do his homework or household chores.

Gilberto mentioned his troubles to a colleague, who asked what he and Jamie did when they were together. "I'm so tired from my work schedule that we just watch videos and eat pizza," he said. "I'm mostly bored by the stuff he likes to play." The problem, the friend told Gilberto, was that he and Jamie weren't doing things together, such as building projects or accomplishing goals. "He said that if I am bored, then something is wrong; that I need to choose activities for us that I love to do, too. Well, I tried it out, and it's great! I took Jamie with me on one of my business trips, and we stopped at a jet manufacturing plant. We had a ball. Now we camp and fish together, too. At home we made a terrarium with ugly bugs in it that his mother hates. We're doing all of the things I love but never had time to do. Now, when we are together, I make sure we make something. When we travel, we pick a small souvenir for him to have in his room to remind him of our time together. He's changed so much, it's hard to believe."

Boys continue to need their mothers. The developmental falsehood about males—that boys must separate from their mothers to grow up strong—is alive and well. Many mothers are afraid to be too involved in their son's lives now, feel sadness at losing contact, and are confused as to what their role should be. We are afraid that loving our sons too much will make them wimps, gay, or worse—tied to mother's apron strings forever. Boys between eight and twelve naturally look more to their fathers, especially if the father-son bond is secure. However, the mother-son bond must be secure, too, for our sons to progress through these often tumultuous ages to adolescence.

The feeling years of a boy's life reveal a shift from the fantasy of childhood to the material reality of a more solid world. No longer is he able to look at a chair and see a castle, a fort, a ship, or a rocket. The chair is a chair, solid and immutable. He may not like the chair as itself, but there it stands. This loss of ability causes intense grief in him, and he acts out in anger at the chair and often at his mother, who is nearby. If we shrink back from his assault with fear, match his anger with our own, overwhelm him with lectures, or try to dominate him with shame or sarcasm, we only add to the intensity of the moment. Feelings are so big and, since he has had no practice at understanding them, the boy himself wonders what all the fuss is about. The question, "Why did you do that?" is met with, "I don't know, Mom. It just happened, and I couldn't control it!"

He probably needs a hug, and he will hate that, too, but he will secretly rejoice that Mom is there offering understanding rather than rejection. The best thing a mother can do now is be available and receptive to her son's feelings. We do not mean that mothers must endure bad language, shouts, insults, or physical violence against herself or the furniture. If it has not happened before, now is the time to let him know how we feel about his behavior and what is acceptable in showing anger. Mothers must be firm but kind leaders during these years, too.

Inner Guidance System

During the feeling years, the elementary-school-aged boy is shifting from the physical body to the emotional body. The passionate, emotional push-and-pull of the younger boy is maturing in these middle years, and the older boy is freer to put more effort into relationships and social skills. He is learning more about life—how he fits into his family, how valued he is by family members, what his unique skills are in relation to the family. This is a confusing time for parents as our sons demand more independence: "But, Rob and John can cross the street to the pool on their own. Why can't I?" We are reminded that they are still young and still in need of our help to master the fundamentals of being a person. This includes safety, telling the truth, money, and relationships with others.

To hear "when you are older" is infuriating to a ten- to twelve-year-old. If crossing that busy street to the neighborhood swimming pool seems too dangerous, stand firm on that. But offer another appropriate responsibility—ideally, one that will boost your son's self-confidence while teaching him more about assuming responsibility for his own safety. For example, the neighborhood park is several blocks away but accessible by quiet streets. Perhaps after you ride there with him and review bicycle-safety rules, he may be allowed to go on his own to play with a friend.

As boys become more independent and spend more time away from their parents, telling the truth about their activities, or about anything else, becomes a problem in some families. Here is an example: Luke, aged nine, called his dad from a friend's house to ask if they could go to a nearby park to play. His dad asked whether an adult would be there, and Luke assured him that his friend's mother would go. Luke's dad later learned that the mother wasn't home at the time and did not accompany the boys to the park, where they played on their own. Luke's parents handled his lying like any other misbehavior. They set up fences by outlining the expected behavior, that is, telling the truth; naming the consequences (in this case, Luke lost the privilege of playing with his friend for one week); and following through with as much kindness and understanding as possible. The principal lesson for Luke was that, with the truth, he would have lost something, but with his lie, he lost out on a whole lot more, including his self-esteem.

Lying can also cover up deeper issues, such as a need for privacy. Privacy issues are significant to boys after age five, and, when it is appropriate, our sons need not be expected to tell us about everything they do.

There is another element of telling the truth that is important for the development of a healthy inner guidance system, one which greatly affects our relationships with others. For the sake of "being nice," many of us have lost contact with our inner messages that tell us the truth about our experiences. Children have a reputation for blunt truth-telling, such as "You sure have a big stomach!" and "I hate your green shirt." In teaching our sons to speak their truth with gracious-ness and kindness, we must be careful not to squash it altogether. For instance, "You don't really feel that way" conveys the message that boys cannot trust their feelings. Learning the art of telling the truth when asked is important in relationships, as in the case of the green shirt. Being able to speak the truth, somewhere between "I hate your green shirt" and "I think it's beautiful," is a skill that a boy in the middle years can learn. Practicing with family members to say something like "Green is not one of my colors. I like your yellow shirt better" helps everyone learn this necessary skill. When more difficult occasions arise for our sons to tell the truth about how they feel, such as to a wife or close friends, they will have learned to trust their inner feelings and to tell the truth about them.

Teaching our sons how to handle and value money is difficult for many parents. Boys in the middle years are beginning to deal with the influence of peers on how they dress, the toys they possess, and the experiences their families can afford. Parenting partners must be clear about their own money values and what is appropriate for their sons to know about the family's financial situation. Discussing the following questions can help parents deal with the money issues their sons will inevitably bring up:

How do I personally feel about money?

How do I feel about our family's financial situation?

What are my values concerning material consumption?

How does our family spend money? On material goods? On experiences, such as travel, entertainment, education?

Who handles the money in our family?

How much should our son know about our financial status?

What values have we communicated to our son about money?

What values do we want our son to hold about money?

Should he have an allowance? How much? Does he need to earn it? How?

What we tell our sons about our finances, and what we do not communicate to them, can form lasting impressions.

◆ JEANNE | During my childhood, money was very tight for my family because of heavy medical expenses. Although my parents gave me everything I needed and most all I wanted, their worry about paying bills communicated feelings of "I shouldn't be buying this" and "There is never enough money," which I have carried with me into adulthood. In this age of dwindling resources, we have tried to teach our son to value simplicity, beauty, sharing, and practicality. This is always an uphill struggle, however, in the world of Legos, Ninja Turtles, and "high top" tennis shoes!

Because a boy's self-esteem is directly connected to his feelings of accomplishment, the ride through the eight-to-twelve years can feel much like a roller coaster—up one minute, down the next. Criticism cuts deeply, especially when he has tried his best to master a task, but fails. The best way to encourage a son to meet greater challenges, we have found, is to acknowledge his efforts first. Nothing discourages him faster than our pointing out his faults or what he did poorly, without our seeing also what he did accomplish. Dan's father complained that he was lazy and a poor worker. He was always quick to find fault with how Dan mowed the lawn or swept the church basement. Rather than complimenting him on doing the job, the father called attention to the small patch of grass Dan had missed or the church pew out of place in the third row. His father's constant criticism about minor lapses led Dan to dread doing any job for him at all. Parents have to remember, a boy in the middle years will strive to do his best; but that will be what can be done best by a nine- or eleven-year-old, not the best of an adult.

It is also important that the task fit the boy. If he is not allowed to explore what he likes, if he is forced to complete chores or participate in activities that he genuinely hates, a boy feels helpless. He then fails to learn to trust his true feelings and to direct his actions from them. Mitchell, aged ten, had been a willing helper at home when he was younger. He liked to feed the family cat, and was proud when he remembered on his own. His feeling box looked like this:

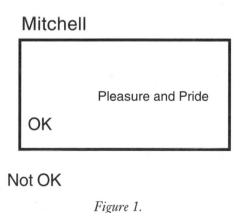

Mitchell

Pleasure and Pride

OK

Not OK

Figure 1.

When he grew older, his mother decided that his younger brother should be given the job of feeding the cat, and she assigned Mitchell the chore of emptying the wastebaskets. When he complained that he didn't like the new job, his mother said, "Oh, you don't really mind it.

Just go on and do it now." Even though Mitchell wants to help at home, his heart isn't in the wastebasket job; he procrastinates and finds other things to do instead. The task has become a power struggle between him and his mother. Mitchell doubts his self-worth and importance to his family, because he is learning that it is not okay for him to have feelings that are different from those of his mother. Now his feeling box looks like this:

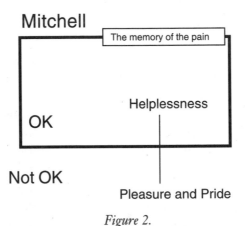

Figure 2.

Below is a blank feeling box. Consider any problems you are having with your son. Explore the possible feelings of your "Tom Sawyer," and whether they are on the inside or outside of his feeling box. Are there behaviors that belong inside or outside the box, too?

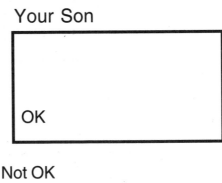

Figure 3.

Next, construct a plan of action for you and your family, to help resolve the feeling or behavior "problem" your son is representing in your family system. For assistance, refer to the feeling-box exercises near the end of chapter 6, the exercises on Learning to Hear the Positive Intent near the end of chapter 8, and the exercise in the Fences section of chapter 9.

Fences

The "Tom Sawyer" boy builds a code of honor. He seeks leaders he can respect and rules that are fair. Secret clubs and rituals become immensely important to him, and he is shocked and disappointed when parents or others do not keep their word. He watches parents closely and is quick to point out any discrepancies between what we do and what we say. He holds us, as well as himself, accountable for following the rules. A double message—that he has to follow certain ethical rules, but we do not—causes him deep confusion and breeds resentment, which takes on greater proportions in the teen years. If he steals or lies, he is ready to understand how this behavior can create problems for himself and others. If he catches us in a lie, even the most trivial "white" lie, his feelings of betrayal mar his trust in us. If the lie pertains to him, his trust in our love for him is undermined.

Kenneth, father of Benji, aged nine, learned this lesson the hard way. Kenneth was divorced from Benji's mother two years ago. He and Benji spent every weekend together, and this time was the highlight of their week. Recently Kenneth met Jan, whom he wants to get to know. At first, he only saw her during the time that he didn't have Benji. Then he began to include Jan in their weekend activities. Benji was quiet and withdrawn on these occasions, but Kenneth decided that Benji needed time to get to know Jan before he opened up to her. Then one weekend Kenneth told Benji that he wouldn't be able to have him visit, because of Kenneth's work. During that week, Benji overheard his mother on the phone express her anger at his dad for lying about the weekend trip that he and Jan were taking. Benji withdrew from his father even more. Although Kenneth apologized, it has taken a long time for Benji to trust again that he is as important to his father as he once had been.

A boy in the transition years wants to know the rules and the consequences of breaking them. When they are laid out clearly in front of him, the eight- to twelve-year-old feels secure. Knowing what to expect and what is expected of him, he then has "moving and doing" room.

Some of the "brick walls" that were necessary for his safety when he was younger still apply in these years. He has not yet mastered the ability to think things through clearly before he acts—he may still, for example, dart into the street after a ball without looking for oncoming cars—so perhaps he still needs to know that, without an adult around, the street is off-limits.

Brick walls may also serve as consequences now, because his mind can grasp concrete cause-and-effect. For example, if a family rule, or brick wall, for an eleven-year-old has been that he walk or ride his bike straight home from school, we could change it to a family rule, or "picket fence," by allowing him to stop off at his friend Ted's house, if he calls us from there to let us know where he is. The consequence of not calling us is that the brick wall of coming straight home from school goes back into effect. The boy younger than eight needed our immediate follow-through for his behavior; his concept of time and space was too limited for us to use an event in the future as a consequence. Now, the eight- to twelve-year-old can project further ahead in time, can predict responses from others (Mom's sure gonna be mad!), and can remember what will happen to him if he doesn't follow through on his agreements.

These agreements are the picket-fence type of family limits and boundaries, rather than verbal agreements, which are more appropriate later, in the teenage years. But in these middle years, our son continues to need reminders and encouragement to hold him to his responsibilities. He is still outwardly directed to please us and to win our approval and attention by doing a good job; his psychological force is barely beginning to inwardly motivate him to complete tasks just for the sake of doing them. Therefore, our sincere praise is vital. We emphasize sincere because he'll know when it's overdone, and will doubt his worthiness for it. Overall, our "Tom Sawyer" needs us close by—leading, guiding, directing, cheering, participating, and giving him more pasture in which to prove himself capable of being himself.

To set appropriate fence limits and consequences, use the following space. Describe the problem or task that you want to address with your son. Create a fence and a consequence that suit his age level and abilities. Refer to chapter 7 on Fences for assistance. Remember, it is important to review fences and consequences frequently, so that your son feels safe and can remain at his optimum learning level.

Problem/Task	Fence	Consequence for Not Following Through
Won't put tools away when finished	Rubber wall	Can't use tools for one week
1.		
2.		
3.		
4.		

Sexuality

If you are like those of us who, before reading anything else, turn first to those sections that directly relate to our son's age group, we suggest that you also read the Sexuality section in chapter 9. Many of the ideas we share there relate to our sons throughout their growing years. If you have not yet broached the subject of your son's sexuality either with him or with your parenting partner, it is never too late to begin.

These are the latency years. Sexuality for the eight- to twelve-year-old is channeled into activity. We do not mean that his projects and activities take the place of sexual interest or exploration, but he does not yet have the biological push toward sexual activity that the adolescent and older teenager experiences. He also continues to demand privacy. Having his own space for his projects and possessions is very important to him, especially if he shares a room with a sibling. He needs his own desk, closet space, chest, and shelves for his toys. A locked box for personal treasures is paramount in fostering his budding sense of who he is in relation to others.

His questions about sex will be more complicated, and require more thought and factual information from his parents. The following are actual questions, anonymously written on index cards, from sixth-grade boys aged ten through twelve. They were addressed to Dr. Sol Gordon, a well-known sexuality educator whose work we introduced in chapter 9, following a speech he gave in an Ohio suburban school system in May 1988.[5] Even those of us most comfortable with the sexuality of our children may gulp at some of these questions.

What is an erection? (age 12)

Is it normal to jack off? (age 12)

I am eleven and I've had sex two times. Should I feel guilty? (age 11)

I haven't had wet dreams. Why? (age 12)

What happens when hair grows down at you peanus? [sic] (age 12)

How long does it take to no [sic] someone's pregnant? (age 11)

What is 4 play? [sic] (age 12)

Why don't I like girls? (age 12)

How masturbation works? (age 12)

Do you have to do it so a girl can have a baby? (age 10)

My friends talk about cum [sic]. What is cum? (age 12)

Our sons deserve truthful answers. Simply because he is asking doesn't mean that a son has tried what he is asking about. There are conservatives among us who presume that giving boys factual information about sex will push them into sexual activities. We strongly believe that, in regard to sexuality, ignorance is not bliss. A boy's ignorance about his body and what is normal leads to guilt, shame, secrecy, anger, and, possibly, to unwanted pregnancy, venereal disease, AIDS, poor sexual relationships in adulthood, and even rape.

Around ten years of age, the most important information for parents to tell their sons is about wet dreams, or nocturnal emissions: that almost all boys have them, that they usually begin between eleven and fifteen, depending on the boy, and that they are normal. Factual information is vital to reassure a boy that there is nothing wrong with him. He needs to know that what his body has released is called semen, and that it will be a pleasurable experience. To save him from embarrassment, it is also a good idea to tell him that wet dreams will leave his sheets wet, and that he can take them off himself and put them in the washing machine. We also agree that it is important to teach boys at this age about menstruation and how a girl's body also changes between eleven to fifteen. When parents honor these changes as normal, healthy signs that their children are growing up, boys will take these changes in stride as part of the journey in achieving manhood.

Parents must talk about masturbation. Between the ages of ten and twelve, masturbation becomes a big issue for boys and for their parents. Mary Calderone, well-known and respected in the field of sexuality education, believes that when parents cannot allow their young sons to discover their bodies as a source of pleasure, these sons will be unable to find satisfaction in their adult sexual relationships.6 Parents will know when the time has come to talk about masturbation. Either a son will ask about it, or we may enter his room just at the right—or wrong!—time. If he asks, we can tell him that masturbation is rubbing his penis to make it feel good, that it is normal, and done in privacy. If we accidentally discover him, we can excuse ourselves for walking in on him, then reassure him that there is no need to be embarrassed, that it is normal, and that we know it feels good. The only thing bad about masturbation is the guilt our son will feel if he thinks he is doing something dirty, shameful, or perverted. If that is how we feel about it, he will feel it, too.

Communication about sexual matters depends upon a solid parent-son relationship based on trust. We agree with sex educators Sol and Judith Gordon that there are more crucial things our sons must know from us than the sexual facts alone. From the Gordons' book, *Raising a Child Conservatively in a Sexually Permissive World*, we have reprinted the following three critical messages from parents to sons that help foster self-esteem and responsibility:

1. *Somehow get across to your children that nothing that will ever happen to them will be made worse by talking to you about it. We've got to open up communication. Sure, there are consequences, but so many children will never tell their parents anything important because of the anticipated reaction of the parents;*

2. *Children are not perfect. They make mistakes, and it's up to us to turn their mistakes into lessons;*

3. *And finally, failure is an event—NOT a person. A person can't be a failure. Eleanor Roosevelt once said, "No one can make you feel inferior without your consent." Children who like themselves grow into adults who like themselves. They don't exploit others, and they are not available for exploitation.*[7]

The Positive Intent

The driving forces for the boy in the transition years of eight to twelve are learning new skills, accomplishing tasks, making things, and seeking adventure and deepening his feeling life. He yearns to contribute to family life in a real, concrete way. He wants to belong to something that is his own—family, team, or secret club. Behind his misbehavior are his efforts to achieve new skills, to succeed at mastery, and to belong. The following are statements typical of this age. We hope our guide will help you understand the positive intent behind your son's words and behaviors. Knowing his positive intent will help you create responses that will foster communication and minimize chaos. Remember, he is beginning to feel deeply about things in a new way.

Statement: I'm never going to play ball again!

Positive intent: I want to be better than I am.

Statement: You're not my boss. I'll do it because I want to, not because you tell me to.

Positive intent: I want more say in what I have to do in our family.

Statement: Yes, I brushed my teeth. (You know he hasn't, because the toothbrush is dry, and the toothpaste is new and unopened.)

Positive intent: I am learning about the problems of lying.

Statement: I washed the mower and put it away, Dad.

Positive intent: I can make things happen without your having to tell me.

Statement: Dad hates me.

Positive intent: I need Dad's attention.

Statement: Mom, you are a stupid jerk.

Positive intent: I am afraid that I can't live without you.

In the following space, you may wish to list some of your own son's typical statements and behaviors. In each case, what positive intent could he be expressing behind his words and actions?

Statement:

Positive intent:

Statement:

Positive intent:

Statement:

Positive intent:

Statement:

Positive intent:

Statement:

Positive intent:

Statement:

Positive intent:

Statement:

Positive intent:

Taking Action

If you have not already done so, we recommend that you read the Taking Action section in chapter 10. Storytelling, playing games, working on projects together, reading great literature aloud, cooking, creating music, and doing arts and crafts are all perfect and appropriate activities for the boy in the feeling years—and are greatly preferable to watching TV. Below are some additional suggestions for boys from eight to twelve.

Emphasize music. Because the focus of development in the emotional body is the maturation of feelings, and the focus of development in the physical body is the lungs and heart, music will especially touch this boy's soul. To foster both his penchant for activity and a love of music, we suggest that you provide him with the materials and assistance to build simple musical instruments. Your local library or music store can help.

Now's the time to start music lessons. If he is interested, the study of an instrument can be of great benefit during the eight-to-twelve years. His ability to learn and understand music will foster self-esteem and nourish his growing soul.

Playing an instrument he likes and music that nurtures your son's soul are key elements here. To avoid power struggles over getting him to practice and wasting money on expensive music lessons, we advise you to listen carefully to what he loves.

I was playing songs I liked by ear on my elementary school's piano at a very young age, so my parents set up lessons with a classical concert pianist from the Old School. The problem was, nobody considered my soul desire or whether the lessons were bringing me joy. At age 12, if I had been allowed to play some Beatles music instead of nothing but classical music, I might have put my heart into the lessons. Instead I just went through the motions of practicing, and pretty much stopped playing once I went off to college. Now I wish I had put more effort into the lessons, and had kept up my music. I look at pieces I used to be able to play, and can hardly imagine I ever was able to play that well.

—Sam, age thirty-eight

Here is a list of resources we found helpful, about how children learn in general, and about how to introduce music specifically:

John Holt's Book and Music Store catalog. A rich stock of books, materials, and instruments for home-schooling families, as well as for parents who take an interest in their children's education. For a subscription write: 2269 Massachusetts Avenue, Cambridge, MA 02140, or call (617) 864-3100.

How Children Learn, by John Holt, New York: Dell Publishing, rev. 1983. Wonderful insight into how kids figure things out on their own before the narrowing influence of "educational experts" takes over. Available from John Holt's Book and Music Store catalog (see above).

Making Music for the Joy of It, by Stephanie Judy, Los Angeles: J.P. Tarcher, 1990. Offers fresh ideas and support for developing a positive relationship with music. Order from John Holt's Book and Music Store catalog.

"Keeping the Beat," by Ellen Babinec Senisi. *Mothering* magazine, Fall 1991, pp. 62-66. Discusses how to make music an integral part of family life. Check local library or write: *Mothering*.

Encourage him to build projects—the larger the better. A boy in the middle years relishes using his large muscles on projects that are usable when he is finished. A treehouse, a fort, or a secret clubhouse are perfect projects to capture his imagination, creativity, and energy. The gift of his own carpentry tools is well worth the expense. See the Needs section under HELP! for resource books with ideas and construction plans.

Enlarge a boy's cooking repertoire. If he started helping in the kitchen as a toddler, the eight-to-twelve year old will now be a more independent cook. He easily makes simple snacks for himself, his siblings, and friends; with occasional help he whips up a batch of chocolate chip cookies; and he prepares easy meals for the family. Guiding him once through the process of planning a menu, checking on ingredients, and the actual cooking steps prepares him to be mostly on his own the next time. To insure success, help him choose foods he knows he and the whole family likes, and make sure the preparations are simple enough for him to accomplish without undue frustration. By eleven or twelve, he may be ready to assume the responsibility for an evening meal each week. Caution: Being responsible for both cooking and clean-up is probably asking too much of our budding cook. Give him a few more years.

Create family dramas. Right about now you may be saying, "Oh, no! This family has had enough drama." What we mean is to create a family play. Your son may have a great talent at acting, and he will love creating the sets and props. There are many story lines to choose from when deciding what you want to perform. Your family might write your own story to be acted out, or choose a childhood favorite. Fairy tales and legends are of great importance to boys of this age, allowing them to identify with the heroic deeds of a white knight or Robin Hood. An excellent book for families interested in theater is *Making Theater*, by Herbert Kohl (New York: Teachers and Writers Collaborative, 1988). You can order it from John Holt's Book and Music Store catalog, 2269 Massachusetts Avenue, Cambridge, MA 02140, or call (617) 864-3100. Check your local library for plays and resources on costumes, props, and sets. Be sure to let us know when you take the show on the road!

Help! Is Out There—Where to Find It

Besides the internal influences of physical, emotional, and psychological change, in the middle years our sons face the outer influences of peers, school, TV, and social events in a broader way than before. The poor condition of the educational system in America, especially for low-income and urban children, demands that parents take an active part in choosing and shaping their sons' education. We suggest that parents read any book by educator John Holt, investigate home-schooling, and explore the Waldorf educational philosophy. Again, we can heartily recommend any of the resources included below. In each section, they are listed in order according to our subjective opinion of their usefulness, beginning with the most useful.

Developmental Tasks

Books

The Child from Five to Ten, by Arnold Gesell, M.D., Frances L. Ilg, M.D., and Louise Bates Ames, Ph.D., San Francisco: Harper & Row, 1946. Detailed descriptions of behavioral and emotional responses of children, in their families, with friends, and at school. Libraries and local bookstores.

In Their Own Way, by Thomas Armstrong, Ph.D., Los Angeles: Jeremy P. Tarcher, 1987. Helps parents discover and encourage their children's personal learning style. Local bookstores.

How Children Fail, by John Holt, New York: Dell Publishing, 1964. Written by a well-known and esteemed educator who truly understood and cared about children. We also recommend the other books written by this much-loved writer. Libraries and local bookstores.

Towards Wholeness, by M.C. Richards, Middletown, Conn.: Wesleyan University Press, 1980. Discusses the educational ideas of Rudolf Steiner and includes a list of Waldorf schools in America. Local bookstores can order it.

The Hurried Child: Growing Up Too Fast, Too Soon, by David Elkind, Reading, Mass.: Addison-Wesley, 1984. Relates how the pressures of growing up too fast affect our children. Local booksellers.

Schooling at Home—Parents, Kids, and Learning, edited by Anne Pedersen and Peggy O'Mara, Santa Fe, N.M.: John Muir Publications, 1990. A collection of ideas about how children learn and about home-schooling by teachers, education consultants, and parent educators. General bookstores.

The Inner World of Childhood, by Frances Wickes, New York: Mentor, 1966. A Jungian approach to child development. Local bookstores.

Journals

ΣΚΟΛΕ, a journal of alternative education by Down-to-Earth Books, a spin-off of the Free School, 72 Philip Street, Albany, NY 12202, (518) 432-1578.

Needs

HearthSong catalog for all sorts of kits, games, looms, and musical instruments. Write: P.O. Box B, Sebastopol, CA 95473-0601, (707) 829-0944.

The American Boys Handybook, by Daniel Beard, Boston: David R. Godine, 1983. A treasury of the lost arts of boyhood. Directions for making kites, knots, soap bubbles, homemade boats, snow houses, sleds, puppets, tricks, and more. Also covers camping, raising wild birds, and caring for dogs. Available from *HearthSong* catalog (see above).

Carpentry for Children, by Lester Walker, Woodstock, N.Y.: Overlook Press, 1985, and Housebuilding for Children, by Lester Walker, Woodstock, N.Y.: Overlook Press, 1988. Full of photos, diagrams, and illustrations for building houses, forts, and other projects out of wood. Order from HearthSong catalog (see above).

Everybody's a Winner: A Kid's Guide to New Sports and Fitness, by Tom Schneider, Boston: Little, Brown & Co., 1976. Filled with noncompetitive games and sports. Local booksellers can order it.

Liberated Parents, Liberated Children, by Adele Faber and Elaine Mazlish, New York: Avon Books, 1975. Includes needs of parents and children. Local bookstores.

How to Father, by Fitzhugh Dodson, Ph.D., New York: New American Library, 1974. Helpful for fathers who want to become involved with their sons. Local bookstores.

All the Best Contests for Kids, by Joan Bergstrom and Craig Bergstrom, Berkeley, CA: Tricycle Press, 1996. Filled with fun and challenge. Local bookstores.

What to Do After You Turn Off the TV, by Frances Moore Lappé, New York: Ballantine Books, 1985. Full of wonderful ideas for the whole family to enjoy together. Try local booksellers.

Inner Guidance System

See suggestions in chapter 10, too.

Self-Esteem: A Family Affair, by Jean Illsley Clarke, San Francisco: Harper & Row, 1978. A practical workbook for nurturing self-esteem among all family members. Try local bookstores.

Peoplemaking, by Virginia Satir, Palo Alto, Calif.: Science and Behavior Books, 1972. A classic on communication and self-esteem. Local booksellers.

101 Ways to Make Your Child Feel Special, by Vicki Lansky, Chicago: Contemporary Books, 1991. Practical things to do to boost your child's self-esteem. Call (800) 677-7760 to order.

Encountering the Self, by Hermann Koepke, Hudson, N.Y.: Anthro-posophic Press, 1989. A sensitive and insightful focus on the ninth year of development in the Waldorf educational philosophy. Available from HearthSong (see above).

The Family Centering Book, by Gay Hendricks, Englewood Cliffs, N.J.: Prentice Hall, 1979. Includes family communication, problem solving, relaxation, meditation, and dreamwork. Local bookstores can order it.

The Radiant Child, by Thomas Armstrong, Ph.D., Wheaton, Ill.: The Theosophical Publishing House, 1985. A practical guide to the spiritual development of children. Local bookstores can order it.

Tales of a Fourth Grade Nothing, by Judy Blume, New York: Dell Publishing, 1972. A story for children about how hard it is being twelve. Local new and used bookstores and libraries.

Superfudge, by Judy Blume, New York: Dell Publishing, 1980. This story continues the misadventures of twelve-year-old Peter and his frustrating family. Local new and used bookstores and libraries.

Fences

When Your Child Drives You Crazy, by Eda LeShan, New York: St. Martin's Press, 1985. Delightful, easily read, supportive of parents, and wise. Local bookstores.

Children: The Challenge, by Rudolf Dreikurs, M.D., New York: E.P. Dutton, 1964. A helpful guide to finding the balance between letting children run wild and stifling them. Local bookstores.

P.E.T.: Parent Effectiveness Training, by Thomas Gordon, New York: Peter H. Wyden, 1970. Good guide to communication. Local bookstores.

Siblings Without Rivalry, by Adele Faber and Elaine Mazlish, New York: Avon Books, 1987. Subtitled: "How to Help Your Children Live Together So You Can Live Too." We're for that! Local bookstores.

Sexuality

See chapter 10 and 12 for other suggestions.

Raising a Child Conservatively in a Sexually Permissive World, by Sol Gordon, Ph.D., and Judith Gordon, M.S.W., New York: Simon & Schuster, 1983. A clear, outspoken guide for talking to our children about sexual issues. Check local bookstores.

Girls Are Girls and Boys Are Boys—So What's the Difference? by Sol Gordon, Ph.D., Fayetteville, N.Y.: Ed-U Press, 1979. Good information for children in the middle years. Local bookstores or Planned Parenthood.

Positive Intent

When Your Child Drives You Crazy, by Eda LeShan. See previous listing.

How to Talk So Kids Will Listen and Listen So Kids Will Talk, by Adele Faber and Elaine Mazlish, New York: Avon Books, 1980. A simple, supportive, effective guide on how to stop yelling at, nagging, and misunderstanding your children. Local bookstores.

Stepparenting, by J. and V. Rosenbaum, New York: E.P. Dutton, 1978. Subtitled "A Sympathetic Guide to Living with and Loving Other People's Children." Local bookstores.

The Couple's Journey, by Susan M. Campbell, Ph.D., San Luis Obispo, Calif.: Impact Publishers, 1980. How to enhance intimate relationships for couples. Local bookstores.

Men, Women and Relationships: Making Peace with the Opposite Sex, by John Gray, Ph.D., Hillsboro, Oreg.: Beyond Words Publishing, 1990. A loving and practical guide for improving relationships between men and women. Local bookstores.

Challenge of the Heart: Love, Sex, and Intimacy in Changing Times, edited by John Welwood, Boston: Shambhala, 1985. Deeply insightful essays by well-loved writers provide challenging reading. Local bookstores.

End Notes

1. Erik H. Erikson, *Identity, Youth and Crisis* (New York: W.W. Norton & Co., 1968), 123-24.

2. Berger, *The Developing Person*, 421.

3. Baldwin, *First Teacher*, 10.

4. Berger, *The Developing Person*, 426-27.

5. Gordon and Gordon, *Raising a Child Conservatively*, 215-16.

6. Ibid., 87.

7. Ibid., 224.

CHAPTER TWELVE

The Mister Cool Years: Thirteen to Seventeen

There's nothing wrong with teenagers that reasoning with them won't aggravate.[1]

—Anonymous

Developmental Tasks

The center of development during the adolescent years is the head, and learning happens through the intellect. These are the thinking years. Our sons no longer think only in pictures, but move into the wider arena of abstract thinking. The feelings that intensified during the years from eight to twelve continue at an all-time high, but most of a teen's attention will be focused on his newfound abilities to criticize and analyze himself, others, and the world around him. When he withdraws into himself, it is not a "pulling away from," but a "stepping back from," so that he can think, absorb, figure out how he feels, and examine what life's events mean personally to him.

> *I don't hate my folks. I just need to be alone. I can't explain it. All my friends understand, but my parents don't. They think I'm going to kill myself or smoke dope in my room. I do like to dye my hair, listen to hard music, and wear an earring, but I am clean, sober, and don't steal. What better kid could a parent want? Sometimes I want to get drunk or something*

just to piss 'em off. But that isn't the way I want to be.
If they keep it up, they will drive me to it.

—Jamie, fourteen

As parents of teenagers, we have to develop a lot of trust—in ourselves, in the parenting we have given so far, and in our sons. Psychologist and theorist Erik Erikson, Ph.D., whose observation of the basic internal conflict in younger boys served to introduce chapter 10, named the process of these adolescent years of growth "identity vs. confusion."[2] Sometimes we wonder whether he meant confusion of the sons or of the parents!

Teenage sons literally try on personalities to see how they fit. One day they are self-assured and know what they want; the next they are depressed, shy, and uncooperative. They will try out The Bully, The Nerd, The Idiot, The Brain, The Social Climber, The Criminal. Some personalities a boy will discard immediately, knowing they do not fit his soul force. Certain experimental behaviors he may keep for a while, depending upon the reactions he gets from his parents or others. Generally, the teenage boy doesn't continue an obnoxious behavior just to spite his parents. If his development and relations with family, teachers, and friends have been fairly predictable and consistent until now, parents can understand that this annoying "costume" a son is trying on causes reactions that are interesting, exciting, or challenging to his inquiring mind. He has become a student of human nature. His heightened sense of justice perceives the paradoxes and contradictions around him, and he tries to puzzle them out.

"I love my Dad, but he talks like a racist." "Mom is kind and gentle, but she lets people run all over her." "My sister is so immature when my friends come over, and I feel ashamed." "My parents say that they support me, but they won't let me find out who I am." This grappling with the incongruities of life is not a logical, rational process. One week, a son argues hotly that seeing "The Rocky Horror Picture Show" at midnight is an experience necessary to his self-esteem, as though it were a matter of life and death. Two months later, that movie is boring. When parents argue back with "Why are you so upset? You'll only change your mind next week" or "When you grow up, you'll understand why I'm doing this," we only provoke anger and resentment. Then the cry "You just don't understand me!" rings loudly in a parent's frustrated ears, and it is true. A boy's unique identity is forming, and a beginning life direction is being set. But we cannot hold him to it. He is a chameleon, changing constantly in response to both the turbulent climate of his inner being and the outer challenges that he strives to meet. We can understand that he is doing what he naturally must do, and we can understand the needs underlying his behavior.

Needs

The adolescent is adrift, pulled constantly between the call of the soul —his inner world—and the call of the outer world. The teenage years require special parental attention to help the growing boy achieve balance: between his inner urge to reflect on the puzzles of life, and the outer drive toward action.

The adolescent boy needs physical activity. The rush of hormonal activity during the teen years causes a great restlessness in many boys. Their bodies are foreign to them, and often a source of embarrassment. They appear to be all arms and legs. Some boys naturally direct their aimless energy into the physical activities of sports and working out at the gym. Their prowess in these areas gives them an acceptable way to move out into the world. They sleep, eat, and breathe football, basketball, and track. The voracious energy of other boys pulls them down into themselves, and they become lethargic, depressed, and withdrawn from the life around them.

All boys need to engage in physical activity during these years. The challenge for parents is to help a son find the activity that suits him best, instead of forcing him into a sport that goes against his nature. The quiet boy who is more likely to be drawn inward by his excessive energy might shudder at the idea of team sports such as football or basketball. Swimming or wrestling, however, may be just what his nature craves. Whether his choice is bicycling, hiking, or pumping iron, the teenage boy must engage his body in physical activity, so that his mind is clear to form and to ponder the questions he will be answering the rest of his life.

Boys require inactivity and silence. The rapid changes in the teenage body and the unfolding of the intellect cause confusion and a sense of isolation. A boy may feel that he is odd; that no one else is embarrassed by unwelcomed erections or feet that seem to have a mind of their own. Most teens tend to pack every waking moment with activities, movement, and sound, to avoid the aching loneliness that pervades these growing years. They must, however, take time to be alone, to be still, and to experience silence. The regular routine of quieting the body and the mind allows space for creativity, ingenuity, inner wisdom, critical thinking, and peace to flourish.

Teenagers will always have their loud music, which inevitably drives parents mad. Each generation has its own version. However, the noise pollution of the technological age from constant, blaring sound—whether from Walkman, TV, boombox, or stereo—is creating a generation of people whose ears and inner senses are deaf to the numinous melodies of their own breathing, frogs at twilight, birds in the early morning, a loved one's laughter, or the voice of the wind.

The teenager is especially vulnerable to overstimulation from activity and sound, because he lives on the brink of catastrophic emotions and nervous energy. His energy drives him to do everything, and his emotions push him to *feel* everything, from the highest high to the lowest low. He uses music and television to drown out the quiet spaces and to fill empty time, but his nervous system needs stillness and rest to avoid overload and burnout.

Encouraging our son to spend time in silence and stillness will be met with resistance if he is already a frenetic teenager who has never developed the habit. It is never too late to begin, but he will not agree to this practice unless we do it, too. We will be fooling ourselves and creating resentment within our son if we insist that he turn off his music to spend time in his room in quiet thought, while we plop down in front of the TV to be lulled into the cultural trance. A timeout to be still and quiet is most effective when it involves the whole family. We don't mean that everyone has to do it at the same time, but it is easier for sons to follow our example. If we devote regular time to the practice of meditation, quiet reflection, rest, sketching, fishing, listening to the sounds of nature, or any other pursuit that allows the stilling of the mind and body, our sons will be more willing to try it as well. It is in stillness that a boy learns to listen to his own soul, and to appreciate the company of his own self. These two abilities are among the greatest gifts that any son can inherit.

Teenage boys need to belong. Boys between thirteen and seventeen are both attracted to and repelled by groups. Peer groups provide a sense of identity that seems so elusive to them during these years. Yet boys suffer great anxiety about whether they belong and whether they are popular or are accepted by their group of choice. The worry over which group to join and the agony of not finding a group that feels comfortable can make adolescence especially painful for boys and difficult for parents.

One important role for parents during the experimentation years involves holding the center, as a mother does for her toddler when he begins investigating the world beyond her lap. We must respect the frustration and honor the agony that our sons feel when faced with joining a group. Because of our empathy, they may be more likely to seek our counsel, or to find temporary refuge from the struggle. The groups they join represent the values they hold and define who they are striving to become. Choosing membership in a particular group is one of the first, major decisions an adolescent faces. He needs to know we are behind him.

This may be particularly difficult if our sons fall in with what we think is the "wrong crowd." Dick, whose son Brent is fourteen, watched him struggle to belong at his new high school. He says, "Our move was a hard one for Brent. He is shy and makes friends slowly, so when he began hanging out with a group of boys I knew were trouble-makers, I was worried. Fred, a close friend, reassured me. He advised, 'Tell him about your concerns. He is young, and still needs your guidance here. He may resist your intervention, but he will probably feel relieved to have your help.'"

Dick says now, "Brent was pretty upset at first, but when I laid everything out he thanked me. I shared my experiences of making friends when my family moved to a new town. Those were some pretty lonely times, so I knew how he felt about being in a new school. I told him that choosing friends was one of the most important decisions he would face in life. He will be known to other people through the friends he has. I said when his friends make trouble, even if he isn't involved, he will be linked with trouble because they are his friends." With his dad's support, Brent decided to stop hanging out with the "troublemakers." Until he made new friends, Dick spent more time with Brent in activities they both enjoyed.

The issue of friends sometimes becomes a power struggle between parents and sons. We may ask ourselves, What will we do if our son chooses—no matter what we say—to be part of a gang or group of kids whose values differ markedly from our own? In such an instance, we must weigh the consequences of our son's choice. If we perceive his involvement with these friends as dangerous, his refusal to heed our warnings warrants our setting fences to protect him. Then we must consider what the fences will be. When faced with the possibility that our son could be injured in a gang fight or arrested for petty burglary, our instinct is to surround him with brick walls and forbid him to see these "bad influences" ever again. For many families this is when the power struggle begins. Determined to see whomever he pleases, a teenage boy might lie, break curfew, and generally be hard to live with. Pat, a single mother, tells how she handled this situation:

> *Alex had just turned fifteen when he met Dillon. I could never understand it, but there was an instant bond between them; they'd have been inseparable if I would have allowed it. The problem was that Dillon's whole family were troublemakers. Dillon had been arrested several times for stealing, his older brother had been accused of rape, and a sister was on probation for drug use. My son too has had problems with the police, and I felt that he just didn't need Dillon's influence, so I said, "No Dillon!" Alex was not to see him, and Dillon was not welcome in our home. Alex and I have been alone since his dad left when he was three, and we've always worked things out pretty well between us. This time was different. Alex didn't say a word to me then, but I knew that I had declared war.*

For the next few months, Alex rarely spoke to me, came in at all hours of the night, didn't do his homework, and stopped seeing to his responsibilities around the house. Finally, I saw a counselor who really understood teenage boys. He suggested I try to see the good things—the positive intent—behind Alex's relationship with Dillon. When I asked Alex why he insisted on seeing Dillon, he said, "Because we're friends, Mom. We care about each other." The counselor helped me understand that this really wasn't Alex's way of getting back at me. I began to look for ways I could accept Dillon in Alex's life. The counselor proposed that I allow Dillon to come to our home, if Alex would agree not to see him other places, except during classes at school. I sat down with the two boys and welcomed Dillon as long as they followed house rules: no smoking, no drinking, music just loud—not blaring—homework done, and leave the room as neat as you found it. So far, things are working out well, and Alex and I are talking again.

—Pat, mother of Alex, fifteen

"Mr. Cool" needs a cheering section. Focusing on the good that is happening in a son's life offers the encouragement he needs to keep trying. His bravado probably needs pumping up from time to time, and although approval from Mom and Dad may be received with a nonchalant shrug, it feels like dew in a desert. Can we ignore some of the things that bug us about his appearance or behavior so that we can focus on what we do like? Now is the time to choose our battles carefully—to cheer our son's efforts and accomplishments, such as staying off drugs, going to school, having a job, abiding by family curfews—and not nitpick over the small stuff, like an earring, messy room, baggy pants, or loud music. The "small stuff" we mention here may be big stuff in your family. The important point is to truly step back, look at our son, and consciously choose what supports his growth and what simply creates power struggles between us and chaos within our family.

Boys need to be seen. All too often parents get stuck in arguments and power struggles with their teenage sons, because we are unable to listen past their strange appearances. We allow the green hair, the nose ring, or the shredded jeans to drown out what our sons are trying to say to us. "My hair isn't green just to piss my dad off," says fourteen-year-old Abe. "I dyed it because it helps me fit in with the people I like to be with. He just can't understand that."

Recently, every communication between Abe and his father had ended in a fight. Dad couldn't hear what Abe had to say, because the green hair bugged him. In therapy they came to an understanding about their feelings, and Abe's dad agreed to stop his criticism of the hair color. Communication improved to the point that Abe's father, a computer analyst, invited him to go on a business trip to a Fortune 500 company. Abe was thrilled, because he is as proficient on the computer as his dad. At his father's insistence, Abe agreed to tuck his hair under a hat. But to his father's surprise, the night before the trip Abe dyed his hair brown. He says, "Once Dad backed off I thought, Hey! What's the big deal. It bothers my dad, and I can always dye it green again. I really wanted to do the computer thing, so I decided to fit into his world a little, and take the pressure off of us. I still have a tube of neon green dye, in case of an emergency."

A son needs his parents to see who he is, beyond our own hopes for him. Pushing him to fulfill a life that we wanted but never got the chance to live can be devastating to a boy's soul. Tom, a forty-year-old father, remembers that when he was a teen, he wanted to be a farmer like his dad. "He wouldn't hear of it. He told me to go to college, and to get a degree in engineering. I did, and for twenty years I have been an engineer. But my heart still longs to grow things and to raise animals. You can guess what I dream of doing when I retire."

Inner Guidance System

According to Waldorf high school and college educator Betty Staley, in her sensitive book about teenagers called Between Form and Freedom, adolescent development has two stages, "negation" and "affirmation." In early adolescence, teenagers oppose everything, which Staley compares to the "no-saying" of the three-year-old.[3] In the later years of adolescence, boys begin to embrace the outer world as an affirmation that they have a place in it, like the four- and five-year-old, who take in life with a joyous "yes!"

During early adolescence, from thirteen to fifteen or sixteen, teens want to see the world through rose-colored glasses. They expect to see beauty and perfection but instead find ugliness, injustices, and human shortcomings. These realities of life leave most boys frustrated, doubtful, and disillusioned. Feelings of anger, hurt, despair, and depression may escalate into cynicism. From their cynicism, teens can be brutally accurate in describing or attacking the injustices they see.

Don | Mothers are especially vulnerable to verbal, and even physical, assaults from sons who feel justified in opposing, blaming, criticizing, and testing everything and everyone in their way, especially those in authority positions. I spend a great deal of time, while counseling mothers and sons, explaining to boys why they frighten their mothers. Not one teenage boy believes me at first. They still see themselves as the little boys that Mommy could pick up and punish. They are not aware that their male force frightens some women. When I give them the feedback that their passion and anger can feel threatening to their mothers, most boys are shocked and attempt to avoid those encounters. A mother who is caught in these hurtful communications with her son can avoid their escalation, by mirroring back to him what she hears him saying (more about this in the section on listening for the positive intent), and by telling him how his statements or actions affect her.

I asked Barry how his political science club meeting had gone. He sort of sneered, and said that the sponsors were a bunch of jerks. I told him not to talk that way about his teachers, and he literally turned red. He then proceeded to lecture me loudly for what seemed like twenty minutes on the racist and hypocritical attitudes of adults, myself included. I was stunned by the force of his anger and bitterness. I agreed with him that some adults do hold racist and hypocritical beliefs.

I also told him that I felt hurt that he lumped all adults together. He calmed down, and we were able to discuss how most of his dad's and my beliefs differed from those attitudes that angered him. I was relieved when he calmed down. I had never seen him in such a state. I didn't know what he could do.

—*Jill, mother of Barry, fifteen*

Parents are often surprised by the power of their sons' emotions. Edward, father of Ed, Jr., fourteen, described his and his wife's reactions this way: "One minute the room we're in is still; our son walks in, and BOOM! a tidal wave hits. After he leaves, we look at each other and wonder where that storm came from." For a mother, sometimes the only way out of the struggle with a son is to physically leave the scene. It is time for the father, or another influential male figure, to step into the fray with his son. A father's presence can have a calming or an intensifying effect on a boy's anger. Either way, a father can model for his son the effective use of the masculine fury.

It is important here to distinguish between masculine fury and rage. According to Shepherd Bliss, well-known conference leader and educator in the men's movement, *fury* is a good word. "It has a mythological connotation," he says, "like the Furies, who in Greek mythology were three avenging goddesses. This was powerful feminine energy. There is a powerful masculine fury, as well. Too often this energy is put down by women or culture as too threatening and turns into rage. Suppressed, this fury as rage is either expressed by men through violence or as passivity. Director John Singleton understood this when, in his movie *Boyz N the Hood*, he named the lead character 'Furious.' If masculine fury is initiated, or socialized, or channeled in a way that is positive for the community, it becomes creative energy. In past times physical labor was the outlet—chopping wood, pitching hay, hauling water. Modern fathers become vital in the lives of their sons to guide them toward peer involvement, such as the Boy Scouts. They can initiate them into the rigors of hiking, climbing trees, or sports like long-distance running, volleyball, and soccer."[4]

We heard the following modern initiation story and offer it as a positive way for fathers to guide their sons' masculine furies: The boys were fourteen, and their families were concerned about the high incidence of drug and alcohol abuse and general troublemaking at the local high school. On a designated night the fathers took their sons into the hills for an overnight camp-out. Around the campfire, the fathers told stories about their teenage years. In the best tradition of the old Storytellers, they shared their adventures—their daredevil stunts, their pranks, their greatest achievements, their meanest failures, their disillusions, their dreams. One father remarked later, "Our sons left those hills with a different respect for being a male, and a new awareness of their fathers as men who were once boys. I think my son now knows that he's going to make it to manhood, and that I'll be with him every step of the way."

When a boy's anger and passion are heard, reflected back in an understanding way, and channeled into positive action by an accepting masculine figure, he gains self-acceptance and mastery over his feelings, and learns to take responsibility for them.

Our friend Alan Connie of North Myrtle Beach, South Carolina, has coached girls' collegiate championship track teams year after year. Guys are always hanging around. He says, "Some of these guys are not as tough as they seem. They look the part; they act the part, but really all they are doing is coming up to you, and in one form or another, saying, 'Boo!' Ever since I figured that out, I just stand my ground, say, 'Chill out, man!' and tease them about something. Most of all, I am firm, but kind. The teenage boys I talk to really struggle with many feelings besides anger. Most of them are looking for a parental figure—someone they can talk to—and all of them are looking for somebody they can trust."[5]

In later adolescence—sixteen to eighteen—a boy uses his growing understanding of how feelings work to reach out to the world. His disillusionment transforms into an acceptance of reality, and he now wishes to help change the injustices he sees, rather than merely criticize them. This is also the time when adolescents begin to search for the truth, and when spiritual, political, and future-career issues become important. The "crushes" of his earlier teen years evolve into personal, more lasting relationships with others. Parents discover that their sons regain their sense of humor and interest in family, although they will still prefer to be with their friends. We can be assured that our maturing sons will become more resilient to the ups and downs in their lives, leaving our homes more peaceful.

⊰ JEANNE | I remember how much smarter my parents seemed to have become when I turned seventeen; I could actually approach them for counsel about matters that troubled me.

Thankfully, times are changing, but the wound that most adolescent boys take with them into manhood is the denial of their deep feelings. We do allow males to feel angry, sexual, and aggressive feelings—they have become part of the male stereotype—but what of the other feelings that naturally make up a male's inner guidance system? It is especially important that teenage boys are allowed to feel and express their hurt, disappointment, fear, sadness, loss, hate, joy, compassion, and excitement.

Most men of today entered manhood with parts of themselves missing, lost to the cultural worship of the intellect. And so it is not surprising that modern leaders find themselves inept at dealing with the problems of pollution, ruin of the rain forests, extinction of animal species, hunger, and poverty. They have not been allowed to feel fear, sadness, loss, appreciation of life, or bliss. Feelings of anger and of the need to conquer, when not balanced by the expression of other human emotions, lead to waste, greed, and unchecked "progress." Below is the feeling box of many modern men, who are cut off from their emotions, except angry, aggressive, and sexual feelings.

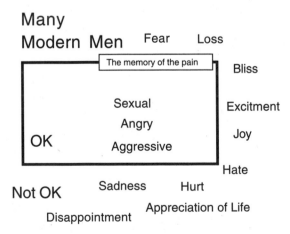

Figure 1.

A boy in the "Mr. Cool" years feels intensely, although he may not be able to name what he feels. When our sons were younger, we were able to name their feelings, and usually something shifted as a result. Their tension was released; they were reassured that we understood. Naming the feeling for an adolescent, however, is often interpreted as our trying to control him. Instead, giving him room to feel without judgment is more effective. When there is an opportunity to talk, our suggesting that he feels sad or afraid or hurt can help him open to more of his inner world of feeling.

≈ ≈ *Don* | As I work with teenagers, the *Feeling Curve* (see chapter 6) is often a hit with them. They understand it immediately, especially the *Clear Thinking Zone*. This has been a great way for families to understand feelings and clear thinking.

Below is a feeling box for your son. Fill it in, then reflect on how your family collaborates on holding those feelings outside the box in their place. What do you need to explore in yourself that will help open the family to a greater variety of feelings? What actions do you need to take? Refer to chapter 6 on the Inner Guidance System for assistance.

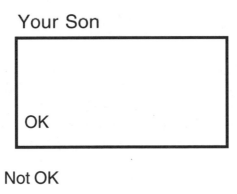

Figure 2.

Fences

Setting fences becomes both harder and easier when sons enter the teen years. A boy is now self-motivated to participate, and he is intensely interested in his inner and outer worlds. He has a stake in how things happen around him. He is able to concentrate deeply on a homework assignment or a task that interests him without being pushed to complete it. Just as passionately, however, he stubbornly refuses to do what is asked of him, because he considers it to be wrong, unfair, or an unreasonable request. Unlike his younger, defiant behavior when pushing against our fences, the adolescent uses his newly developed powers of reasoning; and he can be extremely hard to refute.

A sure way for parents and teenage sons to get in a muddle with each other is for parents to take what their sons do too personally. Adolescent rebellion is usually directed at parents, because we are the closest authority figures around. Part of our job as parents is to be there to reflect back to our sons who they are and who we hope they will become as strong and loving men in the world. Because of this, we feel the brunt of their searching. Most of the time, however, they break through the fences we so carefully built, not to punish us or to get back at us for something we did or didn't do, but because they are motivated by their natural desire to become autonomous. The teenage boy wants to run his own life. He wants to become a man. He finds the weakest links in our fences because he is testing himself just as much as he is testing us.

When a son intentionally or unintentionally breaks the "rules of the house," he needs our feedback about how his actions affect the lives of others. Sometimes he needs more pasture to roam in, and other times he needs less. Fences for a teenager can change from day to day. They must be discussed, reevaluated, and shifted to fit, regularly.

Basic guidelines for setting limits and boundaries with teenagers are:

1. **Only set up fences you can enforce.**

2. **Spend more time in conversation.** Open discussions regularly with your son, but remain in charge. As long as he is still a minor, it is not time for voting.

3. **Be kind**. Firmness and kindness are not opposites. They go hand in hand. Holding the firm line will be more easily accepted by everyone concerned when it is accompanied by kindness.

4. **Always follow through**. Do what you said you would do. This is important modeling for your son. Don't let things slide. If you don't follow through on your commitments, your message to your son is "I don't care about you."

5. **Choose fences after careful thought**. A picket fence, where the consequences are minor, may be appropriate when you ask your son to lock the house when he leaves. If he forgets, usually a reminder is enough to get him on board. Curfews, on the other hand, may require brick walls, because teenage boys are likely to stray and not follow through on time agreements.

6. **Discussions about fences are best done in private**. Respect the adolescent boy's feelings and needs for privacy in these matters. This is not the time to tease or ridicule. Talking about him and the fences you set may be embarrassing in front of his friends or others, and will injure your relationship and the good work that you have done together. His trust in you is a sacred gift that will be hard to recover, once you have broken his confidence.

7. **It is still best that consequences fit the misbehavior**. Boys now have a well-developed sense of time and space, and see the causes and effects of their behavior. Unlike when our sons were younger, consequences can now be set in the future, and they don't necessarily have to mirror the behavior directly. Because of his keen sense of fairness, however, a boy will balk at a consequence that seems out of proportion to the indiscretion, or totally unrelated to what he did or failed to do. Example: Grounding him for two weeks may be a just consequence for not respecting his night curfew; if he cannot be home when he agreed he would, then he may not leave home in the evening at all for a while. Grounding him for two weeks because his grades are not up-to-par, however, may simply cause resentment and rebellion rather than the desired result of better grades.

8. **Before setting a consequence, decide what you want to achieve.** To use the previous example, is it better grades that we want, more of an active interest and involvement in school, or more responsibility and participation in the act of learning? If the goal is better grades, we must find ways to help a son memorize facts; write better, neater papers; hand assignments in on time; answer questions in class; take tests; and so on. Grounding him for two weeks is probably not the best way to achieve these ends. Instead, the situation calls for discussions with him about what he feels the problems are, where his weak spots lie, whether he sees the importance of good grades for his future, and such.

9. **Sometimes letting the consequences fall naturally where they will is the best trade-off in the end.** For example, many, many homes in America with teenage boys go through the battle of the wills, night after night, over homework and getting good grades. Gradually, for the son, the struggle over grades and homework shifts to a fight to preserve some stronghold of will and power. Until he realizes for himself the importance of grades, the value in the ability to study, or the joy of learning something new, no amount of nagging, cajoling, or punishing is going to motivate him to change. A better trade-off, to relieve the destructive tension that this clash of wills creates in families, may be to tell him how important we think schoolwork is, set definite study times, offer to help him in any way we can, be there when he asks for help, and then let go. Sometimes just the letting go brings amazing results.

See chapter 7 to review boundary setting and consequences in greater depth.

Sexuality

These are the years of puberty, when a flood of growth hormones, chiefly testosterone, rockets a boy's growth in all directions. Although boys sprout at different ages, there is now a noticeable change in body and in attitudes about sex. A pubescent boy may feel proud, surprised, or ashamed about the growth of pubic and chest hair, enlargement of his genitals, and deepening of his voice. Sons are sensitive about these new body developments, and we must take care to avoid teasing or ridicule about the changes that are happening to him. It is also important that we respect his need for privacy. Mom is no longer "just Mom." She is a woman, and he is becoming a sexual, adult male. Dad is not "just Dad," but another male, whose body reacts just as his own does. A son's world has changed forever.

For the modern family, sexuality is not so much an event as it is an ongoing process. Today, the first time a parent broaches the subject of sex is usually not the first time the boy has talked about it. Often parents are the last on board. Communication is easier if questions about bodies, loving, touching, and relationships have been freely discussed with a son from birth, as part of the fabric of the family. That being the case, by the time he reaches the teen years there is a foundation of acceptance and understanding from which a boy's sexuality can bloom. Whenever we begin to talk with our sons about their sexuality, it needs to be addressed within the context of relationship—how to treat others, how great it is to feel alive and passionate, and the difference between aggression and assertiveness.

Puberty can be a difficult time for parents, because the changes in our sons and the need to talk with them about sexuality bring back all of the fear, shame, and guilt we suffered when we were teenagers. We want to help our sons avoid the painful experiences we had, but we often don't know how to go about it.

> *I never know what to say to my son about sex. When I was thirteen, my dad came into my room, gave me a jockstrap, and told me that if I put my penis in a girl, she would have a baby, and don't do it until I got married. Closed subject. I don't want to treat my own son that way, but I don't know what to say. We have always been close, but sexual feelings have been a topic we never address.*
>
> *—John, father of Tim, fourteen*

Premodern cultures initiated boys at this age. Their physical awakening took place within a controlled social setting, so that the boy had direct instruction and guidance in the purpose of his sexuality. He was taught how to relate to both men and women. Today, according to Dr. Sol and Judith Gordon, whose frank and insightful book we highly recommend for parents of teenagers, "there is a tremendous amount of sex education that occurs without parental awareness or consent in the lunchroom, the locker room, the bathroom, through graffiti, pornography, sex jokes, and the boasts and bravado of some of the presumed sexually active young people. Young people also receive a great deal of sexual information from movies and television, most of it of a sensationalistic and distorted nature."[6] The Gordons go on to say that while they cannot prove directly that these entertainment programs affect sexual development, their clinical experience indicates that "there is a brutalizing effect in the depiction of excessive violence, especially on boys, as expressed in the lack of a sensitivity to the feelings of others and a persistent need to dominate."[7]

It is time for fathers, or other trusted, adult males, to educate sons about masculine drives and male sexuality. An acquaintance we will call Stephano tells about attending his first men's gathering with poet Robert Bly in the beautiful California woods at the age of fifty. "Robert Bly walked into the center of the circle, and said, 'Now, I'm going to tell you how to sexually please a woman.' I thought, Wow! I've lived all this time, and now finally an older man is going to tell me about sex. It was fantastic!"

Heterosexuality, Homosexuality, and Bisexuality: Identity vs. Confusion

Dr. Erik Erikson's description of the teenage years accurately captures a boy's search to know himself. He looks for how he is alike and different from other members of his family, his friends, and his teachers. Teens experiment with and explore everything from hair color to sexuality, because they are developmentally-driven to discover who they really are as persons, separate and unique. They may or may not engage in or fantasize about same sex or opposite sex relationships. Whatever boys are driven to do, however, they are on a necessary search to find themselves. For some, the truth may be painful and difficult to face, but most boys, at some point in their teenage years, wonder whether or not they are gay or bisexual. The search for truth can be especially painful as a son battles cultural fear, hatred, and ignorance about homosexuality. The locker room jokes and taunts cut deeply into the heart of a young boy in doubt about his sexual orientation. Most of the time, he faces his questions and fears alone, afraid to reveal his thoughts to anyone for fear of humiliation and rejection.

> *I always felt different from others, but during high school, I really felt out of it. The other guys bragged and laughed about girls and how many "hits" they could make. I had lots of friends who were girls, but I didn't get what all the excitement was about. I tried kissing a few times, but I would rather talk or listen to music or just have fun with girls. I was teased a lot about not dating, and some of the names I was called really hurt, especially from guys I really liked. I was very lonely until college where I joined a group of gays. When I admitted I was gay, the world became totally different. I made sense to myself. I felt like a prisoner must feel after chained a long time in solitary confinement.*
>
> *—Jeffrey, twenty-three*

Few of us are prepared when a son comes to us and says, "Mom, Dad, I am gay." Parents experience many inner reactions—anger, fear, denial, hurt, disgust, shame, and guilt. We may ask ourselves, "How can I ever handle this?" Our outward response will not change our son's sexual orientation; if a son is gay, there is nothing we can do to change him. His act of confiding in us is a plea for understanding and support, so our rejection of him only serves to create separation and pain between us. The lifeline of openness from parents to their sons at this crucial time of sexual development may literally save their lives. Here are some facts about homosexuality:

- Children who experience emotional rejection from their parents because of their sexual orientation have high rates of suicide and alcohol/drug abuse.

- A biological (genetic, hormonal, neurological, or other) predisposition towards a homosexual, bisexual, or heterosexual orientation is present at birth in all boys and girls.

- The exact causes of heterosexuality and homosexuality are unknown.

- Homosexuality and heterosexuality are likely to be the result of an interaction of several factors, including genetic, hormonal, and environmental.

- Psychological and social influences alone cannot cause homosexuality.

- Sexual orientation cannot be changed permanently through therapy.

- The American Psychiatric Association states that homosexuality, like heterosexuality, in and of itself, is not a mental or emotional disorder.

- About ten percent of the world's population is and always has been gay, lesbian, or bisexual.[8]

Once the initial shock has registered, we must give ourselves time and room to be human. For some parents, the experience of finding out their son is gay is like facing a death, and we can be led through the stages of denial, anger, grief, and eventually acceptance. The vision of who we thought our son would become has to die, and we must rely on our hearts while navigating this important stretch of parenting. Our son is the same person today as he was yesterday, but now we know him better in his search to be more genuinely himself. At first it may seem hard to imagine, but many parents emerge from this ordeal with a stronger, closer relationship with their sons than ever before. Others who have had to face these issues advise:

- You are not alone. Connect with other parents. (See the *Help! Is Out There—Where to Find It* section at the end of this chapter for a list of resources.)

- Allow yourself all of your feelings. Don't condemn your feelings of embarrassment, anger, or guilt.

- Understand that it took courage for your son to share this issue with you. Match his by being open to what he has to tell you.

- More than ever, your son needs your love, understanding, courage, support, and acceptance.[9]

A person's sexuality is more than a sexual act or sexual feelings. It includes a vitality, creativity, and love that allows a confidence and stability we rely on when we face what life brings us. Our son's ability to grow into a healthy man is not determined by his sexual orientation; rather it is dependent upon his ability to love and act on the world in a life-giving way.

Today teens who are left to find out about sexuality "on the streets," so to speak, are at great risk of contracting AIDS or STD (sexually transmitted disease); causing unwanted pregnancy; and suffering emotional trauma from guilt, pressure to have sex, or unpleasant sexual encounters. Parents must give their sons information about birth control and "safe sex," or condom protection against AIDS. We must be available for questions and able to answer them in a straightforward, accurate, and honest way. It is important to say "I don't know" to what we cannot truthfully answer, and to help find the information our sons need to adjust to a new body and a growing interest in sexual issues. Our openness can help them become sexually responsible, giving, and responsive human beings.

Sexual development commences at different ages and proceeds at varying rates, but puberty in boys generally begins earlier in today's culture than when their parents were children. To understand our sons' sexuality, we must first realize that recent generations are maturing earlier and delaying permanent relationships longer than ever before. Just seventy years ago, men and women married as young as thirteen and started families.[10]

What to expect between ages twelve and fourteen: Twelve-year-olds begin to drop their pencils in class, so that they can bend down to look up a girl's skirt. They may not know what they are looking for, or what they are expected to find, but the mysterious urge to do so is very strong. By thirteen and fourteen, a boy becomes aware of why he wants to see up her skirt, why the magazine pictures of seductive women attract him, and why MTV's dance scene grabs his attention. "Every Sunday since he was small, Mark and I have read the comics together," says George, whose son is fourteen. "Lately, I've noticed that the first thing he goes for when the paper comes is the Macy advertisements of women's underwear. He discreetly pulls it out and heads to his room. I did the same thing with the Sears catalog when I was a boy."

Most boys have their first ejaculation between twelve and thirteen, usually from masturbation or sexual dreams at night. The frequency of wet dreams, or nocturnal emissions, varies with each boy and decreases as he grows older. The important thing here is to let him know that wet dreams are normal, that almost all boys have them, that nothing is physically wrong with him, and what he can do with the messy sheets in the morning. Reassurance that masturbation is normal also remains important.

These early sexual years are exciting and, at times, awkward and uncomfortable. A boy is learning how to live in a body that seems out of control much of the time. After a while, he won't be surprised at his erections related to erotic fantasy, direct stimulation, or "dirty pictures." But an erection just when he steps in front of the class to recite is sometimes too much to bear. A reassuring word from his father or another sympathetic adult male can help a boy come through such experiences with his self-confidence and sense of humor intact.

What to expect by fifteen and sixteen: By now, many teenage boys have developed a regular pattern of sexual activity. Remember that boys develop at their own, natural pace, so there is no need to be alarmed if our sons seem more interested in computers than in girls at this age. A boy's community and family standards often determine how his sexual patterns are acted out—whether he denies his sexual feelings; restricts his activity to solitary fantasy and masturbation, active dreamlife, petting, or foreplay; engages in actual intercourse; or experiments with homosexual activity.

Between fifteen and sixteen, most boys' genitals have reached their full, adult size. Height is very close to what it will be in adult life. Hair has grown on face, genitals, chest, arms, and legs. Erections are now more often related to sexual stimuli—dancing, hugging, or walking and talking with someone they find attractive. "Dirty magazines" and glossy, women's ads are less of a focus. Boys are now more aroused by their own mental fantasies and real-life relationships.

By sixteen and seventeen, a boy's sexual pulse is a feature of his daily life. He becomes aroused from personal contact, erotic pictures and reading materials, and the rhythmic pulse of music. Wet dreams diminish, and some boys are sexually active with girls. Social life is very important, as independence from parental guidance, a drive to affirm talents and abilities, and the desire to be popular claim a boy's focus and concentration. How he acts on his sexual drives varies from solitary fantasy with little to no contact with others, to handholding, to petting, to actual sexual intimacy.

Early one morning I discovered that the motor to our Volkswagen was hot. Then our sixteen-year-old son Matt came down to breakfast looking as though he hadn't slept all night. He claimed not to know anything about the car. I figured something was up. On Saturday, I took him to lunch at a favorite place of ours. I confronted him right out. "Where were you early yesterday morning?" I knew his story was going to be good. He always drives our other car because he can't drive a stick shift, and the Volkswagen "Bug" is rarely used. Matt hemmed and hawed a bit, and finally spit it out. He had driven ten miles in first gear to his girlfriend's house at 3 a.m. He climbed in her bedroom window on the second floor, made out, got back in the Bug, and couldn't find reverse. He pushed the car into the road, drove home in first gear, turned off the motor, rolled it back into place, and crawled into his bedroom window at 5 a.m. His story had to be the truth, because it was so ridiculous. He had used the Bug because it was parked down the hill, away from the house. All I could say was, "Son, you are one of the most determined and inventive people I have ever

known, but please, don't do it again. You could have
gotten yourself shot by me, mistaking you for a robber,
or by your girl's father, finding out it was you and not
a burglar!

—*Fredrick, father of Matt, sixteen*

When our sons are between thirteen and seventeen, education from parents, especially from fathers, must include factual information about pregnancy, birth control, STD, and AIDS, especially if we are approaching a son about sexual matters for the first time. An unfortunate mistake commonly made by parents is to assume that by puberty, our children have learned what they need to know about sex. However, most of their information is sketchy at best, and much of it is inaccurate. The most vital instruction parents can give sons now is to teach them to be sensitive to another's feelings; to respect the word no; and as a colleague of sexuality educators Sol and Judith Gordon told her son, "Don't ever knowingly use your penis as a weapon to hurt somebody."[11]

Parents must also let their sons know how they feel about their sexual activity. Most of us would prefer that our sons wait until adulthood to engage in sexual intercourse, and it is important to communicate that to them. However, some things parents really have no control over, no matter how hard we may try. We can—and we must—educate a son thoroughly about the risks of early sexual involvement, and we can tell him that we hope he waits until he is older to have sex, but we will not be with him in the parked car, or the empty house, or at the party where he makes the final decision. If he does become involved more deeply than we had hoped he would and needs our help, it is also important to let him know that we will continue to love him, no matter what.

Some studies suggest that men reach the peak of their sexual potency in their late teens and early twenties.[12] Whether this is true remains open for debate. Nevertheless, the sexual drive of a young man is strong and foremost in his thoughts. Our sons' sexuality is an especially complex issue in the technological age. When adolescence was shorter and people married young, their sexual drives were easily channeled into the acceptable arena of marriage. Now, with marriage often delayed until the late twenties, sex is becoming a common part of dating relationships. The growing practice of living together before marriage is an option that would have added more grey hairs to the heads of our grandparents. The increasing numbers of young people "coming out of the closet" challenges the sexual values and preferences of parents as well. These issues are not easily solved, and they require that parents remain supportive of and open to conversation with their growing sons. It will be important for us to remember how we felt and thought when we were young and faced with the passion and confusion of the teenage years.

Abe, sixteen, says it well. "I thought I had life all figured out and knew exactly what I would do in most situations. I had my life all planned out. Then I borrowed my buddy's car for a date. It had a back seat that folds out and is very spacious. My date turned out to be someone I liked, and she seemed to like me. We ended up on the tenth floor of a parking garage, using the fold-down seat as our bedroom. The windows are tinted, so you can't see in. That's something I thought I would never do until I was older. Now I'm really confused, but I know that I am not returning to my old way of looking at things. This is too much fun. I am not saying that I am going to become a totally wild and crazy guy. I just realized that I made too many decisions about certain parts of life, before I experienced them. It's all up for reevaluation, but I'm in no hurry to come to any hasty conclusions."

The Positive Intent

A boy in the "Mr. Cool" years is driven to establish a sense of individuality and identity. He constantly wavers between a strong sense of "I *am*!" and an insecure "Who in the heck am I?" Solving this dilemma is crucial to the teenage boy's life direction in work and in personal relationships. Who he is directs his life far more than does his collection of abilities and skills. One's personal identity lies hidden in the soul.

A boy in search of his soul presents a tough challenge to those around him. He is not dependable, because his positions and beliefs change from one day to the next. This can aggravate parents, and it is important that we let our son know how his behavior affects us. The key to this feedback is that we give it in a nonjudgmental and accepting way. We do not have to agree with him; our differences of opinion, when offered openly, can help him clarify his position. On the other hand, our judgment or strong criticism of his beliefs as wrong or immature will only impede his forward movement toward clarity, and will increase the power struggles that are inevitable during these years of exploration. Often, when allowed to explore and have his own ideas and opinions about life questions, a son ultimately adopts the values and deep beliefs held by his parents. The content of arguments changes, but how we communicate with one another is what keeps the parent-son relationship together amid the chaos of disagreement.

Following are examples of statements made by teenage boys and the possible positive intent behind them. We hope that they come close to ones you have heard from your teenage son. They are offered as a beginning point from which to open communication with him (you may wish to review the material in chapter 8 on how to listen for and use the positive intent), but we do not guarantee that they will help you understand him. His feelings, statements, and reactions are usually not logical—that's just not where he is right now. Good luck!

Statement: I'm going to dye my hair blue no matter what you think!

Positive intent: I want to be unique and belong to my group of friends.

Statement: I hate you!

Positive intent: I feel hurt. Or I feel angry with you.

Statement: Dad is a jerk. He never listens to me. He always lectures. I can't stand it.

Positive intent: I need Dad on my side.

Statement: It's none of your business who my girlfriend is or isn't.

Positive intent: I need my privacy. I want more control over my life.

Statement: I can't believe how you think about things. You contradict yourself all the time. (Spoken to Mother)

Positive intent: I am now able to think and see more clearly.

In the space below, we invite you to fill in behaviors or statements typical of your own son, followed by the most likely positive intent behind them.

Statement:

Positive intent:

Statement:

Positive intent:

Statement:

Positive intent:

Statement:

Positive intent:

Statement:

Positive intent:

Statement:

Positive intent:

Statement:

Positive intent:

Taking Action

All parents, no matter what their sons' ages, need support. When we share in parenting groups and with trusted friends and neighbors, it can bring relief, humor, and a new perspective to even the most distressing of family crises. We find it helpful to remember that for many boys, the teenage years are filled with excitement, challenges well met, close friendships, skills gained, and happy adventures. Yet even a happy adolescence has its ups and downs, and we do want to pass on suggestions that can help parents cope during these years. Be sure to check this section in chapters 9 and 10 for suggestions that are still appropriate in the teen years.

Provide a sense of support and security. Your being available, open to questions and honest exploration of feelings, and your staying strongly connected as a family, provide a teenager with a safe haven, where he knows that he is accepted. If a boy knows that he can ask for help without judgment or ridicule, he will be more likely to confide in his parents and to stay connected to his family during these high-pressure years. We know a teenager who had an understanding with his father, that he could call him from wherever he was and ask his dad for a ride home—no questions asked. Teens shouldn't have to "tell all" to their parents; they are entitled to privacy, and this agreement may have saved several lives.

If possible, arrange to be home when he returns from school. It may seem financially difficult, or impossible, but a teenager may need a parent at home just as much as a younger child does. We know a mother who says, "I returned to work after our son turned ten. At fourteen, he needed me to be there when he came home from school. I never thought that we could pay the bills on one salary again, but I'm glad I made the decision to be home while he's a teenager. Our home is more peaceful, and Seth is a lot happier."

Continue to insist that he takes his turn in the kitchen. Most of our sons become extremely busy during the teenage years with activities that take them outside the home. Thinking they should be more independent and aloof from the family, parents often give too much latitude to boys at this time. Although our fourteen-year-old looks adult, he still needs us to set limits and boundaries and to maintain a secure home base where he has responsibilities as a member of the family group. He can assume more cooking chores such as baking, menu planning, grocery shopping, meal preparation, and clean-up. To make things more interesting and challenging give him the opportunity to assume a major part of a holiday dinner, prepare a buffet party for his or your friends, or offer to cook as a gift for a friend in need. Teenage boys especially need to know that despite all the changes they experience in the development of their physical bodies and the expansion of their social horizons, they are important to their families.

Become involved in your son's school and social activities. Many events need chaperones and parental support behind the scenes. Here's a great way to stay in touch with the current styles of dress, hair, language, and music of your son's teenage culture. That's what his world is—another culture—and you may feel that you have landed on another planet if you don't stay current with the latest happenings.

Be politically active in your community, county, or state in defense of young people. Find ways to create constructive things for them to do, such as "hangouts" with live music that do not serve alcohol but do provide activities and refreshments that they like. Help provide jobs that teach skills and boost self-esteem. Find opportunities for teens to gain understanding of and to help people less fortunate than themselves, such as volunteering in nursing homes, soup kitchens, preschools, Headstart programs, juvenile hall, or free health clinics.

Sponsor and/or coach a team sport. Moms and dads involved in the games boys play provide models of leadership their sons carry with them into adulthood. Sports fundamentals, team membership, good sportsmanship, and the spirit of fun are necessary skills in many arenas of life—personal relationships, the workplace, and the community. The participation of parents in sports helps the hesitant boy join a team and supports him to do his best. Remember to choose a sport that everyone enjoys. It may be soccer, baseball, golf, swimming, or whatever a boy loves to do.

Start and/or facilitate discussion groups for teens on topics such as sex, drugs, spirituality, values clarification, how to be a success in today's world, or whatever topic teens want to discuss.

Be on the alert for suicide warning signs. Teenagers are in the greatest-risk category to commit suicide. Here is a list of warning signs from Teens in Action, a national campaign to reduce teen suicide.

- Decreased appetite
- Change in sleep patterns
- Withdrawal from friends and social activities
- Angry outbursts, fearfulness, and touchiness
- Major personality changes
- Frequent physical complaints or tiredness
- Self-destructive behavior
- Preoccupation with death
- Obsessive fear of nuclear war
- Irrational, bizarre behavior
- Overwhelming guilt or shame
- Feelings of hopelessness, sadness, or despair
- Giving away belongings

Drama and the theater provide opportunities for teens to try out various roles and emotions in a structured and acceptable arena. Remember that this is a time when a boy is exploring whom he might want to become. By acting, he can try on anger, compassion, and life situations totally different from his own. Supporting his participation in school or community dramas may give a son just what he needs to work through important life dilemmas. If his interest does not include actual acting, going to the theater or reading the great plays together can provide comparable emotional outlets for him to step outside his own limited experience.

The arts become important as a way to access the teenager's inner being. Beauty and order often calm the emotional turbulence experienced during the teen years, and painting, sculpture, pottery, or drawing can serve as powerful mediums for expression. Organized sports dominate the lives of many boys at this stage, which can be agony for the boy who is not athletically inclined. He may naturally turn to art as an outlet for his frustrations and talents. Parents can support their sons by encouraging acceptable arenas for their creations: theater sets and props, murals for social-service centers that need a lift in decor, banners for parades, decorations for school dances or children's parties, and much more. Artistic talent can even be turned into financial profit by an enterprising young artist with good ideas.

The important role for parents: avoid any judgment that communicates to a boy that he should be doing something else, that he is a failure because he isn't captain of the football team, or that he is wasting his time. Any endeavor that enables a teenage boy to listen to his inner self, and to communicate it to the world in his own way, is worth all the time it takes.

> *I hated sports, even though I'm good at them, and my school made me take PE every year. What I have always loved is art, but my folks never let me take art. The trouble began in junior high, when I decided to be creative another way. I did all kinds of great stuff to get attention. I loved makeup and acting, so I dressed in wild costumes, like a space alien, and walked into class as though nothing was different. Once, I bought this old, junk car for fifty bucks, and painted it all over with grotesque colors and outrageous faces of people about to throw up with their hands over their mouths. Before school, I parked it where you could see it from most of the class windows, and it distracted people all day. I owned the school during my pranks. It was the only time I felt good about myself. Now I do graphic art, day and night. I'd do more if I could. I wasted all those years in school doing what others wanted me to do, just because I was good at it, not because I loved doing it.*

> *—Chuck, nineteen-year-old graphic artist*

Help! Is Out There—Where to Find It

If you are starting here because your son is a teenager, we recommend that you also check the Help! section in chapters 10 and 11. Some of those books are for parents of younger children, but there are many for men and women in general, and for parents of children of all ages. These suggested resources will lead you to others. As with other Help! sections in this book, resources are listed in order based on our subjective opinion of their helpfulness, beginning with the most useful. Good luck!

Developmental Tasks

Between Form and Freedom, by Betty Staley, Stroud, U.K.: Hawthorn Press, 1988. A practical guide to the teenage years with valuable and sensitive insights into the hearts and minds of teenagers. Highly recommended. Order from *HearthSong* catalog.

All Grown Up and No Place to Go, by David Elkind, Reading, Mass.: Addison-Wesley Publishing, 1984. Concerns teens in crisis. Local bookstores.

After All We've Done for Them, by L. Fine, Englewood Cliffs, N.J.: Prentice Hall, 1977. A practical and readable guide to living with teens. Local bookstores.

Identity: Youth and Crisis, by Erik Erikson, Ph.D., New York: W.W. Norton, 1968. Clearly outlines the developmental stages of teenagers. Try local bookstores; they can order it for you.

Needs

Books

Between Form and Freedom (see above).

Summerhill, by A.S. Neill, New York: Hart Publishing, 1960. "The classic work on motivating your child with freedom, responsibility, and creativity." Local new and used bookstores.

Self-Esteem: A Family Affair, by Jean Illsley Clarke, San Francisco: Harper & Row, 1978. A practical workbook that helps families build self-esteem for all family members. Local bookstores.

Go Ask Alice, by Anonymous, New York: Avon Books, 1971. A diary of the real life of a teenage drug addict. Check local bookstores.

Dare to Live, by Michael Miller, Hillsboro, Oreg.: Beyond Words Publishing, 1989. "A guide to the understanding and prevention of teenage suicide and depression." Local bookstores.

Organizations and Networks

National Institute on Drug Abuse
5600 Fishers Lane, Room 10 A 39
Rockville, MD 20857
(301) 443-6245

National Clearinghouse on Alcohol Abuse
P.O. Box 2345
Rockville, MD 20847
(301)-468-2600

Parents, Families, and Friends of Lesbians and Gays (PFLAG)
1101 14th Streer, N.W., Suite 1030
Washington, D.C. 20005
(202) 638-4200
FAX: (202) 638-0243
E-MAIL: PFLAGNTL@AOL.COM

The following organizations provide support, information, and activities for parents and teens:

Boy Scouts of America

Campfire Girls and Boys

YMCA and YWCA

Local church youth groups

Community recreation programs

Teenage support groups

Planned Parenthood

Church-supported counseling services

Association for the Prevention of Teen Suicide

County social services' teen programs

Foster Parents Association

Step Family Association

Volunteer Placement Groups

Inner Guidance System

Values Clarification, by Sidney Simon, Leland Howe, and Howard Kirschenbaum, New York: Dodd, Mead, 1985. Offers questions and situations that require moral and value judgment. A great place for parents to begin to explore with their teens the important questions and dilemmas of life. Local bookstores.

Between Form and Freedom (see previous listing).

Inner Work, by Robert Johnson, San Francisco: Harper & Row, 1986. Using dreams and active imagination for personal growth. Local bookstores.

Fences

How to Survive Your Child's Rebellious Teens, by M. Brenton, New York: Bantam Books, 1979. Focuses on what is possible between parents and teens. Local booksellers.

Children: The Challenge, by Rudolf Dreikurs, New York: E.P. Dutton, 1964. Written for parents of younger children, but the principles work with all ages. Check local new and used bookstores.

Back in Control: How to Get Your Children to Behave, by Gregory Bodenhamer, New York: Prentice-Hall Press, 1983. Helpful in dealing with preteens and teens. Local bookstores.

When Your Child Drives You Crazy, by Eda LeShan, New York: St. Martin's Press, 1985. A sensible and respectful guide for parents. Small section specifically on teenagers. Local booksellers.

Predictive Parenting: What to Say When You Talk to Your Kids, by Shad Helmstetter, New York: Simon & Schuster, 1989. A practical guide for improving family communications. Local bookstores.

Raising Self-Reliant Children in a Self-Indulgent World, by H. Steven Glenn, New York: St. Martin's Press, 1988. One of the best books in print for teaching responsibility and self-motivation to children. Local bookstores.

Sexuality

Raising a Child Conservatively in a Sexually Permissive World, by Sol Gordon, Ph.D., and Judith Gordon, M.S.W., New York: Simon & Schuster, 1983. Honest and straightforward, the Gordons tell it like it is. Local bookstores.

Changing Bodies, Changing Lives, by Ruth Bell and members of the Teen Book Project, New York: Vintage Books, 1981. Covers just about everything a teen wants to know about relationships, sexuality, and growing up. Local bookstores.

Straight from the Heart: How to Talk to Your Teenagers About Love and Sex, by C. Cassell, New York: Simon & Schuster, 1987. Check local bookstores.

The Teenage Survival Book, by Sol Gordon, Ph.D., New York: Times Books, Revised, 1985. Highly recommended. Check local bookstores.

Now That You Know: What Every Parent Should Know About Homosexuality, by Betty Fairchild and Nancy Howard, Orlando, FL: Harcourt Brace, 1989. Mothers of gay children face the falsehoods, misconceptions, and stereotypes to help parents hear what their gay children want to say. Local bookstores.

The Family Heart: A Memoir of When Our Son Came Out, by Robb Forman Dew, New York: Ballantine Books, 1994. A mother's heartfelt memories of her son's revelation that he is gay. Beautifully written; highly recommended. Local bookstores.

The Positive Intent

How to Talk So Kids Will Listen and Listen So Kids Will Talk, by Adele Faber and Elaine Mazlish, New York: Avon Books, 1980. Recommended for younger children, but the principles are very effective with teens. Local bookstores.

Love Is Letting Go of Fear, by Gerald Jampolsky, New York: Bantam Books, 1980. Helps readers understand the positive motivations behind behavior. Local new and used bookstores.

Ask Me If I Care, by Nancy Rubin, Berkeley, CA: Ten Speed Press, 1994. A compelling portrait of today's youth by an experienced high school teacher. Local bookstores.

Uncommon Sense for Parents with Teenagers, by Michael Riera, Berkeley, CA: Celestial Arts, 1995. Clear, insightful; highly recommended for parents of teens. Local bookstores.

End Notes

1. *A Mother's Journal* (Philadelphia, Pa.: Running Press, 1985), 91.

2. Erikson, *Identity, Youth and Crisis*, 131-35.

3. Betty Staley, *Between Form and Freedom: A Practical Guide to the Teenage Years* (Stroud, Gloucester: Hawthorn Press, 1988), 7.

4. Shepherd Bliss, Ph.D., conference leader/educator, phone conversation with Jeanne Elium, Berkeley, Calif., 20 Nov. 1991.

5. Alan Connie, educator/track coach, conversation with Don Elium, Walnut Creek, Calif., 25 June 1990.

6. Gordon and Gordon, *Raising a Child Conservatively*, 90.

7. Ibid., 91.

8. Collected from information compiled by the Federation of Parents and Friends of Lesbians and Gays, Inc. 1101 14th. Street, N.W., Suite 1030, Washington, D.C. 20005.

9. PFLAG, "Our Daughters and Sons: Questions and Answers for Parents of Gay, Lesbian and Bisexual People," from *Can We Understand? A Guide for Parents*, by New York City Parents and Friends of Lesbians and Gays, 1994.

10. Preston Elium, senior citizen, conversation with Don Elium, Salisbury, N.C., 13 Feb. 1991.

11. Gordon and Gordon, *Raising a Child Conservatively*, 115.

12. Ibid., 29.

CHAPTER THIRTEEN

The Graduate Years:
Eighteen to Twenty-Nine

*I have been asked to give this graduating class
a few good words of advice about going out into
the world. Here they are: "Don't go!"*

—From a keynote graduation address to university seniors

In the ancient, initiation cultures, a young man between eighteen and twenty-nine had settled into a productive role within his tribe; knew his responsibilities toward the tribe, the women, the children, and his neighbors; and possessed a clear sense of self. His life was built firmly on regular cycles and the stability of a familiar and consistent world. By this time, he was definitely a man.

Life is different for the modern-day graduate. He is just beginning his journey into manhood. His education gave him an opportunity to explore ideas, but he has had little experience in living his emotional, spiritual, and practical life. He is rarely prepared to make a living. If his childhood was filled with parental acceptance of his feelings, strong guiding fences, and an understanding of his soul, he has a firm foundation from which to start the journey into manhood. But even the best of childhoods does not protect him from his own suffering. He will stumble over the lure of pleasure, money, and flashy trinkets that our culture promises him. All of his book-learning cannot replace wise guidance and lived wisdom.

A healthy, modern man must form his identity in the midst of rapid change and uncertain gender roles. Less constricting roles for men and women have provided opportunities for growth and work not previously available, but what a man is expected to become was radically different just ten years ago, and seems to change daily. Today, a man becomes a man by running head-on into his personal limitations when dealing with life's challenges. How he responds to these unavoidable events forms the healthy man's identity.

> *I entered my manhood when I got divorced. I worked all hours, ignored my family, and it finally caught up with me. I found out the hard way that I can't have it all. I can only manage some of it at a time. Now I am forced to spend time with my children by a "visitation schedule." I hate to say it, but the divorce made me really look at what is important to me. Right now it's my relationship with my kids and my health. I hope I will open up to more in life later, but for now I'm licking my wounds and restructuring my life around what's most important to me.*
>
> —*Harry, forty-year-old divorced father*

Between the ages of eighteen and twenty-nine, young men enter the larger world of life outside the family they grew up in. Some go slowly; some go rapidly. No matter what the speed, modern life sets the stage for adult male initiation. Graduates are plunged into the whole range of human, male experiences: beginning a career, getting married, becoming a father, being fired from a job, having no savings, experiencing divorce or the breakup of an important relationship, being betrayed by one's best friend, becoming physically disabled, facing one's own death, grieving the death of a loved one, experiencing serious illness, succumbing to addiction (overeating, drug abuse, alcoholism, overspending), abusing a child or wife, receiving a promotion, and so on.

"Around age thirty-five," says poet Robert Bly, "a man's way of dealing with the world falls apart. It just doesn't work anymore. It is time for grieving, struggling, and getting in touch with the deep masculine. He loses his hope that he can do the things he wants without going deeper into himself. He has lived a false hope. Now his hope can become more real."[1] As a man faces his limitations, his little-boy dreams of being and doing whatever he wants are crushed. A more realistic view of the world now takes shape. His grandiosity matures into humbleness, and he is able to make a stronger, healthier mark on the world.

Some make this turn willingly; others are pulled into the descent of "deeper" feelings and "clearer" insights through drugs, alcohol, or the abuse of food or money. The first step in the recovery program of Alcoholics Anonymous is to accept that one is powerless over alcohol. When a man gets in touch with where he is truly powerless, he can then know where his life-giving power lies.

It is painful for parents to watch a son struggle with the dark feelings of fear, failure, loss, and grief. We want to rush in, pick him up, dust him off, and shore him up. If we do this, we deprive him of the experience of entering the fire or the darkness and coming out on the other side—alive, whole, and a great deal wiser. Like Theseus, who, to become king, had to defeat the cruel villains hiding along the road to Athens, or Orpheus, who descended into the underworld to win back his soul, a young man must take his own steps to manhood. The consultants and mentors who guide him must be able to walk with him through his despair without taking on his pain, and to applaud his victories without taking the credit. Comedian-philosopher Rob Becker tracks the source of modern man's low self-esteem in his one-man show, "Defending the Caveman." He says, "I want to feel as good about being a man as I did about being a little boy."[2] That goodness comes to a man from the process of defining his own behavioral code of honor: his place in the scheme of things, what he values in life, and the actions he takes to maintain the standards he has set for himself.

As his son hovered on the threshold of manhood, a father named Spencer had to face something much more painful—the abuse he had suffered from his own father. "My son, Nate, is the laziest boy I have ever seen, probably because I never required him to really do anything. When he didn't do what I asked, I gave in to him. I promised him a car if he would graduate from high school. When he did, I gave him the new car, and a credit card plus a thousand dollars. This is embarrassing, but I thought this would help him finally get started in his life. What a fool I was. He took the car, left for a month, spent his credit limit, spent the thousand bucks, got three speeding tickets, and now wants to live at home. Well, I've let him stay. At twenty-one, he's still living the life of a teenager. I've had it, but I don't know what to do. I can't let go of him. That's why I'm in this fathers' support group. I need help."

This father realized that he was trying to protect his son from the painful life he himself had lived with a father who was never there for him. As Spencer faced his own pain, he found the strength to set limits with his son. He gave Nate the gifts of setting his own priorities, facing his own trials, and achieving his own victories. There is really no other way into manhood.

Letting Go

The major task for parents during the Graduate Years is letting go. This can be difficult after the years many a son spends in extended adolescence—college, travel, trying job after job. It is very common for a modern son to return home temporarily, after being on his own. Parents wonder how much to help and whether to help at all. Can we give our opinions and offer him advice? How can we let him suffer when we have the money to end it? Parents who can address their own natural fears and grief about their son growing into adulthood will be better able to support a fledgling son who is slow to leave "the nest."

When I left for college I had big dreams for my future, but my career plans fell flat after I graduated. I got really depressed, and moved back home for nine months. I worked two bum jobs to save up some money, and got counseling. I got myself back together, and went out again for another start. It was strange being home again, but I needed it. I think it was a mixed blessing for my parents. They were used to being by themselves. I actually enjoyed the return. Now, I watch my two-year-old son venture away from his mother, realize how far he has gone, become a little fearful, and run back to her for comfort. I guess I did the same thing.

—John, aged thirty-one

John's story is a familiar one. Emotional turmoil is not the only reason for the modern, young man to return home or stay at home longer. Today's economy presents enormous challenges for the new graduate. High rents and the low salaries of entry-level jobs make it difficult for anyone to successfully launch themselves into the adult world. The task for the young man between eighteen and twenty-nine is to move from a parent-supported state to a peer-challenged stance in the world.

The Challenge of Peers

No initiation culture ever relied on just a mother and a father in the making of a man. The greater world of men and women were always called upon to assist in this task. Modern parents of a graduate must direct him to people, agencies, schools, and counselors that he can rely on to help shape his adult life. Ideally, his parents' role in his life will decrease in importance and transform to that of loving friends and supporters. Now a young man's "mirrors," who reflect to him who he is, are his work colleagues, service club members, men's group members, recovery group members, therapist, teachers, and, best of all, his circle of buddies to whom he looks for male friendship. Elder mentors, whose lived wisdom is a powerful influence, can help guide the younger man in the descent into his own deeper motivations and feelings. The quality of these relationships is crucial to the health of a man in the graduate years.

Taking Action

Understanding our sons during the Graduate Years challenges us to examine our own lives, hopes, and dreams. Our role as kind and firm leaders continues as we cheer from the sidelines. Through our example, our sons learn how to craft the life they want for themselves—what Clarissa Pinkola Estes, Ph.D., Jungian analyst, storyteller, and author, calls the "life made by hand"[3]—the examined life, the life carefully chosen day by day.

Continue to offer support, but don't get taken in. Depending upon the agreements made, parents of sons in the graduate years will find their sons still need advice, financial assistance, moral support, and boundaries. If a young man has returned home from college or lives at home while he works at a job, he must clean up after himself, help cook meals, pay rent for his room, do his own laundry, and so on. Agreements about the rules of the house are best made during a family discussion where all members accept the terms.

Parents must live their own lives. When a son leaves home for college, work, or service, we often face what feels like a crossroads, a pit, a blank, or a question. Whether we have been parents-at-home or involved in our careers for much of our children's lives, this change is a loss we experience either consciously or unconsciously. As our relationship with our son transforms to include his new status, the perspective we hold of ourselves also undergoes a close scrutiny. Who am I now? Where do I go from here? How do I want to live the rest of my life? What are my responsibilities as a parent now? These and other questions lead us to re-evaluate our life path and the journey we have undertaken. Watching our son's bright star lead him onward into his life can be a gift that reminds us of how we were then. Those memories serve as guides to understanding what our son faces as he sets out, and as reminders of what we hoped life held for us. How closely those dreams match what we are living now may be just the nudge we need to follow our own soul's desires.

It helps to trust his judgment and keep our fingers crossed. Many young men make a commitment to a long-term relationship during the graduate years. Because of our own experiences or perhaps because of the nation's track record of divorce and broken relationships, we may be fearful for our sons as they begin to choose a partner. Being out in the world for awhile may help a young man gain understanding of his sexual orientation; for the first time, he may be able to share with us that he is gay. He may choose a mate from a different race, religion, or socio-economic background. He may still seem too young and inexperienced to us to be making such an important, life-long decision at this point. Whomever he chooses will be his decision, however, whether or not we agree with his choice. He deserves our honesty as we share our concerns with him, and he will demand our acceptance— to open our hearts to those he loves.

A new image of mature masculinity is emerging. Health depends upon a life-affirming attitude that leads to action. This definition is not really new. Men have been working for the common good for centuries. The tragedy is that we have devalued the masculine, because we have misunderstood—we have missed—the positive intent behind the action.

Comedian Rob Becker speaks about the caring, life-giving soul of the modern father. "When my wife, Erin, and I visited friends who were expecting their first baby, Erin immediately sat down with the woman, and they began to share their feelings about the pregnancy, birth, and new baby. I hunted down Ross out in the back yard. He had a dazed look in his eyes and a power saw in his hand. 'I'm building a fort,' he said proudly. I said, 'Hey, the baby isn't even born yet, and you are already building him something to play on?' He paused, looked me straight in the eye, and grumbled, 'Are you gonna grab that two-by-four and help me, or not?'[4]

A father's way of caring comes from the urge toward action. Men and boys everywhere are emerging from the sexist-stew of our recent past to redefine a deep, masculine force whose life-affirming urge grows healthy men from the roots of curious, creative, sensitive little boys.

Resources

Let us hope the young man in the graduate years has learned the value of reading for relaxation and enrichment. There are many good books to choose from. We recommend the following for both parents and sons as a place to begin.

Books
CAREER GUIDES

Education for Action: Undergraduate and Graduate Programs that Focus on Social Change, ed. by Sean Brooks and Alison Knowles, Oakland, CA: Food First Books, 1995. A contemporary guide to programs for the common good. Local bookstores.

The 7 Habits of Highly Effective People, by Stephen R. Covey, New York: Simon and Schuster, 1989. A common sense guide for personal change effective in all arenas of life.

What Color Is Your Parachute?: A Practical Manual for Job-Hunters and Career-Changers, by Richard Nelson Bolles, Berkeley, CA: Ten Speed Press, 1996. The best guide to finding a job you love. Local bookstores.

MEN'S ISSUES

Finding Our Fathers, by Samuel Osherson, New York: Fawcett Columbine, 1986. "How a man's life is shaped by his relationship with his father." Local bookstores.

Fire in the Belly, by Sam Keen, New York: Bantam Books, 1991. A personal new look at how men are changing. Local bookstores.

Gods in Everyman, by Jean Shinoda Bolen, M.D., San Francisco: Harper and Row, 1989. Gives insights into modern men through the ancient Greek myths about the gods. Local bookstores.

He, by Robert Johnson, New York: Harper and Row, 1974. A Jungian approach to male development based on the legend of Parsifal and his search for the Holy Grail. Local Bookstores.

In A Man's World: Father, Son, Brother, Friend, and Other Roles Men Play, by Perry Garfinkel, Berkeley, CA: Ten Speed Press, 1992. Offers insights into the mysteries of male behavior. Local bookstores.

Iron John, by Robert Bly, Reading, MA: Addison-Wesley, 1990. A mythopoetic book about men by a distinguished elder and leader of the men's movement. Local bookstores.

SOCIAL ISSUES

In the Absence of the Sacred, by Jerry Mander, San Francisco: Sierra Club Books, 1991. A wake-up call to remember and preserve our deeper, lost values. Local bookstores.

Necessary Wisdom: Meeting the Challenge of a New Cultural Maturity, by Charles M. Johnston, M.D., Seattle, WA: ICD Press and

Berkeley, CA: Celestial Arts, 1991. A profound guidebook for the future to deal with the challenges of our time. Local bookstores.

SEXUALITY

The New Male Sexuality, by Bernie Zilbergeld, New York: Bantam Books, 1992. Insights into men, sex, and pleasure. Local bookstores.

Mars and Venus in the Bedroom: A Guide to Lasting Romance and Passion, by John Gray, New York: Harper Collins, 1995. An intimate and practical guide to good sex. Local bookstores.

Being Homosexual: Gay Men and Their Development, by Richard Isay, M.D., Northvale, NJ: Aronson, Jason, 1994. Outlines the normal path of development for gay men. Local bookstores.

Reinventing the Family: The Emerging Story of Lesbian and Gay Parents, by Laura Benkov, New York: Crown, 1994. An insightful resource for lesbian and gay parents, struggling against monumental odds to create families of love. Local bookstores.

End Notes

1. Robert Bly in a public reading at the Scottish Rite Temple, San Francisco, 9 Mar. 1990.

2. Rob Becker in his one-man show, "Defending the Caveman," San Francisco, At The Improv, 14 Sept. 1991.

3. Clarissa Pinkola Estés, The Red Shoes, an audiotape produced by Sounds True Recordings, Boulder, CO, 1992.

4. Becker, "Defending the Cave Man."

Get the latest from Jeanne & Don!

Free monthly Internet newsletter
Sons & Daughters Online
email your address to: elium@aol.com

To book speaking events
call **(800) 9DADMOM**

Also available from Celestial Arts

RAISING A DAUGHTER
by Jeanne and Don Elium

Following the huge success of *Raising A Son*, the Eliums have turned their attention and expertise to the challenges of raising a daughter in today's world. They address the unique challenge of the mother/daughter relationship, the confusion experienced by fathers, and the special needs of single parents. From infancy through the teen years and on into early adulthood, *Raising A Daughter* is indispensable reading for new and experienced parents alike.   **392 pages**

We are proud to present audio tapes of *RAISING A SON* and *RAISING A DAUGH-TER,* read by the authors themselves. These tapes provide a perfect solution for busy parents who find free time harder and harder to come by. Now you may listen to the wise words of Don and Jeanne Elium while driving to work, or going about daily chores. Or invite other parents over for tea and cookies to gain remarkable insights into the art of parenting.

These tapes are designed for single parents, fathers who are prepared to take a more active role in parenting, and parents in general who seek to realign masculine and feminine energies into a more equal and balanced parenting partnership and family atmosphere.

RAISING A SON: Parents and the Making of a Healthy Man
by Don Elium and Jeanne Elium
Read by the authors

This book-on-tape is a guide for mother and father in the making of a healthy, assertive, and loving man. This seminal work is the first to address the unique challenges that boys bring to families at each stage of their development and the ways that parents can positively guide them.
Three hours

RAISING A DAUGHTER: Parents and the Awakening of a Healthy Woman
by Jeanne Elium and Don Elium
Read by the authors

The often conflicting messages *to* women *about* women make the raising of girls a sometimes daunting responsibility. The Eliums help parents unravel and make sense of all this conflicting information and bring us enlightening insights into the behavior and dreams of our daughters. Covering stages from birth to adulthood, topics include: the unique challenge of the mother/daughter relationship, the confusion experienced by fathers, and the special needs of single parents.
Three hours

Available from your local bookstore, or order direct from the publisher.

Celestial Arts

P.O. Box 7123
Berkeley, CA 94707
(800) 841-BOOK